Pandas in 7 Days

Utilize Python to manipulate data, conduct scientific computing, time series analysis, and exploratory data analysis.

Fabio Nelli

www.bpbonline.com

FIRST EDITION 2022

Copyright © BPB Publications, India

ISBN: 978-93-5551-213-0

To View Complete
BPB Publications Catalogue
Scan the QR Code:

Dedicated to

All those who are constantly looking for awareness

&

in a special way to My wife and my son

About the Author

Fabio Nelli has a Master's degree in Chemistry and a Bachelor's degree in IT & Automation Engineering. He is currently working professionally at many research institutes and private companies, presenting educational courses about data analysis and data visualization technologies. He also completes his activity by writing articles on the web (in particular on his website, meccanismocomplesso.org) and in-depth books on the subject.

About the Reviewers

Purna Chander Kathula is a Data Manager and a Python Developer who guides teams working on complex Data Engineering tasks, building data pipelines, easy handling of heavy lifting jobs, legacy data ingestions, Validations, Data Analysis, and Visualizations. His expertise lies in building tools and frameworks that validates structured, semi structured, and unstructured data. He is Coursera-certified in "Applied Data Science with Python" from the University of Michigan. He has authored two books, "Instant Sikuli Test Automation" and "Hands-on Data Analysis and visualization with Pandas". He lives with his family and two children, and loves watching fiction movies and spending time with family and friends in his free time.

Pragnesh Prajapati is a Data Scientist with extensive experience in building AI products. He is currently working as a Senior Data Scientist at Cerebulb (India) Private Limited to develop predictive analytics products for industries like sugar, cement, and mining. He is also working as an Mlops Solution architect in a freelance capacity to develop Mlops solution for big data architecture.

He completed his B.E graduation in Electronics and Communication where he was exposed to IOT devices. He has taken 12+ online courses related to ML, Python, Deep learning, MLOPS, and AWS.

He started his professional journey as an Embedded Consultant in Amnex Info Technologies, primarily working on IOT devices, and later worked as a machine learning consultant in the R&D Department. He has worked on IOT, Machine Learning, and Deep Learning products.

He started mentoring and tutoring students in 2021, and worked with an Edu-tech company as a data science tutor.

In his free time, he likes to learn new technologies (for instance, quantum machine learning), listen to podcasts, and play guitar.

Acknowledgments

My gratitude also goes to the team at BPB Publications for being supportive enough to provide time to finish the first part of the book and also allow me to publish the book in multiple parts. Because image processing is a vast and active area of research, it was impossible to deep-dive into different classes of problems in a single book, especially if I am attempting to not make it too voluminous.

Preface

This book will cover the topics of data analysis with the Pandas library in a simple and understandable way. The concepts will be gradually treated with many practical examples and explanatory images in order to facilitate and speed up learning. The book will be structured in two parts. The first part will deal with illustrating all the basic concepts of the Pandas library, with basic data structures, examples of methods, and other data manipulations typical of data analysis. The second part will show the application part of the Pandas library in the real world of data, that is, those available in the external world. We will learn how to find data, and how to acquire it from normal external sources (data sources). Many problems produced by real data will be presented and methods on how to solve them will be illustrated. Finally, we will briefly show how to view our results through graphs and other forms of visualization, and how to save or document them by generating reports.

In parallel, the book can also be seen in its separation into 10 chapters. The first two chapters serve to introduce the topic of data analysis and illustrate the characteristics that make the Pandas library a valid tool in this regard. The following 7 chapters correspond to the 7-day course that will be used to learn Pandas in all its features and applications, through a whole series of examples. All topics will be reviewed individually, each with its own examples. The last chapter, on the other hand, will direct the reader on possible paths to take once the book is completed and continue with their training as a data scientist or other professional applications.

The details of the 10 chapters are listed as follows:

Chapter 1 - Pandas, the Python library, gives a brief overview of the Pandas library and data analysis.

Chapter 2 - Setting up a Data Analysis Environment, explains how to install Pandas on various platforms and the different ways of working (workspaces).

Chapter 3 - Day 1 - Data Structures in Pandas library, provides an introduction to the basic data structures of the Pandas library, followed by the declaration, data upload, and other related concepts.

Chapter 4 - Day 2 - Working within a DataFrame, Basic Functionalities, discusses the basic commands and operations to be performed on Series and DataFrames, such as the selection and extraction of some data and the evaluation of statistics.

Chapter 5 - Day 3 - Working within a DataFrame, Advanced Functionalities, explains the advanced commands and operations for data analysis. Selections by grouping, multiindexing, and other more elaborate techniques are explained in this chapter.

Chapter 6 - Day 4 - Working with two or more DataFrames, discusses the Commands and operations involving multiple DataFrames. Comparison, joins, Concatenation, and other operations are also discussed in detail.

Chapter 7 - Day 5 - Working with data sources and real-word datasets, includes different data formats available in input and output – real world data, their importance, their characteristics, and the need to process them. Data sources such as databases and web (HTML and data sources available online). Cleaning and processing of data before analysis. Some practical examples on research, pre-processing, data cleaning, and then analysis of the real data acquired.

Chapter 8 - Day 6 - Troubleshooting Challenges with Real Datasets, explains that the real data, that is acquired from external sources, are never ready to be processed. They must first be preprocessed (cleaned) and then the data formats must be standardized with each other. Despite these preliminary operations (pre-processing), the loaded data can present significant problems such as empty fields, incorrect data, or difficult to work with as textual values.

Chapter 9 - Day 7 - Data Visualization and Reporting teaches us that once we have analyzed the data and obtained our results, they will need to be visualized in some way. Python with the Matplotlib library offers remarkable visualization tools. The chapter includes discovering Jupyter Notebooks, interactive data analysis, and reporting.

Chapter 10 Conclusion - Moving Beyond, provides a brief conclusion on the possibilities that open up once you become familiar with the Pandas library. The Data Scientist profession today, applications, and other Python libraries to use are discussed in this chapter.

Code Bundle and Coloured Images

Please follow the link to download the
Code Bundle and the *Coloured Images* of the book:

https://rebrand.ly/b34fcf

The code bundle for the book is also hosted on GitHub at **https://github.com/ bpbpublications/Pandas-in-7-Days**. In case there's an update to the code, it will be updated on the existing GitHub repository.

We have code bundles from our rich catalogue of books and videos available at **https://github.com/bpbpublications**. Check them out!

Errata

We take immense pride in our work at BPB Publications and follow best practices to ensure the accuracy of our content to provide with an indulging reading experience to our subscribers. Our readers are our mirrors, and we use their inputs to reflect and improve upon human errors, if any, that may have occurred during the publishing processes involved. To let us maintain the quality and help us reach out to any readers who might be having difficulties due to any unforeseen errors, please write to us at :
errata@bpbonline.com

Your support, suggestions and feedbacks are highly appreciated by the BPB Publications' Family.

Did you know that BPB offers eBook versions of every book published, with PDF and ePub files available? You can upgrade to the eBook version at www.bpbonline.com and as a print book customer, you are entitled to a discount on the eBook copy. Get in touch with us at :

business@bpbonline.com for more details.

At **www.bpbonline.com**, you can also read a collection of free technical articles, sign up for a range of free newsletters, and receive exclusive discounts and offers on BPB books and eBooks.

Piracy

If you come across any illegal copies of our works in any form on the internet, we would be grateful if you would provide us with the location address or website name. Please contact us at **business@bpbonline.com** with a link to the material.

If you are interested in becoming an author

If there is a topic that you have expertise in, and you are interested in either writing or contributing to a book, please visit **www.bpbonline.com**. We have worked with thousands of developers and tech professionals, just like you, to help them share their insights with the global tech community. You can make a general application, apply for a specific hot topic that we are recruiting an author for, or submit your own idea.

Reviews

Please leave a review. Once you have read and used this book, why not leave a review on the site that you purchased it from? Potential readers can then see and use your unbiased opinion to make purchase decisions. We at BPB can understand what you think about our products, and our authors can see your feedback on their book. Thank you!

For more information about BPB, please visit **www.bpbonline.com**.

Table of Contents

1. **Pandas, the Python Library** 1
   Structure 1
   Objective... 2
   A bit of history... 2
   Why use Pandas (and Python) for data analysis? 4
      A trust gained over the years 5
      A flexible language that adapts to any context..........................5
      Automation, reproducibility, and interaction...........................6
   Data Analysis 7
      What is data analysis? 7
      The data scientist 7
      The analysis process 8
   Tabular form of data 10
      Tabular form of data.. 10
      Spreadsheets.. 11
      SQL tables from databases 12
      Pandas and Dataframes 13
   Conclusion 14
   References 14

2. **Setting up a Data Analysis Environment** 15
   Structure... 15
   Objective... 16
   The basic procedure 16
      Installing Python 16
      Installing Pandas and the other libraries................................. 18
      Installing Jupyter Notebooks 19
      Considerations...20
   Anaconda 20
      The Anaconda distribution 20
      Installing Anaconda 21

Installing Anaconda on Linux systems...22

Conda and the Anaconda command line shell 23

Creating and managing environments with Conda...................................24

Conda – Create an environment with a different Python version 26

Conda – Export the environments...27

Creating and managing packages (and libraries) with Conda 27

Jupyter Notebook...29

Creating a Notebook on Jupyter..30

First steps on a new Jupyter Notebook 32

Working online on development environments: Replit...............................37

Replit...37

Creating a Python workspace for data analysis on Replit......................38

Conclusion 41

Questions...42

3. Day 1 - Data Structures in Pandas library...45

Structure...45

Objective...45

Introduction to the Series 46

A Series as a sequence of data...46

The Index() constructor..50

The name attribute of Series...51

Various ways to build Series 52

The Series() constructor 52

Creating a Series from a NumPy array 53

Creating a Series from a scalar value 57

Creating a Series from a dictionary 58

Creating a Series from a list of tuples 60

Creating a Series from a 2-element array list...60

Introduction to DataFrames...61

The DataFrame as an indexed data table...61

The DataFrame() constructor 62

Other constructor arguments 64

Access the various elements of the DataFrame with iloc[ ] and loc[ ] ..67

Various ways to build DataFrames...70

Creating a DataFrame from a Numpy ndarray 70

Creating a DataFrame from a Series dictionary......................72

Creating a DataFrame from a ndarray dictionary 74

Creating a DataFrame from a structured array or a record array..........76

Creating a DataFrame from a list of dictionaries......................79

Creating a DataFrame from a list of Data Classes......................80

Creating a DataFrame from a list of Named Tuples 81

MultiIndex DataFrame......................81

Creating a MultiIndex DataFrame from a dictionary of tuples 82

Conclusion 85

Questions......................85

4. **Day 2 - Working within a DataFrame, Basic Functionalities** **87**

Structure 87

Objective......................88

Viewing Data 88

Direct printing of the DataFrame values......................88

The head() and tail() methods 91

Selection 92

Selection by Subsetting......................92

Subsetting by index or by position......................93

Indexing Operators and Indexers......................95

loc[ ] – Selection by Labels......................98

iloc[ ] – Selection by location 100

Indexer ix[ ]......................101

at[] and iat[] – Selection by value......................102

Selection on dtype 102

Filtering 104

The Boolean condition......................104

Filtering on the lines 105

Filtering on columns 107

Application of multiple conditions 108

Boolean reductions 110

Filtering with isin() 112

Editing114

Adding, inserting, and deleting a column in a DataFrame..................114

Adding, inserting, and deleting a row in a DataFrame 118

Adding new columns with assign() 123

Descriptive Statistics..125

The describe() method 125

Calculation of individual statistics..128

The standardization of data...130

Transposition, Sorting, and Reindexing...131

Transposition 131

Sorting...132

Sorting by label 133

Sorting by values..135

Reindexing..137

Reindexing using another DataFrame as a reference 140

Conclusion 141

Questions..142

5. **Day 3 - Working within a DataFrame, Advanced Functionalities............145**

Structure...145

Objective...146

Shifting..146

The shift() method 146

Reshape..149

The stack() and unstack() methods 149

Pivoting..153

Iteration 154

Iteration with for loops...155

Methods of iteration 158

Application of Functions on a Dataframe.......................................162

The levels of operability of the functions 162

Applying NumPy functions directly on DataFrame............................163

Applying functions with the apply () method...................................164

Applications of functions with the pipe() method 167

Chaining pipe() and apply() methods..169

Applying functions with arguments with the pipe() method................171

The applymap() and map() methods...172

Transforming 173

The transform() method...173

Transform() does not aggregate elements......................................176

Transform() works with a single column at a time.........................177

Aggregation..178

The agg() method 178

Grouping 181

The groupby() method 181

The groupby() method for indexes 185

Grouping with Transformation 187

Grouping with Aggregation 188

Apply() with groupby() 189

Categorization..189

Specifying a category column 190

Conclusion 193

Questions...194

6. **Day 4 - Working with Two or More DataFrames 197**

Structure..197

Objective..197

Add data to a DataFrame 198

The append() method 199

Appending multiple Series 202

The concat() function 202

Concatenations between DataFrame and Series that are not

homogeneous 204

Multiple concatenations 205

Joining between two DataFrames 206

The merge() method 206

The LEFT Join 207

The RIGHT Join...208

The OUTER Join...209

The INNER Join...209

Arithmetic with DataFrames...210

Two homogeneous DataFrames as operands 210

Two non-homogeneous DataFrames as operands.......................212

Operations between a DataFrame and a Series.......................214

Flexible binary arithmetic methods..216

Flexible binary methods and arithmetic operators.................217

Differences between arithmetic operators and flexible binary methods...
219

Arithmetic operations between subsets of the same DataFrame.........224

Arithmetic operations between subsets of different DataFrames.......225

The relative binary methods...227

Boolean operations 228

Boolean operations between two DataFrames 229

Flexible Boolean binary methods......................................230

Aligning on DataFrames 231

The align() method...231

Aligning with the Join modalities 232

Conclusion 235

7. Day 5 - Working with Data Sources and Real-World Datasets..............**237**

Structure..238

Objective..238

Files as external data sources..238

Read and write data from files in CSV format 239

Preview of the content being written to file 242

Some optional to_csv() parameters 243

Read and Write Microsoft Excel File 244

Read data from HTML pages on the web 247

Read and write data from XML files......................................250

Read and Write data in JSON 257

Write and read data in binary format 260

Final thoughts on saving data to file 262

Interact with databases for data exchange 262

SQLite installation...263

Creation of test data on SQLite....................................264

Other data sources 266

Working with Time Data 267

    Date Times 267

    Time Deltas 273

    Create arrays of time values 276

    Import Date Time values from file..279

Working with Text Data 281

    The methods of correcting the characters of the string........284

    Methods for splitting strings...287

    Methods for concatenating columns of text 289

    Separate alphanumeric from numeric characters in a column 290

    Adding characters to the rows of a column 293

    Recognition methods between alphanumeric and numeric characters....

    294

    Searching methods in strings..295

Conclusion 296

8. Day 6 - Troubleshooting Challenges with Real Datasets 299

Structure..299

Objective..300

Handling Missing Data...300

    How NaNs are formed 301

    Other operations that generate NaN.....................................304

Working with Missing values 308

    Find and count the missing values...308

    Drop missing values...309

    Filling in of Missing Values..310

    Fill Forward or Backward..311

    Interpolate 313

    Conversion of data types in the presence of NaN 314

Other common operations for correcting newly imported DataFrame 317

    Data Replacing...318

    Data Duplicated...319

    Renaming Axis Indexes 321

Tidy Data...325

    Methods for inversion of Stacked Data 326

Example with the stack() method 327

Example with the melt() method 329

Columns that contain values, not variables...330

Several variables in the same column 331

Columns that contain multiple variables 334

Variables in both rows and columns...336

Groups of Variables in the columns..338

Names of columns with multiple variables 339

Conclusion 342

9. Day 7 – Data Visualization and Reporting...345

Structure..345

Objective..346

Matplotlib..346

Making a Line Plot with Matplotlib..347

Making a Scatter Plot 350

Making a Bar Chart 353

Making a Pie Chart 354

Making a Box Plot..356

Using the data in a DataFrame with Matplotlib................................357

Introduction to Seaborn..369

Reporting...376

Data Profiling and Reporting..377

Reporting in HTML and PDF 380

Conclusion 384

10. Beyond Pandas 387

Structure..387

Objective..388

Where to learn more about Pandas?..388

The official Pandas documentation..388

Participate in the development of the Pandas library...................389

What can you learn after Pandas? 390

The Data Scientist...391

The knowledge of the Data Scientist...392

The Task of a Data Scientist 392

The goals of a Data Scientist..392

Data Scientist and R...392

Statistical analysis with StatsModels 393

Machine Learning with Scikit-learn 394

Image Processing and Deep Learning 396

Big Data 398

The Data Engineer, a new professional figure 400

Conclusion 400

Questions..400

Index **403**

CHAPTER 1
Pandas, the Python Library

Before starting to work directly with seven chapters in seven days, it would be beneficial to introduce the Pandas library. In this chapter, you will see how this library developed in Python – one of the most successful programming languages – was born, and then in a few simple words, we will summarize what it is for and what it does.

Pandas is designed specifically for data analysis and is intricately linked to this discipline. So, in this chapter, you will be shown a brief overview of the steps that involve data processing and data analysis in general. These concepts will be resumed in the following chapters with practical examples.

Structure

In this chapter, we will cover the following topics:

- A bit of history
- Why use Pandas (and Python) for data analysis?
- Data analysis
- Tabular form of data

Objective

After studying this chapter, you will have an overview of how the Pandas library can serve in data analysis, on what type of data it works (a tabular form of data), and what are its strengths that have made it a great success in these recent years, making it an indispensable tool.

A bit of history

In 2008, developer **Wes McKinney**, employed at AQR Capital Management (a global investment management company based in Connecticut (USA)), began work on creating a tool that would allow quantitative analysis to be performed on financial data. In those years, there was already an excellent development of projects on R, a programming language designed to carry out statistical analyzes, and many companies made extensive use of the commercial software based on the use of macros or scripting on data spreadsheets (spreadsheets such as Microsoft Excel).

But McKinney was looking for something new. The R language was quite difficult for the layman and took an enormous time to learn. As for the commercial software, these had a cost and were also very limited to their basic functionality. The Python language was emerging in the scientific environment, a very flexible and easy-to-learn programming language. Python was free, easy to learn, and could virtually interface with anything – thanks to the integration of many modules and libraries in continuous development.

Already in 2009, McKinney had in hand a module of functions and new data structures that formed the prototype of a library that would later become Pandas. Before leaving the company he worked for, he managed to convince the management to grant the open-source right to the library. And in 2012, another McKinney colleague at AQR Capital Management joined the project, Chang She, to become the second-largest contributor to the bookstore.

Figure 1.1 shows in sequence, significant events in the history of the Pandas library:

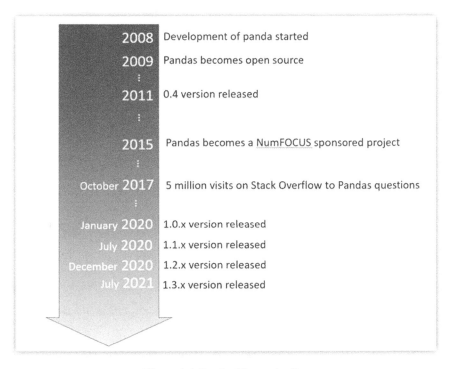

Figure 1.1: *Pandas library timeline*

Thus, was born the **pandas** module, a specific Python library for data analysis. The goal was to provide the Python developers with efficient data structures and all the functionality necessary to carry out the data analysis activities with this language in the best possible way.

The choice of using the tabular form as structured data (like spreadsheets) and integrating functionalities similar to those used by the SQL language to manipulate and generate database tables, was the key to the success of this library. Much of the functionality of the R language and macros available in commercial software were implemented in Python and integrated into the **pandas** library, making it an even more powerful and flexible tool.

The choice to use Python as a programming language allows you to take advantage of many libraries that greatly expand the scope of application of our analysis projects. One of these libraries is for example the NumPy library. This powerful tool for scientific computing, once integrated into the project, allowed the implementation of indexing and element selection tools with high performance, compensating in a good part of the computational speed problems of the Python language compared to other programming languages, such as C and Fortran.

Figure 1.2 shows how choosing a Python library like Pandas allows you to take advantage of many other technologies, such as NumPy:

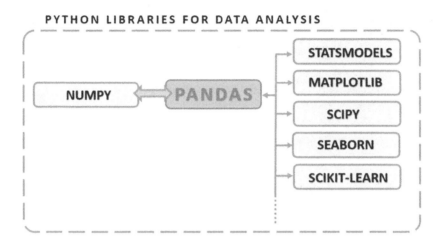

Figure 1.2: *Pandas and other Python libraries for data analysis*

In 2017, because of the great diffusion of Python in academic and professional environments, there was a growth of interest in the **pandas** library and its potential, becoming a reference tool for all those involved in the data analysis sector. Moreover, it was precisely in those years that we began to talk about Data Science almost everywhere.

Taking advantage of the wave of success, **pandas** have developed enormously in recent years, resulting in the release of numerous versions, thanks to the contribution of more and more developers.

Today, many data scientists in the major private companies that analyze data (Google, Facebook, JP Morgan) use Pandas. This library is, therefore, the perfect tool for data analysis – powerful, flexible, easy to understand, can be integrated with many other libraries, and is, therefore, an indispensable tool to know.

The Pandas library is the free software developed under 3-Clause BSD License, also known as Modified BSD License, and all releases and documentation are freely available and can be consulted on the official website (**https://pandas.pydata.org/**).

Why use Pandas (and Python) for data analysis?

As shown earlier, the choice of using Python as the programming language for developing Pandas has led to the undisputed success of this library. Since its first appearance in 1991, Python has spread almost exponentially, becoming today one of the most used programming languages. The merit of this is due precisely to the great flexibility of this language and its ability to integrate libraries into its code that have extended its applicability to many areas of work.

In this section, we will see in detail the following factors that led to choosing Pandas and the Python language as a tool for data analysis and data science in general:

- A trust gained over the years
- A flexible language that adapts to any context
- Automation, reproducibility, and interaction

A trust gained over the years

As for data analysis, thanks to the **pandas** library, Python soon entered into competition with other programming languages and analysis software such as R, Stata, SAS, and MATLAB. Python, however, being a free product, has spread easily, and due to its enormous potential, it has been able to gain wide trust from all the users. Although at first it was seen as a tool for "do-it-yourself" calculation, over the years, Python has proven to guarantee excellent results and be a valid tool in both the academic and the industrial fields. In fact, today Python enjoys the utmost confidence in the world of data science, and this is largely due to libraries such as Pandas, which have guaranteed its feasibility, providing all the necessary tools to carry out a work of analysis and calculation of the highest level, at virtually no cost.

A flexible language that adapts to any context

In many organizations, it is common to find projects or processes in which several programming languages or calculation software are involved at the same time. Since they work strictly in specific fields (sometimes too specific), each of them must be applied only to one or more steps of data processing. But they never manage to cover the entire structure of a project.

Therefore, to start a project, it is necessary to set up a certain number of development and work environments, in addition to developing interfaces or ways of exchanging information and data between them.

But why keep so many works and development environments when just one might be more than enough? It is at this point that Python takes over, a language so flexible that it adapts to many applications and can be used in many areas. In more and more organizations, this language has gradually replaced all pre-existing technologies (web server, calculation, programming, notebooks, algorithms, data visualization tools, and so on) unifying them under a single language.

Automation, reproducibility, and interaction

Pandas is a library based on a programming language. But why not instead choose an application that has already been developed, tested, and therefore, does not require development and programming skills? By choosing Pandas, you will find yourself forced to deal with the programming activities that require time and skills, however simple and intuitive programming in Python can be. So, why choose Pandas?

It is a question of automation, reproducibility, and interaction. Programming languages are gradually replacing large applications that offer everything ready and tested. Applications are environments, even though they are powerful, feature-rich, narrow, and fixed. In fact, they can offer thousands of features, but often never a one that fits your needs completely.

Choosing a programming language, you leave a free hand to those who use it. In this case, the developer or data scientist will choose and develop a work environment that will fully meet their needs. Python provides a large number of libraries, full of ready-made tools, thus, allowing it to work even at a high level, with algorithms and procedures already implemented within. Therefore, the data scientist will be free to use ready-made tools by integrating them into their personal work environment.

Large applications with ready-made work environments require the continuous presence of a user who interacts with them, selecting items, entering values, and performing continuous checks on the results to then choose how to continue the analysis and processing of the data. Pandas, being a library of programming languages, is instead a perfect automation tool. Everything can be automated. Once the procedure is established, you can convert everything into lines of code that can be executed as many times as you want. Furthermore, given that the operations, choices, and data management will be carried out by programs that strictly follow the commands read from lines of code, and not from real-time operations by humans, reproducibility will also be guaranteed.

But why then choose Python and not another programming language like Java or C++?

Python is a language that differs from the latter in that it is an interpreter language. The developed code does not need to be written in the form of complete programs, which then must be compiled to run. The Python code can also run one line at a time and see how the system responds to each of them, and depending on the result, make decisions or modify the following code. You could then interact with the data analysis process. So, the interaction has been added, which is one of the aspects that has made the use of software and applications advantageous compared to programming languages.

Data Analysis

With the previous two sections, you will have become aware of the qualities that make Pandas and Python an indispensable tool for data analysis. The next step is to take a quick look at what the latter is. In the following section, we will have a quick overview of data analysis and some concepts that will then serve to better understand the purpose of many features in the Pandas library.

What is data analysis?

Data analysis can be defined as the disciplinary area in which a series of techniques are applied to collect, handling, and process a series of data. The ultimate goal will be to obtain the necessary information from these data in order to draw conclusions and support decision-making.

Therefore, using calculation techniques and tools, we will start with the raw data extracted from the real world, which will undergo manipulations (cleaning, sorting, processing, statistics, views) in order to gradually convert them into useful information for the purpose set at the beginning of the analysis. The objective of the analysis will, therefore, be to evaluate hypotheses, validating or refuting them (scientific world), or to provide information to be able to make decisions (especially in the business and financial world).

Thus, it is clear that data analysis is a fundamental tool for the academic environment, and more so for the business environment, where making correct decisions can be very important for investments.

The data scientist

Given the importance of data analysis, more elaborate techniques and tools have developed over time, hand-in-hand with the development of information technologies. With the increase in the amount of data available, the use of increasingly powerful and efficient tools becomes indispensable.

Today, the tools in this area are many, offering multiple possible approaches to the development of a data analysis environment. It is, therefore, up to the data scientist to choose the right tools among the various technologies available that can meet the objectives set for the analysis.

The data scientist, in addition to having the skills related to calculation techniques and data analysis processing, must also have a broad knowledge of all the available technologies that will allow him to set up a good work environment, essential to obtain the desired results.

This professional figure is gradually taking shape in the last 5 years, becoming increasingly important in many areas of work.

The analysis process

However, regardless of the choices of the technologies or tools used, there are general lines on which the data analysis process is based. The data scientist, or anyone who needs to carry out data analysis, must be clear about the main steps into which the data processing technique is divided.

Therefore, to better understand the aims of the **pandas** library, it is important to broadly know how a typical data analysis process develops. Once the structure of the process is clear, it will be easy to understand where and when to apply the different methods and functions that the **pandas** library offers.

In *Figure 1.3*, the main steps that make up the data analysis process are shown:

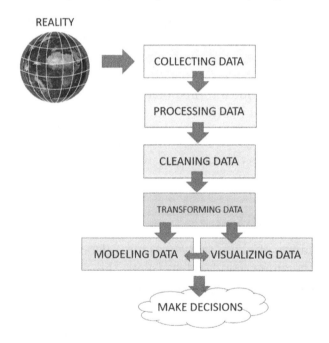

Figure 1.3: *The various steps of the data analysis process*

As shown in *Figure 1.3*, there is a precise sequence of operations that make up the data analysis process. Let's see every single step in detail, as follows:

- **Data collection**: Once you have assessed the nature of the necessary data (numbers, text, images, sounds, and so on) and the characteristics required to meet the objectives of our data analysis, we proceed with the collection.

The data sources can be most varied. There are organizations that make a lot of data available online, already partially processed and organized, but the data are not always so easy to find. Sometimes, it is necessary to extract raw data such as fractions of text, the content of web pages, images, and audio files. And therefore, it will be important to prepare a whole series of procedures and technologies to extract the data from these heterogeneous sources to be collected and subsequently processed. Lately, with the advent of the **Internet of Things (IoT)**, there is an increase in the data acquired and released by devices and sensors.

- **Data processing**: The collected data, even if in part already processed, are still raw data. Data from different sources could have varied formats and certainly be internally structured differently. It is, therefore, essential to make the data obtained as homogeneous as possible, converting them all into the same format, and then processing them to collect them together in a structured form more suited to us. As for Pandas and other data analysis technologies and relational databases, the data will be collected by typology through a tabular structure – a table formed by rows and columns, where often the data will be distributed on columns that identify particular characteristics, while on the rows will be the collected samples.

- **Data cleaning**: Even though the collected data has been processed and organized in a structured form suited to us, such as a tabular data structure, they are not yet ready for data analysis. In fact, the data will almost certainly be incomplete, with empty parts, or contain duplicates or errors. The data cleaning operation is, therefore, required in which you must manage, correct errors where possible, and integrate the missing data with appropriate values. This phase is often the most underestimated, but it is also the one that can later lead to misleading conclusions.

- **Transforming data**: Once the data has been cleaned, integrated, and corrected, it can finally be analyzed. It is in this phase that the actual data analysis is concentrated. Here, the analyst has at his disposal a multitude of techniques to manipulate structured data, acting both on the structure itself and elaborating new values from those already present. Everything must be aimed at focusing the data or at least preparing them to be able to extract the useful information you are looking for. At this point in the process, it may be obvious to the analyst that the data obtained at the time may not be sufficient or not suitable. You will then have to go back to the previous steps of the process to search for new data sources, delete useless information, or recover the previously deleted data.

- **Modeling data**: The previous step is aimed at extracting information that must then be enclosed in a model. The mathematical, conceptual, or decision-making model will be based on hypotheses that can be evaluated here, thanks to the information extracted during the data analysis. The model can, therefore, be validated or refuted, or at least its knowledge be increased, so as to decide whether to return to the analysis in the previous steps to deepen the model and extract new information or start with a new analysis or definitively close the process of analysis and make decisions directly.

- **Data Visualization**: The data modeling process often needs to be assisted with data visualization. The data are often reported in very large quantities, and it will be very difficult for the analyst to identify the characteristics (trends, clusters, various statistics, and other characteristics) that are hidden inside by reading only rows and columns. Even reporting and evaluating the results of statistical processing often runs the risk of losing the bulk of the information. The human being has a greater ability to extract information from graphic diagrams and, therefore, it is essential to combine the analysis process with good visualization of the data.

Tabular form of data

You saw in the previous section that data must be processed in order to be structured in tabular form. The **pandas** library also has structured data within it that follow this particular form of ordering the individual data. But, why this data structure? In this section, we will see how to answer this question, introducing the following topics.

Tabular form of data

From my point of view, I could say that the tabular format has always been the most used method to arrange and organize data. Whether for historical reasons or for a natural predisposition of human rationality to arrange the data in the form of a table, we find the tabular format historically in the collection of the first scientific data written by hand in previous centuries, and in the accountants' accounts of the first merchants and banks, which in current technologies have internal database tables storing terabytes of data. Even calendars, recipe ingredients, and other simple things in everyday life follow this structure.

The tabular format is simply the information presented in the form of a table with rows and columns, where the data is divided and sorted following the classification logic established by the headings on the rows and columns.

But it is not just a historical question. The reason for the widespread use of this form of organizing data is mainly due to the characteristics that make it ideal for calculating, organizing, and manipulating a large amount of data. They are also easily readable and understandable, even for those with no analysis experience.

It is no coincidence that most of the software used in offices makes use of tools for entering, calculating, and saving data in tabular form. A classic example is spreadsheets, of which the most popular of all is Microsoft Excel.

Spreadsheets

A spreadsheet is an application on a computer whose purpose is to organize, analyze, and store data in tabular form. Spreadsheets are nothing more than the digital evolution of paper worksheets. Accountants once collected all the data in large ledgers full of printouts, from which they extracted the accounts. Even the goods in a warehouse were recorded in paper registers made up of rows and columns, in which dates, costs, and various descriptions were reported.

Such a tool has followed the evolution of the times, becoming an office software like spreadsheets, of which the most famous version is precisely Microsoft Excel.

Spreadsheets are programs that operate on data entered in cells within different tables. Each cell can contain both numbers and text strings. With appropriate formulas, you can perform calculations between values contained in areas of selected cells and automatically show the result in another cell. By modifying the values in the operand cells, the value in the cell intended for the result will also be modified in real-time. Spreadsheets, compared to paper worksheets, in addition to organizing the data in tabular form, introduce a certain degree of interaction, in which the user is able to select the data visually, insert calculation formulas, and view the results in real-time.

Figure 1.4 shows how Spreadsheets are the digital evolution of Paper Worksheets, adding new useful properties:

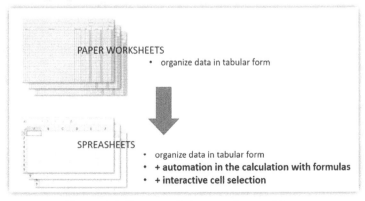

Figure 1.4: *Paper worksheets and spreadsheets*

The leap forward was enormous, while retaining the tabular structure.

SQL tables from databases

Another technology that has enormously marked the evolution of data management is relational databases. Spreadsheets share many features with databases, but they are not quite the same. A table extracted from an SQL query from a database can somewhat resemble a spreadsheet. Not surprisingly, spreadsheets can be used to import large amounts of data into a database and a table can be exported from the database in the form of a spreadsheet. But the similarities end there.

Database tables are often the result of an SQL query, which is a series of SQL language statements that allow you to extract, select, and transform the data contained within a database, modifying its format and its original structure to get a data table. Therefore, while the spreadsheets introduce excellent calculation tools applicable to the various areas of the data table, the SQL tables are the result of a complex series of manipulations carried out on original data, based on selections of data of interest from a vast amount of data.

Figure 1.5 shows how the SQL Tables started from the characteristics present in the Paper Worksheets, to adapt to relational databases, showing new and powerful properties:

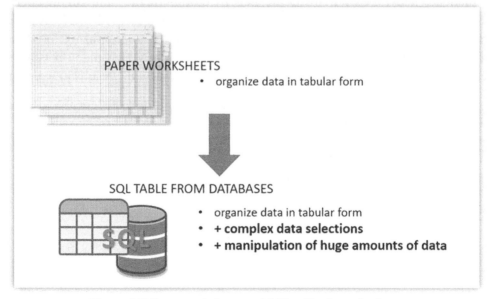

Figure 1.5: *Paper worksheets and SQL tables form databases*

Pandas and Dataframes

The idea of being able to treat data in memory as if it were an SQL table is incredibly captivating. Likewise, selectively interacting on data selections by applying formulas and calculations as is done with spreadsheets can make the tabular data management powerful.

Well, the **pandas** library introduced DataFrames as structured data, which makes all this possible. These objects that are the basis of data analysis with Pandas, have an internal tabular structure and are the evolution of the two previous technologies. By combining the calculation features of spreadsheets and the way of working of SQL languages, they provide a new and powerful tool for data analysis.

Furthermore, by exploiting the characteristics of the Python language discussed in the previous sections, we also add aspects of automation, flexibility, interaction, and ease of integration with other technologies, which the two previous technologies only partially cover.

Figure 1.6 shows how many fundamental properties of Spreadsheets and SQL Tables can be found in the DataFrame, the main data structures of the Pandas library:

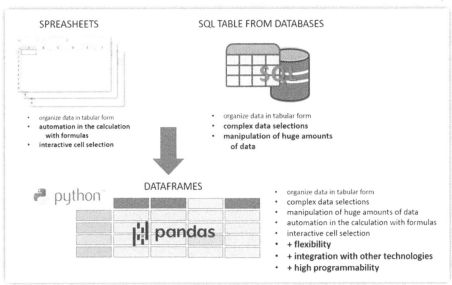

Figure 1.6: *Pandas take the best of all technologies*

By introducing the DataFrame, Pandas make it possible to analyze data quickly and intuitively. We will resume the DataFrame in *Chapter 3, (Day 1) Data Structures in Pandas Library* deepening the characteristics of this type of object, and we will see how to create and manage them in the Python language with a series of practical examples.

Conclusion

In this chapter, we had a quick overview of some fundamental concepts that will be useful to fully understand the **pandas** library. The general framework that is deduced will help contextualize the various topics introduced in the following chapters. In fact, each chapter will cover a series of topics that can be included in the practice of data analysis in one or more steps of the process. It is, therefore, clear that it is important for the reader to keep in mind the general scheme of a typical process of data analysis.

Pandas is a Python library, and therefore, it is essential to have at least a knowledge of how it came about, and why it was built with this programming language. That's why we talked about this language in a few lines, and how it has contributed enormously to the success and spread of this library.

Pandas are designed to be powerful and efficient tools. Taking up the concepts of data in tabular form, spreadsheet, and database with their SQL tables, we tried to highlight what are the characteristics that make it so. It is important to understand how it was born and what reasons led to its realization in this form.

In the next chapter, we will learn how to set up a work environment that best suits the data analysis activity with Python and Pandas. We will also learn how to install different tools and various development environments including the Anaconda distribution and Notebook Jupyter.

References

Meet the man behind the most important tool in data science (https://qz.com/1126615/ the-story-of-the-most-important-tool-in-data-science/)

CHAPTER 2
Setting up a Data Analysis Environment

Before proceeding further with the chapters that specifically deal with the Pandas library, it will be beneficial to have a work environment to develop the examples given in the book and practice. In this chapter, we will deal with the installation part of Pandas and other libraries used in the book and the setting up of an appropriate work environment – as appropriate as possible to the data analysis activity. In this regard, various possibilities will be illustrated, which the reader can choose from according to their tastes and availability. In particular, Anaconda will be shown, a specific distribution for data analysis, which allows you to install a work environment quickly and practically with Python, Pandas, and all the other tools necessary on almost all platforms available today (Windows, Apple , Linux).

Structure

In this chapter, we will cover the following topics:

- The basic procedure
- Anaconda
- Working online on development environments: Replit

Objective

After studying this chapter, you will have a complete environment not only for carrying out the examples in this book, but also a workspace for carrying out any data analysis tasks with Pandas and Python.

Furthermore, during the installation of the various components, you will become familiar with the concepts of package and environment managing, essential for working efficiently on multiple projects at the same time.

Finally, you will have the possibility of being able to choose different possibilities, including Anaconda, a powerful distribution specific for data scientists, the rudimentary installation of individual packages, and the possibility of working completely remotely without having to perform any installation.

The basic procedure

In this section, we will learn the basic procedure in which all installations will be carried out individually and manually without using specific tools. In this case, the development environment that we will create will be highly generic and basic.

Installing Python

Pandas is a library developed to work with the Python language, and therefore, you will first need to install the Python language in our PC, and then, subsequently Pandas and the other libraries covered in the book. At the time of writing this book, the latest version of Python released was 3.9, although updates of previous versions such as 3.8, 3.7, and 3.6 are also released in parallel.

Python 3.x vs Python 2.7

At present, there are still many references to the Python 2.7 version both in the literature and in many examples distributed on the Internet. Despite this spread, the Python 2.7 version is no longer supported as of 2020. It is, therefore, a good practice to consider Python 3.x versions. All new versions of the data analysis and scientific computing libraries have been released for this version, and it is unthinkable not to use this version. All the examples in this book refer to Pandas 1.3 and Python 3.8 or higher.

Python can be installed in a multitude of ways. The most rudimentary method is to go on the official website of this programming language (https://www.python.org/) and download the latest release available, as shown in *Figure 2.1*:

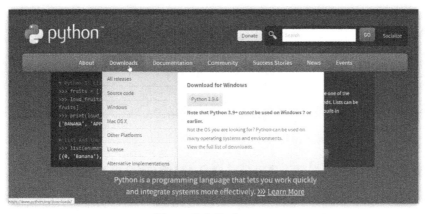

***Figure 2.1:** Python.org*

By loading the main page on the browser, it is generally suggested to download the installer corresponding to the platform used, with the latest released version of Python. You can download the installer on your PC and then run it. Otherwise, from the menu, you can choose the desired operating system – Windows, Mac OS X, or other, (Python releases are already integrated in Linux) – and download the installer, which once executed, will install all the basic tools for the program in Python on our PC.

When you click on the installer, a window similar to the one shown in *Figure 2.2* will appear on the screen:

***Figure 2.2:** Python Installer on Windows*

Once Python is installed, you can open the Python shell, where you can enter the Python commands line-by-line interactively, or use the IDLE to develop programs with several lines of code to run all together, as shown in *Figure 2.3:*

Figure 2.3: Python Shell

Installing Pandas and the other libraries

Now that we have Python on our computer, we just need to start installing the Pandas library. To do this, we need **pip**, a tool made available by **PyPI**, **The Python Package Index** (https://pypi.org/), which is nothing more than the online repository where all the libraries importable on Python are present, including Pandas.

From the command line of your operating system, run the following command:

On Windows:

py -m pip install pandas

On Mac OS:

python3 -m pip install pandas

Immediately, the downloading of Pandas and dependencies (other libraries necessary for its operation) like NumPy will start, as shown in *Figure 2.4* (you won't need to install it separately):

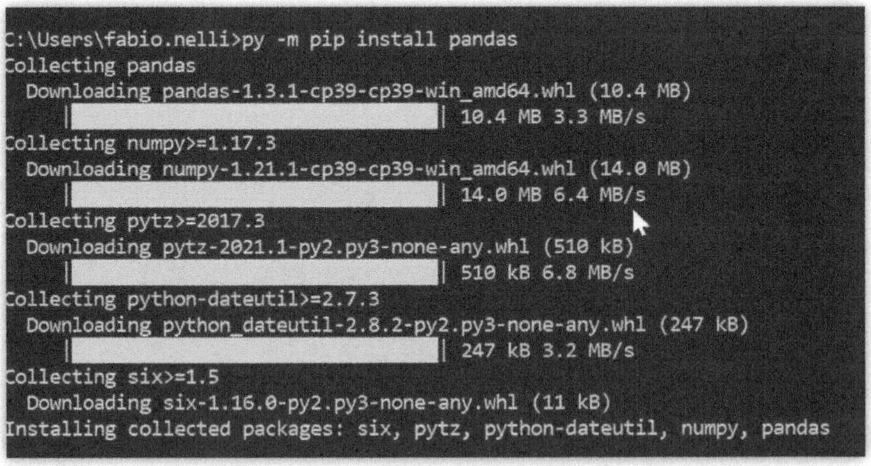

Figure 2.4: Pandas installation

We will do the same thing with the matplotlib and seaborn graphics libraries, as shown as follows:

On Windows:

```
py -m pip install matplotlib
py -m pip install seaborn
```

On Mac OS:

```
python3 -m pip install matplotlib
python3 -m pip install seaborn
```

To check if everything went well, open the Python console, and run the following command:

On Windows:

```
py
```

On Mac OS:

```
python3
```

Next, we will import the three newly installed libraries, as follows:

```
>>> import pandas
```

```
>>> import matplotlib
```

```
>>> import seaborn
```

If you do not receive error messages, the installation of the three libraries will have gone correctly, as shown in *Figure 2.5*:

```
C:\Users\fabio.nelli>py
Python 3.9.6 (tags/v3.9.6:db3ff76, Jun 28 2021, 15:26:21) [MSC v.1929 64 bit (AMD64)] on win32
Type "help", "copyright", "credits" or "license" for more information.
>>> import pandas
>>> import matplotlib
>>> import seaborn
>>>
```

Figure 2.5: import libraries in Python shell

Installing Jupyter Notebooks

Now, the next step is to install Jupyter. The installation of **Jupyter Notebooks** is really simple, because it does not differ at all from any other library. As we did previously for the other libraries, it will be sufficient to enter the following commands via the command line:

On Windows:

```
py -m pip install jupyter
```

On Mac OS:

```
python3 -m pip install jupyter
```

The download of all the necessary packages, both Jupyter and the dependencies, will start immediately, and then the installation will begin.

As for the use of Jupyter, we will see it in detail in the following section. However, if you don't want to wait, you can check **jupyter** online, without installing it on your computer. Go to the page **https://jupyter.org/try**.

Considerations

However, this basic form of installation can be useful for those who want to work from scratch and for simple programming that requires the development of small programs in Python. For those who work in the professional field, they must work in environments that make development and analysis more comfortable and provide the management tools that facilitate the management of activities as much as possible. For those who want to work with data analysis, it is advisable to work with Anaconda. In the following section, we will see what Anaconda is, and how to install it on your system.

Anaconda

Anaconda (https://www.anaconda.com/) is an open-source distribution specifically designed to be used in data analysis. Distributed by Continuum Analytics, it is available free of charge at a basic level for students, researchers, and individual users (Individual Edition). However, as a professional product, it is sold in different packages (depending on the level of use). The higher editions (paid subscription) provide additional tools such as teamwork, managing a large scale of data, and increasing the performance of work systems.

In the following section, we will learn more about this useful work tool and learn how to install it and set up a development system suitable for our data analysis activity with Pandas.

The Anaconda distribution

Within the Anaconda distribution, you can work with two different programming languages – R and Python. These two languages are, in fact, found to be most suitable for data analysis and other related activities such as Machine Learning.

In our case, we are only interested in the Python part. Furthermore, all the packages used in the book – such as NumPy, Jupyter, and Pandas, but also matplotlib and seaborn – are included in the distribution.

Anaconda is, therefore, the most suitable tool for those who want to practice data analysis with Python, in particular with the Pandas library. Furthermore, becoming familiar with this environment, and its development and analysis tools is crucial for those who want to undertake the profession of data scientist.

In fact, Anaconda, in addition to providing a development and analysis environment in Python in an easy and intuitive way, also provides other tools that help the data scientist in the following ways:

- The management of packages and libraries to be installed
- Scientific and statistical calculation
- Large-scale data processing
- Predictive analysis

In fact, it includes many tools for machine learning.

Installing Anaconda

Opening a browser and loading the **Anaconda Individual Edition** download page (HTTPS://WWW.ANACONDA.COM/PRODUCTS/INDIVIDUAL), you will be suggested the most suitable installer for your system, as shown in *Figure 2.6*:

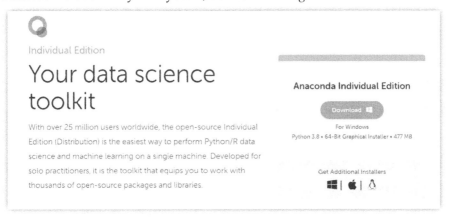

Figure 2.6: Anaconda Individual Edition download page

But if it's not what you are looking for, you can search the website to find the distribution that best matches your needs, choosing the particular operating system (MacOS, Linux, or Windows), the system bits (32 or 64 bit), and the version of Python you want to work with.

Installing Anaconda on Linux systems

On Linux, the installation must be done manually by downloading an executable file such as `Anaconda3-2021.05-Linux-x86_64.sh`. Once this is downloaded, it will need to be launched from the shell.

It will ask you to confirm the location where you want to install all the files. In my case, it is the following:

```
~ / anaconda3
```

The installation will take a few minutes, after which, you will have all the same tools available on other platforms within the directory.

For example, to launch the Anaconda navigator, enter the following commands:

```
cd ~ / anaconda3
./anaconda-navigator
```

The graphics application will open on the screen.

Once you have found the installer corresponding to the system you are working on, perform the installation. Once the Anaconda installation is complete, you will find a series of applications on your PC. To get an overview of all the tools that the Anaconda distribution has to offer, launch **Anaconda Navigator**. A screen will appear in which the available applications will be shown depending on the edition level you have chosen, as shown in *Figure 2.7*. Here, you can decide to install the ones that will be most convenient for your business, and then once installed, launch them individually:

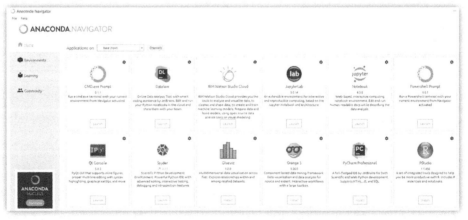

Figure 2.7: *Anaconda Navigator for Individual Edition*

Once the application is open, you will find yourself on the Home screen. As you can see in *Figure 2.7*, there are a good series of applications in the Individual Edition that will be useful for data analysis and development of projects with Python and Pandas, including Jupyter Notebook. In addition, there are other applications for developing programs in Python such as Spyder and other specific tools for data analysis and visualization.

In addition, in the Anaconda Navigator, you can select other screens, as shown in *Figure 2.8*:

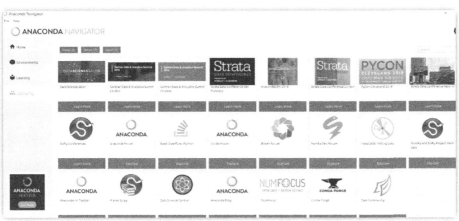

Figure 2.8: *Anaconda Navigator – Community Panel*

In particular, in the **Individual Edition**, you can navigate a real package manager in the **Environments** screen; in the Learning screen, you will find the tutorials and courses where you can learn the topics covered by Anaconda; and in the Community screen (shown in *Figure 2.8*), there are many links to connect to forums, events and particular sites where you can exchange information and actively participate in the Python data analytics community.

Conda and the Anaconda command line shell

In addition to Anaconda Navigator, which is an excellent visual tool to be able to launch and install the various applications in the distribution, there is also Conda.

Conda is the real package manager that underlies the distribution and is a very useful tool for the following:

- Python package management
- Management of work environments

Both of these activities will be very useful for our work, and for this reason, we will dwell on these aspects, deepening them further, in order to guarantee you the tools to be able to work in the best way.

Conda is an application that is run on the command line through a series of commands that perform various operations. We temporarily leave the graphical environment and launch the Anaconda command line prompt. You can do this from Anaconda Navigator by clicking on the appropriate application on the HOME screen, as shown in *Figure 2.9*:

Figure 2.9: *Icon for launching CMD.exe from Anaconda Navigator*

By pressing the **Launch** button under the corresponding icon, a shell will open which integrates all the Anaconda tools, including **conda**, from which you can run all the command lines of distribution, as shown in *Figure 2.10*:

```
C:\windows\system32\cmd.exe

Microsoft Windows [Versione 10.0.19041.1110]
(c) Microsoft Corporation. Tutti i diritti sono riservati.

(base) C:\Users\nelli>
```

Figure 2.10: *CMD.exe prompt*

Creating and managing environments with Conda

Once you open the shell to enter the commands that we will need for our operations, you will notice that next to the prompt, there is **(base)**. This tells us the environment we are currently working on, which is the default base one.

But what are environments? Well, we can define an environment as a workspace in which a particular version of Python and a set of packages with certain versions can be set up in isolation without interfering in the least with the basic work environment (that of Operating System).

Having different environments allows us to work simultaneously with different work environments, each set up independently and differently (with different versions of Python and packages installed) without creating conflicts between the different versions (and dependencies) and without ever running the risk of overwriting.

Working with multiple environments in this way allows us to develop certain projects, which often relate to a certain version of Python, or which use certain versions of packages.

Furthermore, the environments created with **conda** can then be saved, cloned, and even exported to be used on other systems in order to simplify the reproducibility of the analysis methods developed, regardless of where we work.

So, in addition to the basic environment, it is possible to create new ones, thanks to **conda**. On the command shell, enter the following command to create a new environment that we will call **mypandas**:

```
(base) > conda create --name mypandas
```

The system will carry out a series of checks, and then will ask for confirmation to proceed, as follows:

```
Proceed ([y]/n)? y


Preparing transaction: done
Verifying transaction: done
Executing transaction: done
```

We can know all the environments present on our Anaconda distribution by entering the following command:

```
(base) > conda env list
```

All the environments present on the system will be listed, as follows:

```
# conda environments:
#
base                   *  C:\Users\nelli\anaconda3
mypandas                  C:\Users\nelli\anaconda3\envs\mypandas
```

As you can see, the new environment just created is also present.

Conda – Create an environment with a different Python version

When you are creating environments, a useful option is to create them with different versions of Python. This is possible by specifying the version of Python to use when creating a new environment.

For example, look at the following command:

```
conda create -n myoldpandas python=3.6
```

This will create a new environment based on Python version 3.6.

But we are still working on the basic environment; to work on what we have just created, it is necessary to activate it. To do this, enter the following command:

```
> conda activate mypandas
```

The prompt will now appear as follows:

```
(mypandas) >
```

As you can see from the prefix, you are now working within the new environment.

To exit the environment and return to the basic one, it is necessary to deactivate it. Enter the following command:

```
> conda deactivate
```

At this point, you will return to the default environment, as shown as follows:

```
(base) >
```

Often, after working for a long time on your environment and having enriched it with several packages, the need will arise to create a similar new one. Instead of creating a completely new environment and redoing all the operations, it is possible to clone the already existing one. This way, you will save yourself a lot of work.

To clone an environment already present on your system, enter the following command:

```
> conda create --name mypandas2 --clone mypandas
```

Now, you will have a perfect clone of your environment, as shown as follows:

```
(base) >conda env list
# conda environments:
```

```
#
base                    *   C:\Users\nelli\anaconda3
mypandas                    C:\Users\nelli\anaconda3\envs\mypandas
mypandas2                   C:\Users\nelli\anaconda3\envs\mypandas2
```

Another useful operation is to remove an environment that is no longer practical. This operation is also very simple. Enter the following command:

```
> conda remove --name mypandas2 --all
```

The aforementioned environment will be permanently removed from the system, as shown as follows:

```
(base) >conda env list
# conda environments:
#
base                    *   C:\Users\nelli\anaconda3
mypandas                    C:\Users\nelli\anaconda3\envs\mypandas
```

Conda – Export the environments

When you reach a certain level of activity and join a development team, you will find it necessary to share the environments with others, or load a ready-made one on your system. For this kind of work, **conda** allows you to export and import the environments generated on Anaconda.

To export an environment present on our system, first activate it and then launch the following command:

```
conda env export > mypandas.yml
```

Conda will generate a YML file that will contain all the information needed to reproduce the environment in another environment. A file is a great format to be able to email this information or save it on a USB stick.

To learn more about the subject, I suggest you visit the following official website:

https://conda.io/projects/conda/en/latest/user-guide/tasks/manage-environments. html.

Creating and managing packages (and libraries) with Conda

As mentioned in the introduction of this section, **conda** is not only an environment manager, but also an excellent package manager. In fact, once we have created a work environment, with a certain version of Python, we will still use Conda to install all the packages we need.

In fact, Conda is a valid tool for managing Python packages. Also, through the command line, you can download the different packages available in the distribution, and then install them, and remove them later, when no longer needed. It will be necessary to look for the version of the package that best suits your environment and that which will take care of the different dependencies.

In our case, we will install Pandas and all the libraries covered in the book in our environment **mypandas** created earlier. So, let's activate our environment, as follows:

```
> conda activate mypandas
```

Once the environment is activated, we immediately install the **pandas** library by entering the following command:

```
(mypandas) C:\Users\nelli>conda install pandas
```

A series of information about the package, its version, and dependencies will appear on the screen. It will then ask you for confirmation to proceed with the installation of Pandas, as follows:

```
Proceed ([y]/n)?
```

Press **y** and proceed with the installation. Conda will first download the package and all the dependencies and then move on to the actual installation. The operation will take a few minutes. The Pandas installation will also include the NumPy installation since it is a package necessary for its operation.

If you try to install it later, the following message will appear:

```
(mypandas) C:\Users\nelli>conda install numpy
Collecting package metadata (current_repodata.json): done
Solving environment: done


# All requested packages already installed.
```

Conda will inform you that the library is already installed and present in your environment.

Now, let's take care of installing all the other libraries we will need throughout the book, as follows:

```
(mypandas) > conda install matplotlib


(mypandas > conda install seaborn
```

```
(mypandas > conda install jupyter
```

Now that we have all the necessary packages installed, let's finish by adding some information about the other useful commands for managing the packages with **conda**.

Anaconda is a large distribution and contains many packages, but it may not necessarily contain all of them. If, by chance, during the installation of a particular **conda** package, you cannot find the package in the distribution, you can always install it with **pip**.

Still, within the environment, you can run **pip** to install the package you need, as follows:

```
(mypandas) > pip install package_name
```

Another **conda** command that you require to remove a package that is no longer needed, or incorrectly installed, is given as follows:

```
(mypandas) > conda remove package_name
```

Jupyter Notebook

Jupyter Notebook will be the necessary tool that we will work on throughout the book. This is because it is ideally suited for all data analysis activities. In a Notebook, you can manage the code interactively, seeing the results in real time, and at the same time, adding textual and descriptive parts like in a real workbook.

So, let's get out of the shell and go back to **Anaconda Navigator**. If you have noticed correctly, there is a drop-down menu at the top. Opening it, you will see that there will be a list of all the environments in the distribution, including **mypandas** that we created earlier. Select it and you will see that Anaconda Navigator will show you all the applications installed in this environment, as shown in *Figure 2.11*:

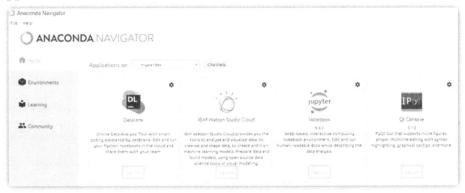

Figure 2.11: mypandas environment in Anaconda Navigator

As you can see, Jupyter Notebook is present in the applications available within the environment. Click on the **Launch** button of Jupyter Notebook to open the application.

A page will open automatically from the browser on your computer. If not, you can load Jupyter Notebook by going to the address `localhost:8888/tree`, as shown in *Figure 2.12*:

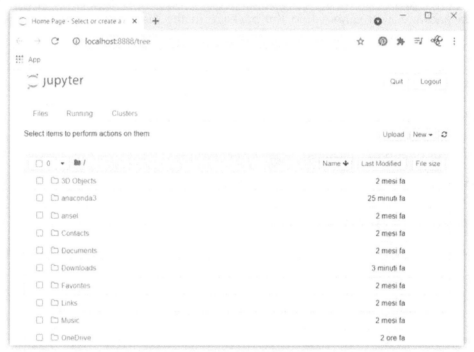

Figure 2.12: Jupyter Dashboard

The starting page is the file system view. This will vary from system to system, depending on which root directory is set on Jupyter. As you can see from the *Figure 2.12*, there is a list of folders that correspond to those in the operating system. Navigate to select the directory where you want to save your Notebook and any attached files.

Creating a Notebook on Jupyter

To create a special directory, click on the **New** button on the right, and from the drop-down menu, select **Folder**, as shown in *Figure 2.13*:

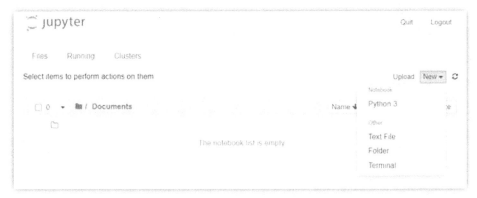

Figure 2.13: Create a folder in Jupyter Notebooks

A new **Untitled Folder** directory will be created. It must, therefore, be renamed. Select the new directory and click on the **Rename** button, as shown in *Figure 2.14*:

Figure 2.14: Rename a folder in Jupyter Notebooks

A dialog box will appear where you can enter the new folder name. Enter myPandas or any other indicative name you prefer, as shown in *Figure 2.15*:

Figure 2.15: Enter the folder name in Jupyter Notebook

Click on the **Rename** button to save.

Now that we have created a directory, we can create a **Notebook** within it. In the list of files, there is the new directory. Click on it to enter. Then, once inside, click on the

New button, and from the drop-down menu that will appear, select **Python 3** under **Notebook**, as shown in *Figure 2.16*:

Figure 2.16: *Create a new Notebook in Jupyter Notebooks*

Immediately, another panel will open on the browser, in which a new page corresponding to the newly created Notebook will be loaded, as shown in *Figure 2.17*:

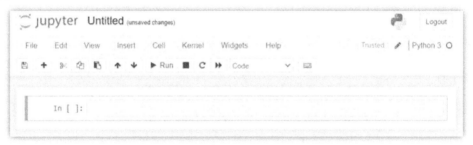

Figure 2.17: *A new Jupyter Notebook*

First steps on a new Jupyter Notebook

The Notebook page is a real development application complete with buttons and workspace. The upper part presents a menu with several buttons, while the lower part has an empty block.

There are two types of blocks in Jupyter Notebooks. One to insert the Python code and one to insert the Markup language formatted text. You can create many blocks of both types, similar to the paragraphs of the pages of a book. Some paragraphs will contain text, in which you will add notes, descriptions, and titles of what you are doing, and others will contain some Python code to execute.

For those who are already familiar with Python, note that the blocks of Jupyter Notebook used for the code correspond to those of IPython and, therefore, inherit the same interactive features.

The users insert pieces of code within a block, which can be executed individually (that is, independently of the other code blocks in the notebook), and directly observe the execution result that will be shown on the document immediately after the block. At this point, the user can continue with the creation of other blocks, and then return later to modify the code in the block and re-execute the single block again, observing the new results.

This interactive method will be essential for those who work with data analysis, since it will often be necessary to retrieve parts of the data and reprocess them as the analysis continues, or to review the previous operations and calculations following the insights received later.

To better understand how it works, let's see some basic operations. For example, the default block that appears in a new notebook is used for code. It can be understood from the text **In [ ]:** present at the beginning. This label, which is the same as in IPython, indicates that the block is in Input (code to be executed), while the space between the empty square brackets indicates that it has not yet been executed.

Write the following commands in it to import the two libraries – Pandas and NumPy – needed to start all our work, as shown in *Figure 2.18*:

```
import numpy
```

```
import pandas
```

Figure 2.18: Importing libraries in a new Jupyter Notebook

Then, to execute the code of the selected block (highlighted by an outline rectangle), click on the **Run** button in the menu.

The number 1 will appear inside the square brackets, which indicates that the block has been executed and, therefore, the two libraries imported into the notebook. The numbers that will appear inside the square brackets will indicate the sequence of the blocks executed. Furthermore, a new empty block will be created at the bottom, used for the Python code.

At this point, we can add some text to see how the text blocks work. Select (if not already) the new empty block and click on the pop-up menu, where the **Code** item is shown and select **Markdown**. This drop-down menu is used to change the type of block. Selecting **Markdown** will convert it to a formatted text block, as shown in *Figure 2.19*:

Figure 2.19: *Creating a Markdown block in Jupyter Notebook*

At this point, by selecting Markdown, you will see the **In []:** label disappear from the left. The block is now ready to contain some formatted text.

Enter the following text:

```
# My First Notebook
## from chapter 2 example

*italic text*
**bold text**

* first item
* second item
* third item


1. enumerated item
2. enumerated item
3. enumerated item
```

Owing to the particular sequences of characters, the notebook is able to understand how the text must be formatted, changing its font and size. For example, depending on the number of # characters you bring before a paragraph, you will have the different levels of heading (1 for the title, 2 for the subtitle, 3 for a paragraph head, and so on). Whereas, if you use the * characters, you can tell the text whether it should be in italic or bold, or if it should show a list, as shown in *Figure 2.20*:

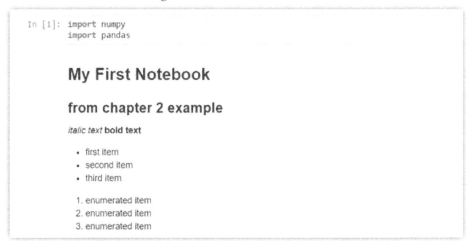

Figure 2.20: Inserting formatted text into a Jupyter Notebook

To make the entered text effective, press the **Run** button as you did previously for the code. It will appear in place of the block, the corresponding text appropriately formatted, as we can see in *Figure 2.21*:

Figure 2.21: Formatted text in a Jupyter Notebook

If we want to go back to making changes to the text just entered, simply click twice on it, and the text block ready for editing will immediately reappear.

Now that we have added some text with a title and a subtitle, it would be better to move it before the code block. In a Jupyter Notebook, the order of the blocks can be changed at any time. Select the block to be moved (highlighted by an outline rectangle) and then press the buttons on the menu with the up and down arrows to move it in the relative direction. In our case, we will press the arrow upwards, as shown in *Figure 2.22*:

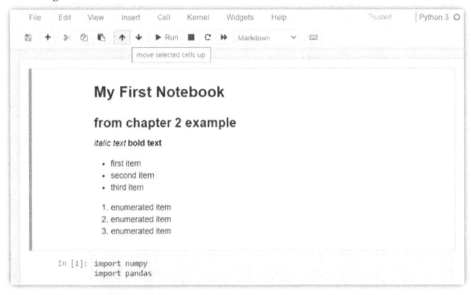

Figure 2.22: Changing the order of the blocks in the Jupyter Notebook

Now, you can continue to insert the Python code and text into your notebook following the same procedures shown earlier. At the end, you will have to save the notebook to be able to go back to work later. So, let's give the Notebook a title by clicking on the top where **Untitled** is written, as shown in *Figure 2.23*:

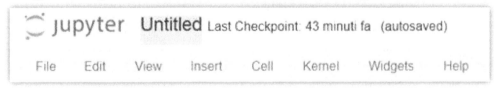

Figure 2.23: Entering the Title in a Jupyter Notebook

A dialog box will appear where you enter the new name of the notebook. For example, enter `My first notebook` and save by clicking on the `Rename` button.

There are many commands available in this application, and it is impossible to see them all in the context of this book. For further information, it is recommended to visit **https://jupyter-notebook.readthedocs.io/en/stable/notebook.html**. However, there are many tutorials on the Internet that explain how to use Jupyter Notebook at any level.

Working online on development environments: Replit

Currently, there are also **integrated development environments** (**IDEs**) that work online and, therefore, allow you to create highly customized environments (as we saw with Anaconda) by choosing both the programming language and the libraries to be included in the environment.

One of them is Replit (**https://replit.com/**), whose name stands for *read-evaluate-print-loop*. The strength of these IDEs is precisely that of not having to worry about installing software and setting up a work environment on our PCs, but finding one that is already available online, and is easily customizable. The only requirement is a browser and a connection to the Internet, specifications that are present on any system – even in low-cost mobile phones.

Replit

Replit supports over 50 programming and markup languages, including Python. For this reason, we have chosen it as an example in this book. Today, remote programming is increasingly common, and the ability to work on our projects, wherever you are and with any PC or mobile phone without having to leave traces on them, is truly an attractive option.

Replit allows you to work through a page loaded on a browser, on several windows at the same time, in a similar way to any IDE software installed on our computer. *Figure 2.24* shows the Replit development environment as it appears on the browser:

Figure 2.24: *The Python workspace in Replit (online IDE)*

In addition, Replit, like other similar online IDEs, have other useful tools, in particular an integration with GitHub, which allows you to import the code directly from it, and to distribute our projects in a simple and immediate way.

If you don't like Replit, you can use other similar online IDEs, such as Glitch (**https:// glitch.com/**) which have similar functions. The choice is varied, and therefore, you can choose the online IDEs as you prefer. There are also some integrated tools that allow you to transfer the code and projects from one online IDE to another. For example, from Replit, it is possible to import codes developed on Glitch.

You should always take this into consideration; however, these applications have a basic set of operations at a free level, but they become paid if we want to access a wide range of services offered (same thing for Anaconda).

Creating a Python workspace for data analysis on Replit

On Replit, we can create our own custom workspace based on Python, importing all the libraries we need. First of all, you need to open a browser and load the main page, then press the **Sign-Up** button and make your account registration. It will be useful if you already have Google accounts available. Just click on them to directly access the workspaces, as shown in *Figure 2.25*:

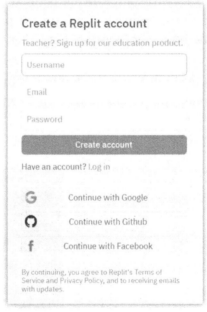

Figure 2.25: Sign up to Replit

Once you have created an account or are using your existing account on Google, GitHub, or Facebook, you can access a menu page, where you can choose the programming languages on which to create an online workspace, or access your previously created workspace, or choose from projects developed by other audiences that are useful for learning. There is also the possibility to connect to a GitHub repository and, thus, download the codes.

For the purposes of our book, you will create a new Python-based workspace by clicking on the **Python** button as the language to use, as shown in *Figure 2.26*:

Figure 2.26: *Choice of programming language to use*

Once you click on the **Python** button, a dialog box will appear where you can choose whether to create a new workspace (in Replit, they are called **repl**) or import the code from GitHub. Enter the reference name of the workspace to be created in the text box on the right and click on the blue **Create repl** button at the bottom, as shown in *Figure 2.27*:

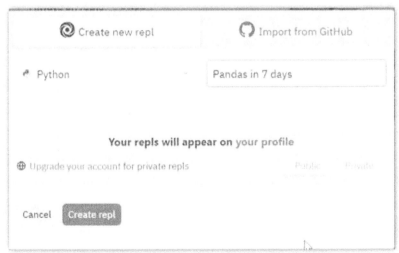

Figure 2.27: *Settings to create the workspace on Replit*

At this point, the new workspace will be loaded on your browser. It is very simple and intuitive to use. The IDE is divided into three panels, the one on the left is a sort of manager (file manager, package manager, database manager, and so on). In the center, there is space for entering the code. On the right is the classic Python interactive console. Refer to *Figure 2.28*:

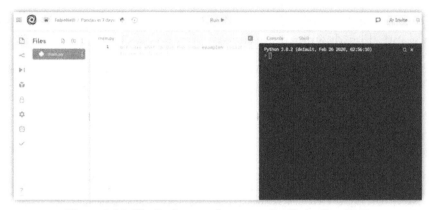

Figure 2.28: *The Python workspace on Replit (online IDE)*

At this point, we begin to install all the packages needed to work with the examples in the book – Pandas, Numpy, matplotlib, and so on. Look at the panel on the left (the manager to be clear) and click on the box-shaped icon (package manager). Then enter **pandas** in the text box to search for the library. Various results will appear in the search. Choose the **pandas** library (at the time of writing the book, it was version 1.3.1). Install the library. As you can see in *Figure 2.29*, the dependencies of the library are shown, including NumPy. These packages will be automatically installed along with Pandas:

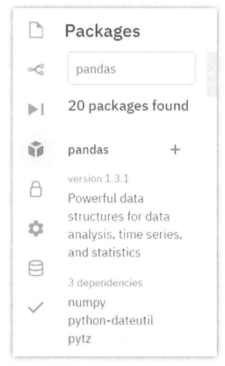

Figure 2.29: *Installing pandas library in Replit workspace*

The installation progress will appear on the console in the right panel. As you can see in *Figure 2.30*, the other necessary packages are also installed or updated if they are already present in the workspace:

```
--> python3 -m poetry add pandas
Using version ^1.3.1 for pandas

Updating dependencies
Resolving dependencies...

Writing lock file

Package operations: 2 installs, 2 updates, 0 removals

  • Updating numpy (1.20.3 -> 1.21.1)
  • Updating python-dateutil (2.8.1 -> 2.8.2)
  • Installing pytz (2021.1)
  • Installing pandas (1.3.1)
[]
```

Figure 2.30: Replit console during the pandas installation

Do the same with the matplotlib and seaborn library.

You have now completed the setup of your remote development environment and you can start working with the examples shown in the subsequent chapters of the book.

Conclusion

In this chapter, we saw the different ways in which to set up our work environments. We first saw the basic procedure, the general one that requires the installation of Python and each individual package manually. Then we saw that there is a distribution designed specifically for those who work with data analysis, known as **Anaconda**. This distribution provides many tools that greatly facilitate the management of development and work environments, allowing you to manage environments and packages. You can create several development environments with different versions and settings at the same time. Finally, the possibility of fully working remotely was shown, using special sites that distribute the already developed work environments online, without having to install anything on your computer. One of these is **Replit.**

Now that you have an environment to work in, you can move on to the next chapters of the book, and start this Pandas study path in 7 days, reading sequentially the corresponding 7 chapters. This path will gradually lead you to the way of working with data analysis

Questions

1. What are the differences between working directly with Python manually installed on the system and using a distribution like Anaconda?

2. Why is it preferable to work within Python environments?

3. What are the advantages of working with Jupyter Notebook as a data scientist?

Multiple Choice Questions

1. Which is the library that Pandas uses internally to enhance numerical computing performance?

    A. SciPy

    B. Statsmodels

    C. NumPy

2. Which of these is the Anaconda package manager?

    A. pip

    B. conda

    C. apt-get

3. Which of these are the Python libraries for data visualization?

    A. Seaborn, matplotlib

    B. Numpy, SciPy

    C. Statsmodels, scikit-learn

4. Which of these is the Jupyter Notebook text block formatting language?

    A. HTML

    B. XML

    C. Markdown

5. Which of these features is not possible with remote work environments like Replit?

    A. Creating an environment

    B. Exporting an environment

    C. Cloning an environment

Answers

1: C; 2: B; 3: A; 4: C; 5: B

Key Terms

Python, Pandas, NumPy, Jupyter Notebook, Anaconda, Conda, package manager, Python environments, Replit.

References/Further Readings

- https://docs.python.org/3/library/
- https://packaging.python.org/tutorials/installing-packages/
- https://pandas.pydata.org/docs/
- https://docs.anaconda.com/
- https://jupyter-notebook.readthedocs.io/en/stable/notebook.html
- https://docs.replit.com/
- https://numpy.org/doc/
- https://seaborn.pydata.org/
- https://www.meccanismocomplesso.org/en/scipy-a-python-library-for-mathematics-science-and-engineering/
- https://matplotlib.org/stable/contents.html
- https://www.meccanismocomplesso.org/en/data-science-section/

## CHAPTER 3

Day 1 - Data Structures in Pandas library

Here is the first chapter corresponding to the first day of our goal of learning Pandas in 7 days. With this chapter, we will begin to use the library, becoming familiar with the fundamental objects on which to carry out all the activities related to data analysis – the data structures. Pandas mainly provides two types of data structures to work on – Series and DataFrame.

Structure

In this chapter, we will cover the following topics:

- Series
- Index
- DataFrames
- MultiIndex DataFrames

Objective

After studying this chapter, you will gradually become familiar with the type of objects, discovering with continuous examples, how they are structured and all the ways to define them within the Python code. Being familiar with structured objects such as Series and DataFrames is essential to be able to confidently face the following chapters.

Introduction to the Series

In this section, we will deal with the first type of structured data – the Series. This type is the simplest and, as we will see in the following sections, it can be considered as one of the "bricks" on which to build the more complex DataFrame. We will see how a Series is structured and discuss the different ways in which it can be defined, all with practical and simple examples.

NOTE:

Before proceeding with this chapter, it is necessary to set the work environment on which to run the examples present. You can use any system presented in *Chapter 2, Setting up a data analysis environment.* **Here, we will use a Jupyter Notebook on Anaconda, where we have created a** mypandas **environment.**

Open a new Notebook on Jupyter and insert the following code in the first cell:

```
import numpy as np
import pandas as pd
```

In this way, we imported the libraries necessary to be able to execute the commands in this chapter.

A Series as a sequence of data

A Series is nothing more than a sequence of data similar to better known types of data such as a list in Python or a Numpy array.

Refer to the following example:

```
In []:   lst = [ 5 ,9 ,11, -1, 4 ]
         nar = np.array([ 5 ,9 ,11, -1, 4 ])


In []:   print(lst)
         print(nar)


[5, 9, 11, -1, 4]
[ 5  9 11 -1  4]
```

Series is a type of structured data and, therefore, has an additional feature compared to the previous types. An additional array of length corresponding to that of the Series values has inside label values that identify the elements corresponding to the array of values. This array is called index.

We then create a Series with the simple **Series()** constructor of the Pandas library, as follows:

```
<In []:    ser1 = pd.Series([ 5 ,9 ,11, -1, 4 ])


In []:    print(ser1)


0      5
1      9
2      11
3      -1
4      4
dtype: int64
```

Figure 3.1 is a graphic representation of the Series, **ser1** that has just been created:

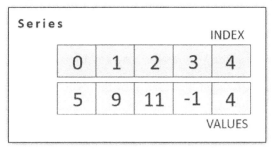

Figure 3.1: *Series structure*

As we can see from the output text format and from *Figure 3.1*, the internal structure of a Series is based on two different arrays. On the right, we have an array of values, called values, which contains the input data, passed as an argument in the constructor. On the left, we have instead a self-generated array, called index, in which there is a sequence of integers ranging from 0 to N-1, where N is the length of the data array, values.

In fact, we can separately obtain the two arrays with the values and index attributes of the Series, as follows:

```
In []:    print(ser1.values)
```

```
[ 5  9 11 -1  4]
```

```
In []:    print(ser1.index)
```

```
RangeIndex(start=0, stop=5, step=1)
```

Furthermore, the values contained within the Series are individually accessible. If you specify the position of the element (index) you want to access inside the square brackets, you will get the corresponding value – pretty much the same way you access values inside a Numpy arrays in Python.

So, to access the value of the third element of the Series just defined, you will write the following code:

```
In []:    print(ser1[2])
```

```
11
```

And similarly, if you want to access the third element of an **ndarray,** you will write the following code:

```
In []:    print(nar[2])
```
```
11
```

With this evidence, it could be assumed that the operating mechanism of index is largely similar to the implicit indexes in a Numpy array. But in reality, its features are considerably greater. In fact, the array index can be enhanced to our liking through an array of labels, in the same way as the array values are enhanced.

We then define a new Series plus an array of labels to add as index. For simplicity, we will use simple alphanumeric characters as labels, as shown as follows:

```
In []: ser2 = pd.Series([5, 9, 11, -1, 4],
                    index = ['a','b','c','d','a'])
In []: print(ser2)
```

```
a     5
b     9
c     11
d     -1
a     4
dtype: int64
```

In the index array, there are two identical labels **a**.

Therefore, the values within the index do not have an ordinal value as in the NumPy array, but a semantic value, that is, the labels must somehow report the class of belonging of the corresponding value in the values array – a concept of class closely linked to data analysis, which will prove very useful later, and not a narrow concept of an ordered index typical of mathematical calculations.

It is precisely for this reason that the selection in a Series of all the elements (values) belonging to a class can be carried out in a really simple way. That is, the elements that correspond to a certain label **e** could be considered as belonging to the same class. And then you can select them and extract their values from a Series, specifying only the corresponding label, without absolutely knowing their position inside.

In our small example, the values belonging to the class labeled with **a** can be obtained simply by inserting this label between the square brackets, as shown as follows:

In []: print(ser2['a'])

a   5

a   4

dtype: int64

In addition, the values of the index array can be defined at any time. For example, you can later overwrite the default values generated by the **Series()** constructor, as follows:

In []: print(ser1)

0   5

1   9

2   11

3   -1

4   4

dtype: int64

In []: ser1.index = ['a','b','c','d','a']

In []: print(ser1)

a   5

b   9

c   11

d   -1

a   4

dtype: int64

As we can see, the sequence of numeric values assigned by default have been totally overwritten with the elements of the array assigned directly to index.

The Index() constructor

An alternative, and perhaps cleaner, way of working is to separately define the index array with the **Index()** constructor and use it later by passing it as an argument in the **Series()** constructor or subsequently assigning it to the index attribute, as follows:

```
In []: idx = pd.Index(['a','b','c','d','a'])
       ser3 = pd.Series( [5, 9, 11, -1, 4], index = idx)


In []: print(ser3)
```

a   5

b   9

c   11

d   -1

a   4

dtype: int64

The result is practically the same, but the separate management of the creation of the index array can be useful in projects with many lines of code, especially when this can be reused several times to enhance different Series or other data structures.

NOTE:

Series, the correspondence between Index and Values

An implicit concept is taken for granted in the examples. The correspondence between the elements of the index and value arrays within a Series is very important and is not fully managed automatically. It is, therefore, up to the user to manage it correctly.

It is, in fact, implicit that the number of elements of index and values must always be the same. With the use of constructors to create a Series, the order of the input elements for both arrays will be used to make the correspondence between them. Incorrect handling by the user will lead to errors.

For example, define an index array with fewer elements than the values entered in the Series constructor, as follows:

```
idx2 = pd.Index(['a','b','c','d'])
ser4 = pd.Series( [5, 9, 11, -1, 4], index = idx2)
```

It will give ValueError as an error message.

The name attribute of Series

Another feature of Series as structured data is the possibilityis the possibility to assign an additional name to them as an attribute, in addition to that of the variable itself. In this regard, the name attribute, belonging to the **Series** object, is enhanced with a string, as follows:

In []: ser1.name = "First series"

    print(ser1)

a   5

b   9

c   11

d -1

a   4

Name: First series, dtype: int64

From now on, the Series will feature this name.

Even the internal index array of the Series can, in turn, have a specific name through the name attribute, as follows:

```
In []:  ser1.index.name = "Characters"
        Print(ser1)
```

Characters

a   5

```
b      9
c      11
d      -1
a      4
Name: First series, dtype: int64
```

The name of the index array will appear at the top before the Series values are printed.

Various ways to build Series

In the previous section, we saw the basic characteristics of the Series as structured data. In this section, we will deepen the subject by seeing together many ways of building the Series.

The Series() constructor

The `Series()` constructor (as well as the `DataFrame()` constructor) is a very powerful tool, which is able to adapt to many types of input data. This makes it possible to use as input values several common types of structured data, often used in data processing..

Being able to use data types such as tuples, NumPy arrays, and dictionaries allows you to integrate the Pandas library into many other Python applications that work and generate data in these common forms. It is, therefore, important to know and be familiar with how to use these types of data to generate the Series.

We have seen that the simplest form of declaring a Series object is to use the constructor with a single argument, which will match the input data, as shown as follows:

```
pd.Series(input_data)
```

Actually, it accepts many arguments which, if not expressed, assume default values, including **index** and **name** that we saw in the previous section, as shown as follows:

```
pd.Series(data=None, index=None, dtype=None, name=None, copy=False,
fastpath=False)
```

With **dtype**, it is possible to force the type of data entered in the Series. For instance, refer to the following:

```
In []: ser4 = pd.Series([5, 9, 11, -1, 4],
                index = ['a','b','c','d','a'], dtype=float)
```

```
        print(ser4)
a       5.0
b       9.0
c       11.0
d       -1.0
a       4.0
dtype: float64
```

It forces the conversion of the incoming integers **(int64)** to floating point **(float64)**.

Creating a Series from a NumPy array

The objects most used in practice as data input for Pandas data structures such as the Series, are the NumPy arrays. In fact, the NumPy library is the most used in scientific computing, and mainly makes use of this type of data. It is, therefore, important to know how to convert a NumPy array into a Series.

In this regard, let's define an example **ndarray** with some values inside, as follows:

```
In []: nda = np.array([7,5,4,1,-11])

        print(nda)

        print(nda.dtype)


[   7    5    4    1 -11]

int32


In []: ser5 = pd.Series(nda)

        print(ser5)


0       7

1       5

2       4

3       1

4       -11
```

```
dtype: int32
```

The type of data contained within the **Series (dtype = int32)** is maintained within the values of the Series. If we want to convert them to another type, we can force the conversion at the constructor level, by adding the **dtype** explicitly as an argument, as follows:

```
In []: ser5 = pd.Series(nda, dtype=np.int64)

        print(ser5)
```

```
0      7

1      5

2      4

3      1

4    -11
```

```
dtype: int64
```

Numpy Arrays passed by reference and by copy

When passing the NumPy arrays as data input within a **Series()** constructor, it is necessary to pay attention to the fact that no copy is made from the NumPy array to the values array of the Series (step by reference). The array values will be the same NumPy array and, therefore, any changes made on it will affect the Series, as shown as follows:

```
In []: n = np.array([1,2,3,4])

        ser = pd.Series(n)

        print(ser)
```

```
0    1

1    2

2    3

3    4
```

```
dtype: int32
```

By varying the value of an element of the NumPy array used to build the Series, the corresponding value in the Series itself will be varied, as shown as follows:

```
In []: n[3] = 0
       print(ser)
```

```
0    1
1    2
2    3
3    0
```

```
dtype: int32
```

The same goes for the opposite. By varying the value within the Series, the corresponding value in the NumPy array will be varied at the same time, as shown as follows:

```
In []: ser[3] = 5
       print(ser)
       print(n)
```

```
0    1
1    2
2    3
3    5
```

```
dtype: int32
```

```
[1 2 3 5]
```

To overcome these consequences, we will use the copy option set to True passed as the argument of the **Series()** constructor, as shown as follows:

```
Int []: n = np.array([1,2,3,4])
        ser = pd.Series(n, copy=True)
        print(ser)
```

```
n[3] = 0

print(ser)
```

```
0    1

1    2

2    3

3    4

dtype: int32

0    1

1    2

2    3

3    4

dtype: int32
```

But the most interesting aspect is to take advantage of the many data generating functions available in the NumPy library, which allow you to automatically obtain arrays full of values, useful for easily populating the Series.

For example, it is possible to create an array containing random values between 0 and 1, with the **randn()** function of the random module of NumPy, which accepts as an argument the number of values to be generated, as shown as follows:

```
In []: ser6 = pd.Series(np.random.randn(5))
print(ser6)
```

```
0     0.923559

1     0.629791

2    -0.920411

3     0.573092

4    -0.160999

dtype: float64
```

The values obtained will vary with each run.

Another similar function that is widely used is the **numpy.arange()** function which allows you to generate a sequence of values based on certain rules set as an argument, as shown as follows:

```
numpy.arange([start, ]stop, [step, ], dtype=None)
```

For example, let us generate a NumPy array containing a sequence of five integers from 1 to 5, as follows:

```
In []: ser7 = pd.Series(np.arange(1,6))

       print(ser7)
```

```
0    1

1    2

2    3

3    4

4    5
```

```
dtype: int32
```

There are many other similar functions in NumPy, as well as the **zeros()** function which generates an array containing all 0 values. Let's look at it, as follows:

```
In []: ser8 = pd.Series(np.zeros(4))

       print(ser8)
```

```
0    0.0

1    0.0

2    0.0

3    0.0
```

```
dtype: float64
```

Creating a Series from a scalar value

A way to enhance a Series similar to the previous one seen with **zeros()** is to use a single scalar value as the input data. In this case, however, specifying a single scalar in the following way is not sufficient:

```
In []: ser9 = pd.Series(4)

       print(ser9)
```

```
0    4
```

dtype: int64

In fact, we have the creation of a Series with a single element containing the inserted scalar as the argument. To have an effect like that obtained with the **zeros()** method, the array index must also be entered in the constructor. It will be the length of the index array that will tell the constructor how many elements the array values are populated, as shown as follows:

```
In []: ser9 = pd.Series(4, index= ['a','b','c','d'])
        print(ser9)
```

```
a    4
b    4
c    4
d    4
```

dtype: int64

Creating a Series from a dictionary

Even more complex types of data, such as dictionaries, can be used as data inputs, as follows:

```
In []: d = { 'a': 12, 'b': -1, 'c': 7, 'd': 3 }

        ser10 = pd.Series(d)

        print(ser10)
```

```
a    12

b    -1

c    7

d    3
```

dtype: int64

The particular **key:values** structure in pairs allows us to define the values of the array and the index at the same time. The Series constructor is, therefore, able to recognize the various pairs of values within the **dict** (dictionary) by assigning the keys to the index array and the relative values to the values array.

Dictionaries are complex data, and you must often deal with multiple key-value pairs. It can happen that we are only interested in a part of them, a set of keys, present within the dictionary. With the Series constructor, we can select directly within the dictionary which values to incorporate, specifying an index array containing the keys we are interested in, as shown as follows:

```
In []: idx = pd.Index(['a','b','c'])

        d = { 'a': 12, 'b': -1, 'c': 7, 'd': 3 }

        ser12 = pd.Series(d, idx)

        print(ser12)
```

```
a       12

b       -1

c       7
```

dtype: int64

But, what if a key was present in the index array that was not present in the dictionary? The **Series()** constructor in this case still inserts an element with that value in the index, but in the corresponding element of values there will be the value NaN (missing value). This particular value indicates that the field is empty and we will often find it in subsequent chapters of the book.

In a similar way to the previous code, we define an index with three labels and then subsequently a dict. But this time, one of the labels will not be defined within the dict, as shown as follows:

```
In []: idx = pd.Index(['a','b','e'])
        d = { 'a': 12, 'b': -1, 'c': 7, 'd': 3 }
        ser13 = pd.Series(d, idx)
        print(ser13)
```

```
a       12.0
b       -1.0
e       NaN
```
dtype: float64

Since the key **e** is not present inside the **dict**, and therefore, is not finding a value to use, the **Series** constructor will assign the NaN value (missing value) to the corresponding label.

Creating a Series from a list of tuples

Another type of data that we often find ourselves working on is a list of tuples. Also, from this type of data, it is possible to generate a Series, as follows:

```
In []: t = [('a',5),('b',2),('c',-3)] #list of tuples
        idx, values = zip(*t)
```

In order to do this, we need to use a zip() function that allows us to iterate within the list to separate the first terms from the seconds of the tuple into two arrays, which we will use as index and values in the constructor, as shown as follows:

```
In []: ser11 = pd.Series(values, idx)

        print(ser11)
```

```
a     5

b     2

c    -3

dtype: int64
```

Creating a Series from a 2-element array list

A similar structure to the previous one is that of a list of arrays containing two elements, as shown as follows:

```
In []: t = [['a',2],['b',4],['c',3]]
        idx, values = zip(*t)
        ser12 = pd.Series(values, idx)
        print(ser12)
```

```
a    2
b    4
c    3
dtype: int64
```

Also, in this case, the conversion to Series is easily solved, thanks again to the `zip()` function, which selects the first elements of the arrays as labels to be inserted in index, and the second elements as data to be inserted in values.

Introduction to DataFrames

Once you have seen the Series, it's time to deal with the DataFrame, a more complex structured data. The DataFrames are very important, since they are the central nucleus around which the whole Pandas library revolves. It is, therefore, important to understand how they are structured within them and learn how to correctly define them within the Python code.

The DataFrame as an indexed data table

A DataFrame is a more complex data structure than the Series, and it can be considered, in simple terms, as the extension in two dimensions of the structure of a Series. Starting from a Series that is now familiar to us, we can, therefore, think of a DataFrame as a set of Series of the same length, and all having the same array index in common, unified in a column to form a table, as shown in *Figure 3.2*:

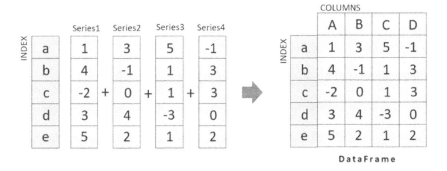

Figure 3.2: DataFrame

But in addition to this useful simplification, we need to add an additional array of labels called **columns**. This array will have a length equal to the number of columns inserted in the DataFrame and each element will correspond to a certain column, equal to a real index.

Therefore, within a DataFrame, there are two different types of indexing that work simultaneously, index for the rows of the table of values and columns for the columns.

The DataFrame() constructor

Similar to Series, the Pandas library provides a **DataFrame()** constructor that allows you to define a **DataFrame** object starting from a series of input values, as follows:

```
In []: df1 = pd.DataFrame([[1, 2, 3], [4, 5, 6] ,[7, 8, 9]])

       print(df1)
```

```
   0  1  2

0  1  2  3

1  4  5  6

2  7  8  9
```

As you can see, by passing only the internal values, the **DataFrame()** constructor is able to autonomously populate the two vectors index and columns, and it does so by inserting a sequence of integers from *1* to *N - 1*, where *N* is the length of index and columns respectively.

If instead we want to have a DataFrame with all the label values defined for both columns and index, then we must specify them directly as arguments of the constructor, as shown as follows:

```
df1 = pd.DataFrame([[1, 2, 3], [4, 5, 6] ,[7, 8, 9]],

                   index = ['a','b','c'],

                   columns = ['A','B','C'])

       print(df1)
```

```
   A  B  C

a  1  2  3

b  4  5  6

c  7  8  9
```

Now we have the index and columns arrays enhanced by labels.

To be able to access these values directly, you can call the attributes as index and columns, as shown as follows:

```
In []: df1.index
```

```
Index(['a', 'b', 'c'], dtype='object')
```

```
In []: df1.columns
```

```
Index(['A', 'B', 'C'], dtype='object')
```

Both attributes return an **object** of type Index.

However, if we want to have only the values contained in the DataFrame, we can recall the values attribute, as shown as follows:

```
In []: v = df1.values
       print(v)
       type(v)
```

```
[[1 2 3]
 [4 5 6]
 [7 8 9]]
```

```
numpy.ndarray
```

This attribute returns a two-dimensional Numpy **ndarray**.

Viewing DataFrames in Jupyter Notebook

Throughout the book, to make the sample code in the various chapters as universal as possible, we will always use **print()** to display the contents of all variables, including DataFrames.

But Jupyter Notebook has a touch of respect for this type of object. In fact, if you simply report the instance of a DataFrame, it will be displayed in an attractive graphic format, as shown in *Figure 3.3*:

```
In [112]: df1
Out[112]:
              A  B  C
          a   1  2  3
          b   4  5  6
          c   7  8  9
```

Figure 3.3: Jupyter Visualization of a DataFrame without print()

Other constructor arguments

If we take the formal definition of the constructor on the Pandas library documentation, we see the following:

```
pandas.DataFrame(data=None,

                 index=None,

                 columns=None,

                 dtype=None,

                 copy=None)
```

We can see that the arguments that the constructor accepts are the same as those of the **Series()** constructor, except for the additional presence of the columns argument. The Series did not need this argument since the columns are not present in that data structure. As for the rest, the same speeches made previously apply.

With the **dtype** argument, it is possible to force the conversion of the type of data passed as values. For example, if we want the values within the DataFrame to be 64-bit floating points, it will be necessary to add this type to the **dtype** argument, as follows:

```
In []: df1 = pd.DataFrame([[1, 2, 3], [4, 5, 6] ,[7, 8, 9]],
                 index = ['a','b','c'],
                 columns = ['A','B','C'],
                 dtype= np.float64)
       print(df1)


     A    B    C
a  1.0  2.0  3.0
```

```
b   4.0   5.0   6.0
c   7.0   8.0   9.0
```

As we can see from the result, even though the values passed into the DataFrame are all integers, the constructor has converted them to floating point numbers.

The **copy** argument is implicitly set to **False** within the constructor. So, if we don't explicitly specify it as an argument, and we use a two-dimensional **ndarray** to value the DataFrame, we will make a pass by reference. That is, the values will not be copied but it will be the **ndarray** passed as an argument to be incorporated within the DataFrame. If we modify the **ndarray** externally by modifying a value, we will modify the corresponding value in the DataFrame at the same time and vice versa, as shown as follows:

```
In []: nda = np.array([[1, 2, 3], [4, 5, 6] ,[7, 8, 9]])

        df2 = pd.DataFrame(nda,

                            index = ['a','b','c'],

                            columns = ['A','B','C'])

        print(df2)


      A   B   C

a   1   2   3

b   4   5   6

c   7   8   9


In []: nda[1] = [4,0,6]

        print(nda)


[[1 2 3]

 [4 0 6]

 [7 8 9]]
```

```
In []: print(df2)
```

```
   A  B  C

a  1  2  3

b  4  0  6

c  7  8  9
```

As you can see, if you do not pay attention to the exclusive use of one of the variables, or if it is not a well-desired strategy, you risk finding the values modified without being aware of them and, thus, making unexpected errors during the analysis of the variables data.

But why is the passage by reference preferred by default?

It must be said that despite the examples in this book, DataFrames tend to be large objects that occupy large memory spaces. The same is true for **ndarray** passed as an argument to the constructor.

In this case, carrying out the passage by reference means saving a lot of memory space by avoiding unnecessary copies.

To avoid this, we can force the constructor to make a copy of the **ndarray** passed as an argument. So, the copy is then set to **True**. In this case, the values within the DataFrame will be completely independent from those of the ndarray and changing the latter will have no impact on the values within the DataFrame, as shown as follows:

```
In []: nda = np.array([[1, 2, 3], [4, 5, 6] ,[7, 8, 9]])

       df2 = pd.DataFrame(nda,

                          index = ['a','b','c'],

                          columns = ['A','B','C'],

                          copy=True)

       print(df2)
```

```
   A  B  C

a  1  2  3
```

```
b   4   5   6

c   7   8   9
```

```
In []: nda[1] = [4,0,6]

       print(nda)
```

```
[[1 2 3]

 [4 0 6]

 [7 8 9]]
```

```
In []: print(df2)
```

```
    A   B   C

a   1   2   3

b   4   5   6

c   7   8   9
```

As we can see from the preceding result, now the DataFrame is completely independent from the ndarray used to value it.

Access the various elements of the DataFrame with iloc[ ] and loc[ ]

Now that we have seen how a DataFrame is structured and how it can be created through the use of a constructor, a common operation to learn is how to access its internal elements through selections. Although we will deal with the selection of the elements of a DataFrame in depth in the *Chapter 4, Day 2 - Working within a DataFrame, Basic Functionalities*, it is very important to have at least the fundamental bases for accessing these elements in order to start working with this type of object.

We have seen that the index and columns attributes allow us to access the Index objects as substructures of the DataFrame, in the same way as the values attribute which returns us the values contained as an ndarray.

But very often, we want to select certain subsets of values contained within the DataFrame, to be able to view and modify them in a simple way. For this purpose, there are two selectors, **iloc** and **loc**, which help us enormously in this purpose.

The iloc selector allows us to select the values of a DataFrame, specifying the row and column through the corresponding numerical indexes (sequence of integers starting from 0), as shown as follows:

```
iloc [ row number, column number ]
```

```
So, first, let's define a DataFrame as follows:

df2 = pd.DataFrame(nda,
                   index = ['a','b','c'],
                   columns = ['A','B','C'],
                   copy=True)

     print(df2)


   A  B  C

a  1  2  3

b  4  5  6

c  7  8  9
```

We will be able to access a single value by specifying its row and column number in **iloc[]**, as shown as follows:

```
In []: df2.iloc[0,1]
```

2

This selector is also useful if we want to select an entire row or an entire column, as shown as follows:

```
In []: print(df2.iloc[0]) #select first row

       print(df2.iloc[:,1]) #select second column

A     1
```

```
B    2

C    3

Name: a, dtype: int32

a    2

b    5

c    8

Name: B, dtype: int32
```

As you can see, by expressing a single number, this will be understood as the row number to select, while if we want to select a column, then it will be necessary to insert the character **:** for the row number (in this case it means all the rows) and then the number of the column to be selected. Here, with this character, we are introducing the concept of slicing that we will see in the *Chapter 4, Day 2 - Working within a DataFrame, Basic Functionalities.* For now, be content to consider it as **select all**.

The **loc[]** selector works in a similar way, except that it accepts as arguments, the labels present in both index and columns to make the selections. So in this case, we will enter the label of the row and column of the values we want to select, as shown as follows:

```
In []: print(df2.loc['a','B'])


2


In []: print(df2.loc['a']) #select first row
       print(df2.loc[:,'B']) #select second column


A    1
B    2
C    3
Name: a, dtype: int32
a    2
b    5
c    8
Name: B, dtype: int32
```

Various ways to build DataFrames

In the previous section, we saw what DataFrames are and how they are made. We also started using the `DataFrame()` constructor to create them. In this section, as we had done in parallel for the `Series()` constructor, we will see together the different ways of building a DataFrame depending on the types of input data used to enhance them.

Creating a DataFrame from a Numpy ndarray

We have already seen in the previous section, using the values attribute, that the values within a DataFrame are nothing more than a two-dimensional Numpy ndarray. It is, therefore, clear that the simplest and most intuitive way to enhance them is to use previously created **ndarray**, as shown as follows:

```
In []: idx = np.array(['a','b','c'])

       col = np.array(['A','B','C'])

       nda = np.array([[1, 2, 3], [4, 5, 6] ,[7, 8, 9]])

       df3 = pd.DataFrame(nda, index=idx, columns=col)

       print(df3)
```

```
   A  B  C

a  1  2  3

b  4  5  6

c  7  8  9
```

But the most interesting thing is to use the NumPy functions that generate values automatically in a similar way to those we used to populate the Series. Only in this case, we need two-dimensional arrays. In the Series, we used **np.arange()** to generate an array with a sequence of integers. If we concatenate the **np.reshape(x, y)** method, it is possible to generate a two-dimensional array having x rows and y columns from this sequence.

In this regard, the previous case would have been more elegant to define it in the following way:

```
In []: df3 = pd.DataFrame(np.arange(1,10).reshape(3,3),

                          index=idx,

                          columns=col)

        print(df3)
```

```
   A  B  C

a  1  2  3

b  4  5  6

c  7  8  9
```

The same is true for the **np.zeros()** method. Here, too, **np.reshape(x, y)** is concatenated to convert the sequence of 0 generated into a two-dimensional array suitable to be accepted as the input given by the **DataFrame()** constructor, as shown as follows:

```
In []: df4 = pd.DataFrame(np.zeros(9).reshape(3,3),

                          index=idx,

                          columns=col)

        print(df4)
```

```
     A    B    C

a  0.0  0.0  0.0

b  0.0  0.0  0.0

c  0.0  0.0  0.0
```

It is possible to generate an array of random numbers using the **np.rand.rnd()** function. And then by concatenating this function to **np.reshape (x, y),** you can convert it to a two-dimensional array, as shown as follows:

```
In []: df5 = pd.DataFrame(np.random.randn(9).reshape(3,3),

                          index=idx,

                          columns=col)

        print(df5)
```

```
       A         B          C
a   1.138277   1.479283  -0.445134

b   1.199514   0.386425   0.150183

c   0.670408  -0.536880  -0.278374
```

Thanks to the use of these automatic value generating functions, it is possible to initially populate large DataFrames; impossible to do (or at least very boring) manually, is writing the array by hand.

Creating a DataFrame from a Series dictionary

At the beginning of this section, to facilitate the understanding of the internal structure of a DataFrame, we had given the example that a DataFrame could be thought of as the union of some Series, having the same index and the same length.

Well, this example is just what we described. A DataFrame can be built through the use of a **dict** in which the key-value pairs are represented by column labels as key and the Series as values, as shown as follows:

```
In []: ser1 = pd.Series([1,4,7], index=['a','b','c'])

       ser2 = pd.Series([2,5,8], index=['a','b','c'])

       ser3 = pd.Series([3,6,9], index=['a','b','c'])

       d = { "A" : ser1,

             "B" : ser2,

             "C" : ser3}


In []: df6 = pd.DataFrame(d)

       print(df6)


   A  B  C
a  1  2  3

b  4  5  6

c  7  8  9
```

Now, let's move on to a more complex, but general example. Let's say that the series we want to use are not all of the same length and that they also contain, or not, other key values that we do not consider, as shown as follows:

```
In []: ser1 = pd.Series([1,4,7,-3,-1], index=['a','b','c','e','f'])

        ser2 = pd.Series([2,5,8], index=['d','b','c'])

        ser3 = pd.Series([3,6,9,0], index=['a','b','c','d'])

        d = { "A" : ser1,

              "B" : ser2,

              "C" : ser3}

        df7 = pd.DataFrame(d)

        print(df7)
```

	A	B	C
a	1.0	NaN	3.0
b	4.0	5.0	6.0
c	7.0	8.0	9.0
d	NaN	2.0	0.0
e	-3.0	NaN	NaN
f	-1.0	NaN	NaN

As we can see from the result, the **DataFrame()** constructor is able to work very well with dictionaries. It is perfectly able to take into consideration all the index labels of the Series, even if not in all, and based on these, align all the corresponding values in a table. If the labels are not present in the corresponding column, it will insert a NaN value (missing values), thus, managing the lack of information. Furthermore, the constructor can do this work even if the index labels present in one Series follow a completely different order in the others. From this behavior, we understand the potential of a constructor such as **DataFrame()**.

If, on the other hand, we do not want to take into consideration the other labels, but want to keep only the values of those labels established by us, we can carry out a filtering at the manufacturer level, without subsequently "cleaning" the unwanted information. This can be done by specifying only the labels we want in the constructor as the index argument, as shown as follows:

```
In []: df7 = pd.DataFrame(d, index=['a','b','c'])

        print(df7)
```

```
   A   B  C

a  1  NaN  3

b  4  5.0  6

c  7  8.0  9
```

However, there remains a missing value to manage. As you can see, working with more general cases, we approach the case of real data in which problems of missing or incorrect data can often arise. We will see in the following chapters, in particular in *Chapter 6, Day 4 - Working with two or more DataFrames*, how to manage this kind of inconvenience.

Creating a DataFrame from a ndarray dictionary

A very similar case to the previous one is to use ndarray dictionaries or generic lists. Same rules and same behavior, except that in this case, we added an **ndarray** to populate the index, since **ndarray** do not contain this type of information, as shown as follows:

```
In []: nda1 = np.array([1,4,7])

        nda2 = np.array([2,5,8])

        nda3 = np.array([3,6,9])

        idx = np.array(['a','b','c'])

        d = { "A" : nda1,

              "B" : nda2,

              "C" : nda3}

        df8 = pd.DataFrame(d, idx)

        print(df8)
```

```
   A  B  C

a  1  2  3
```

```
b  4  5  6

c  7  8  9
```

Pass-by-copy with Dictionaries

The DataFrame() constructor has a completely different behavior with Dictionaries than the Numpy arrays. In fact, if a value of type **dict** (dictionary) is passed as data input, it will make a copy of all the values contained within it without any passing by reference. This is so regardless of whether there are **Series** or **ndarray** within the dict.

In fact, in the case of a Series dictionary (see the previous section Creating a Series from a dictionary), if we modify an internal value of a Series, the dictionary will be changed in turn, which is not the case for the DataFrame, as shown as follows:

```
In []: ser1['a'] = 0

       print(d)

       print(df6)


{'A': a    0

b    4

c    7

dtype: int64, 'B': a    2

b    5

c    8

dtype: int64, 'C': a    3

b    6

c    9

dtype: int64}


     A  B  C

a  1  2  3
```

```
b   4   5   6

c   7   8   9
```

We find the same consistent behavior in the case of a dictionary of **ndarray** (see the previous section *Creating a DataFrame from a ndarray dictionary*). Here too, by changing the value of a **ndarray**, the dictionary will be changed, while the DataFrame generated by it will not. See the following:

```
In []: nda1[0] = 0

        print(d)

        print(df8)



{'A': array([0, 4, 7]), 'B': array([2, 5, 8]), 'C': array([3, 6, 9])}



    A   B   C

a   1   2   3

b   4   5   6

c   7   8   9
```

Creating a DataFrame from a structured array or a record array

There are data structures in Numpy called structured arrays and record **arrays**. They are very similar and are often confused with one another. They have a complex structure, as follows:

```
In []: str_array = np.array([(1, 2, 3), (4, 5, 6), (7, 8, 9)],

                    dtype=[('A', '<f8'), ('B', '<i8'),('C','i4')])

        print(str_array)



[(1., 2, 3) (4., 5, 6) (7., 8, 9)]
```

It is a list of N tuples with M values inside, each of which can be of a different type, which will be defined in the constructor through **dtype**. In this topic, we will pass another list of M tuples of two values, where the first will be a label and the second will be the type of data.

To better understand this concept, it may be helpful to take a look at the graphical representation of the structured array in *Figure 3.4*:

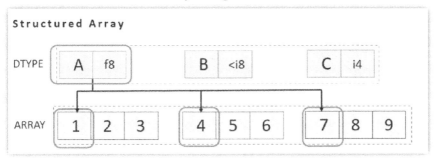

Figure 3.4: *Structured Array*

To access the elements within the structured arrays, see the following:

```
In []: print(str_array['A'])
       print(str_array[1])
```

```
[1. 4. 7.]
(4., 5, 6)
```

It is, therefore, possible to select within the tuples, thanks to the label that defines a particular value in the internal sequence. Insert the label inside the square brackets to make the selection, obtaining a list of all the elements that share the data defined in **dtype**. If you want to access a single tuple within the list, we behave as with a classic array, indicating the index of the element between the square brackets.

There is, therefore, a certain indexing with labels, which is a bit of a prelude to the DataFrame. And it's easy to mentally convert this structure into a DataFrame, as shown in *Figure 3.5*:

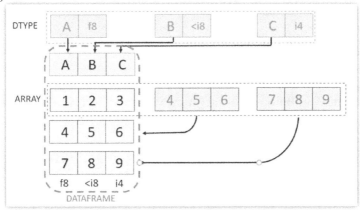

Figure 3.5: *Conversion from structured array to DataFrame*

The following is pretty much what happens, when passing a structured array to the `DataFrame()` constructor:

```
In []: df9 = pd.DataFrame(str_array)

       print(df9)
```

```
     A  B  C

0  1.0  2  3

1  4.0  5  6

2  7.0  8  9
```

As we can see, this is exactly what is shown in *Figure 3.5*. The constructor takes the tuples with their values inside and converts them into the rows of the DataFrame to which it will assign, by default, the labels in index (Index object of pandas) with a sequence of integers from *1* to *N-1*, where N is the number of tuples. The labels passed in **dtype** will populate the elements of the columns array (pandas Index object). Within each single column, the type of data will be that defined in the **dtype** of the structured array. If we want to value the labels in index, specify them directly in the DataFrame() constructor, as follows:

```
In []: df9 = pd.DataFrame(str_array, index=['a','b','c'])

       print(df9)
```

```
     A  B  C

a  1.0  2  3

b  4.0  5  6

c  7.0  8  9
```

As far as record arrays are concerned, the speech is perfectly the same. This type of structured data always belongs to the NumPy library, and is defined as follows:

```
In []: rec_array = np.rec.array([(1, 2, 3), (4, 5, 6), (7, 8, 9)],

                    dtype=[('A', '<f8'), ('B', '<i8'),('C','i4')])

       print(rec_array)

[(1., 2, 3) (4., 5, 6) (7., 8, 9)]
```

As you can see, the definition is perfectly the same, and the internal structure does not vary absolutely from the one represented in *Figure 3.3*. The only difference is that you can access the labeled values, not by recalling the label in the square brackets, but as a real attribute, as shown as follows:

```
In []: print(rec_array.A)
```

```
[1. 4. 7.]
```

As for the `DataFrame()` constructor, it will also accept this type of data without problems, behaving in the same way as it does with the structured arrays, as shown as follows:

```
In []: df10 = pd.DataFrame(rec_array, index=['a','b','c'])

        print(df10)
```

```
     A   B  C
a  1.0   2  3
b  4.0   5  6
c  7.0   8  9
```

Creating a DataFrame from a list of dictionaries

We have seen that the combination of data types, nesting them one inside the other, can generate a large variety of structured data in Python. Another very common combination in which data can be found is that of a list of dictionaries, as shown as follows:

```
In []: list_dicts = [{ 'A': 1, 'B': 2, 'C': 3},

              { 'A': 4, 'B': 5, 'C': 6},

              { 'A': 7, 'B': 8, 'C': 9},]

        print(list_dicts)
```

```
[{'A': 1, 'B': 2, 'C': 3}, {'A': 4, 'B': 5, 'C': 6}, {'A': 7, 'B': 8,
'C': 9}]
```

Also in this case, we can think of a conversion into a DataFrame through its constructor, provided that the elements inside it are properly structured to meet our needs, as shown as follows:

```
In []: df11 = pd.DataFrame(list_dicts, index=['a','b','c'])

       print(df11)
```

```
   A  B  C

a  1  2  3

b  4  5  6

c  7  8  9
```

Creating a DataFrame from a list of Data Classes

In addition to structured data made with Python primitives such as dictionaries, lists, and tuples, there are other types of data, provided by other Python modules that could be useful for populating DataFrames. One of these are the Data Classes. This type of data was introduced in Python 3.7 in 2017 with the document PEP557 (**https://www.python.org/dev/peps/pep-0557/**), and was included among the types of data manageable by the **DataFrame()** constructor from Pandas version 1.1.0.

To make use of these objects within the Python code, it is necessary to import the **dataclasses** module. In our case, we will only import the **make_dataclass** constructor, as shown as follows:

```
In []: from dataclasses import make_dataclass
```

As an example, create a **Data** Class which you will refer to as **Dataset** type, and then use it to define the values of the DataFrame rows through a list, as shown as follows:

```
In []: Dataset = make_dataclass('Dataset', [('A', int),('B', int),('C', int)])

       df12 = pd.DataFrame([Dataset(1,2,3),

                            Dataset(4,5,6),

                            Dataset(7,8,9)], index=['a','b','c'])

       print(df12)
```

```
   A  B  C

a  1  2  3

b  4  5  6

c  7  8  9
```

Creating a DataFrame from a list of Named Tuples

The other types of data very similar to the previous one are the Named Tuples. As the name implies, you can create certain tuples by giving them a particular name. These tuples, once defined by a name, can then be inserted into a list to populate the DataFrame.

To use Named Tuples, you need to import them from the collections module, as shown as follows:

```
In []: from collections import namedtuple

In []: Dataset = namedtuple('Dataset', 'A B C')

       df13 = pd.DataFrame([Dataset(1,2,3),

                            Dataset(4,5,6),

                            Dataset(7,8,9)], index=['a','b','c'])

       print(df13)
```

```
   A  B  C

a  1  2  3

b  4  5  6

c  7  8  9
```

MultiIndex DataFrame

To conclude the chapter, we will introduce a particular extension of the DataFrame. In fact, the ones we have seen so far have an internal structure with one index level per row and one index level per column.

But the Pandas library allows you to further extend this structure by inserting higher levels of indexing, both by row and by column. When you have a DataFrame with these characteristics, it is generally referred to as **MultiIndex DataFrame**.

Creating a MultiIndex DataFrame from a dictionary of tuples

We have seen that the combinations of types to generate structured data are many in Python, and they can reach very complex levels of structuring. Some of these can still be interpreted correctly by the **DataFrame()** constructor. If the structure is multi-level hierarchical, it can still be converted to a MultiIndex DataFrame.

An example of how the DataFrame() constructor can generate a MultiIndexed DataFrame is with a dictionary of tuples with a nested two-level structure, as shown as follows:

```
dict_tuples = {('X', 'A'): {('x','a'): 1, ('x','b'): 4, ('x','c'): 7,
                            ('y','d'): 0, ('y','e'): 0},
               ('X', 'B'): {('x','a'): 2, ('x','b'): 5, ('x','c'): 8,
                            ('y','d'): 0, ('y','e'): 0},
               ('X', 'C'): {('x','a'): 3, ('x','b'): 6, ('x','c'): 9,
                            ('y','d'): 0, ('y','e'): 0},
               ('Y', 'D'): {('x','a'): -1, ('x','b'): -3, ('x','c'): -5},
               ('Y', 'E'): {('x','a'): -2, ('x','b'): -4, ('x','c'): -6}
               }
```

The complex structure of this dictionary of tuples is still interpretable by the **DataFrame()** constructor and is passed as data input; it will generate a MultiIndex DataFrame, as shown as follows:

```
In []: multidf = pd.DataFrame(dict_tuples)

       print(multidf)

       X              Y

       A  B  C    D     E

x a    1  2  3  -1.0  -2.0

  b    4  5  6  -3.0  -4.0

  c    7  8  9  -5.0  -6.0

y d    0  0  0   NaN   NaN
```

```
e  0  0  0  NaN  NaN
```

As we can see in the output representation, as a result, the labels of index (a, b, c, d, e) and columns (A, B, C, D, E) are grouped under other indices (x , y) and (X, Y) respectively. Using the **iloc[]** and **loc[]** selectors, it is possible to extract a DataFrame with a single index level from this MultiIndex DataFrame, as follows:

```
In []: print(multidf['X'].loc['x'])
```

```
   A  B  C

a  1  2  3

b  4  5  6

c  7  8  9
```

However, while remaining within the MultiIndex DataFrame, some selections can be made by accessing different subsets. For example, if we want to access the values of a single column, it will be sufficient to specify within the square brackets, first the higher-level columns label, and then the lower level one, as shown as follows:

```
In []: print(multidf['X']['A'])
```

```
x  a    1

   b    4

   c    7

y  d    0

   e    0
```

```
Name: A, dtype: int64
```

Also, for MultiIndex DataFrames, there are columns and index attributes; only in this case, they will return a **MultiIndex** object, instead of **Index**, as shown as follows:

```
In []: print(multidf.columns)
```

```
       print(multidf.index)
```

```
MultiIndex([('X', 'A'),

            ('X', 'B'),
```

```
                    ('X', 'C'),

                    ('Y', 'D'),

                    ('Y', 'E')],
             )
MultiIndex([('x', 'a'),

            ('x', 'b'),

            ('x', 'c'),

            ('y', 'd'),

            ('y', 'e')],
           )
```

If, on the other hand, we want to see the labels divided by level, we can use the levels attribute, as follows:

```
In []: print(multidf.columns.levels)

       print(multidf.index.levels)
```

```
[['X', 'Y'], ['A', 'B', 'C', 'D', 'E']]
```

```
[['x', 'y'], ['a', 'b', 'c', 'd', 'e']]
```

However, the use of MultiIndex DataFrame can be very complex. It is preferred to extract a simple DataFrame containing the values we need from this type of object, as shown as follows:

```
In []: dfn = print(multidf['X'].loc['x'])

       print(dfn)
```

```
   A  B  C

a  1  2  3

b  4  5  6

c  7  8  9
```

Conclusion

In this chapter, we saw the structured data that are the basis of the pandas library – Series and DataFrame. With some examples, we have also seen how they are structured internally and how to use indexes and columns for indexing.. We also presented how their **Series()** and **DataFrame()** constructors are able to construct these objects, receiving common types of data such as lists, tuples, and dictionaries as inputs and in different combinations of them. Finally, we concluded with a brief mention of the most extensive case of structured data – the MultiIndex DataFrame.

In the next chapter (the second day of our course), we will begin to work with DataFrame, discovering many possible operations and calculation tools.

Questions

1. What are the differences between a Numpy ndarray and a DataFrame?

2. How is a DataFrame structured internally?

3. In light of what we have learned, what makes a DataFrame better than a spreadsheet or SQL table?

Multiple Choice Questions

1. What is meant by Index, Series, and DataFrame?

   A. Constructors

   B. Methods

   C. Objects

2. What is meant by Index(), Series(), and DataFrame()?

   A. Constructors

   B. Objects

   C. Methods

3. Within a DataFrame, which of the following elements must have the same type of data?

   A. Rows

   B. Columns

   C. Values

4. We construct a DataFrame using an ndarray 'nd1' as the data input. What guarantees me an independent copy of the data?

    A. nd2 = nd1 and, then I use nd1 as input data

    B. copy = True as argument of constructor DataFrame()

    C. Passing directly nd1 as input data. The constructor will copy its values leaving nd1 independent.

5. Which of these statements is true about MultiIndex DataFrame?

    A. MultiIndex DataFrames have two indexing levels per row and two indexing levels per column.

    B. MultiIndex DataFrames can have infinite indexing levels, both per row and per column

    C. MultiIndex DataFrames are made up of multiple DataFrames, each having a different index.

Answers

1: C; 2: A; 3: B; 4: B; 5: B

Key Terms

- Series
- Ndarray
- Index
- DataFrame
- Constructors
- MultiIndex DataFrame

References

- *Python for Data Analysis. Data Wrangling with Pandas, NumPy, and IPython, McKinney, OReilly*
- *Python Data Analytics With Pandas, NumPy, and Matplotlib, Fabio Nelli, Apress*

    https://pandas.pydata.org/docs/user_guide/index.html

CHAPTER 4

Day 2 - Working within a DataFrame, Basic Functionalities

After having learned how to define and build a DataFrame, in this chapter, we will address some of their basic features, largely applicable also to the Series. Through a series of basic operations and examples of some concepts related to them, we will discover how the DataFrame can be modified in its structure and content as we wish. All operations are aimed at a common purpose – preparing the DataFrame on which we are working and the data within the manipulation (which we will see in the *Chapter 5, Day 3 - Working within a DataFrame, Advanced Functionalities*).

Structure

In this chapter, we will cover the following topics:
- Viewing
- Selection
- Filtering
- Editing
- Descriptive Statistics
- Transposition, Sorting, and Reindexing

Objective

After studying this chapter, you will be able to see and understand the content of a DataFrame (**viewing** and **statistics**), select appropriate parts (**subsetting**) or filter its elements based on appropriate conditions (**filtering**), add new ones (editing), and finally modify the structure (**reindexing** and **transposition**). All will be aimed at focusing on that part of the DataFrame on which we will later want to operate (manipulation) – which we will discuss in the next chapter.

Viewing Data

In this section, we will see how to view the data within a DataFrame in a simple and direct way, both with the classic **print()** function, and using appropriate methods made available to the Pandas library.

Direct printing of the DataFrame values

The first thing that comes naturally to us, after creating a new DataFrame, is to be able to see its contents. We already saw in the previous chapter that this can be done by simply using the **print()** function.

After creating any DataFrame with the **DataFrame ()** constructor and assigning it to a variable, it will be sufficient to pass the latter as an argument to the **print()** function, as shown as follows:

```
In[ ]: import numpy as np

       import pandas as pd
```

```
In[ ]: dfr = pd.DataFrame(np.random.rand(100).reshape(20,5))

       print(dfr)
```

```
          0         1         2         3         4
0   0.191256  0.170541  0.142903  0.984159  0.100340

1   0.767157  0.241995  0.704391  0.048797  0.380394

2   0.524190  0.391752  0.471562  0.582821  0.438586

3   0.482197  0.842324  0.425179  0.025220  0.268374
```

4	0.613918	0.031072	0.777962	0.682337	0.044402
5	0.152923	0.039114	0.488992	0.375734	0.041075
6	0.591187	0.130946	0.460390	0.647393	0.997631
7	0.052332	0.799502	0.921812	0.556729	0.072723
8	0.365278	0.848417	0.011146	0.160439	0.899374
9	0.594452	0.884869	0.457250	0.622870	0.377015
10	0.754178	0.132307	0.876525	0.431657	0.303924
11	0.888541	0.246831	0.484676	0.521972	0.978563
12	0.711728	0.928700	0.404088	0.562801	0.522832
13	0.231189	0.818645	0.096971	0.414662	0.945034
14	0.345317	0.007435	0.698157	0.775030	0.539030
15	0.424671	0.138965	0.693826	0.496616	0.836236
16	0.835626	0.524158	0.586314	0.525488	0.377256
17	0.678388	0.530112	0.338357	0.955739	0.282579
18	0.621372	0.038738	0.945889	0.727736	0.222806
19	0.281437	0.380723	0.960103	0.016986	0.629478

As you can see, all the contents of the DataFrame will be displayed in text form, including the indexes with their labels. However, the printout will keep the tabular format respecting the row-column correspondence with their labels.

np.random and random values

Throughout the book, we will use randomly generated values and, therefore, the reader will be warned that in these cases, there will be no correspondence between the values reported in the book and those obtained by running the examples (which will be different each time). The generation of random numbers to enhance DataFrame is a very common (and also useful) practice. In these examples, the reader is invited to pay attention to the process and functionality and not to the reported values.

A more eye-catching mode is the one that is built-in in Jupyter Notebook. That is, the ability to view the content of a DataFrame in print formatting, similar to an image of a book, using a particular font and spacing the colors of the table rows to make it more readable, as shown in *Figure 4.1*. This particular formatting can be obtained on Jupyter Notebook, by simply writing the instance name of the DataFrame, as follows:

```
In[ ]: dfr
```

Refer to Figure 4.1:

	0	1	2	3	4
0	0.713321	0.407743	0.272693	0.591089	0.778127
1	0.033181	0.007454	0.692392	0.383027	0.485039
2	0.323282	0.219315	0.141534	0.701166	0.106942
3	0.527240	0.297825	0.436417	0.075872	0.119068
4	0.061217	0.547924	0.653361	0.864192	0.601082
5	0.052252	0.643673	0.473189	0.611888	0.824488
6	0.461120	0.325087	0.793557	0.290149	0.404572
7	0.997146	0.506639	0.884892	0.110393	0.606124
8	0.724040	0.459088	0.184363	0.064830	0.901350
9	0.449625	0.946444	0.433300	0.508719	0.502080
10	0.386052	0.156612	0.300951	0.315361	0.648082
11	0.389872	0.686016	0.491354	0.561517	0.548997
12	0.643087	0.611485	0.400492	0.656925	0.067662
13	0.474193	0.121560	0.962377	0.549798	0.704303
14	0.095282	0.267752	0.762813	0.620844	0.067957
15	0.951379	0.987939	0.869214	0.724106	0.805649
16	0.682436	0.949039	0.428778	0.902600	0.735342
17	0.991081	0.664901	0.953110	0.462377	0.017509
18	0.265634	0.609697	0.099757	0.734682	0.730406
19	0.002649	0.706732	0.573928	0.310536	0.536113

Figure 4.1: DataFrame as displayed on Jupyter Notebook

In this chapter, the DataFrames that we use are small in size, so this simple direct printing approach of a DataFrame is functional. In reality, in real case studies, the DataFrames created will be enormous in size with hundreds (sometimes thousands) of rows and dozens of columns. It is immediately clear that the direct display of an entire DataFrame is at least burdensome on the part of the system being used, and useless (because it is illegible) for those who are using it. So, the approach to be used will be different from the common `print()`.

The head() and tail() methods

To have a sufficient view to roughly understand the structure of a DataFrame and get an idea of the data it contains, the Pandas library provides us with the two methods **head()** and **tail()**. By calling these methods on a reference DataFrame, the first five lines are printed, with the **head()** method, or the last five lines with the **tail()** method, as follows:

```
In [ ]: dfr.head()
```

Refer to *Figure 4.2*:

	0	1	2	3	4
0	0.713321	0.407743	0.272693	0.591089	0.778127
1	0.033181	0.007454	0.692392	0.383027	0.485039
2	0.323282	0.219315	0.141534	0.701166	0.106942
3	0.527240	0.297825	0.436417	0.075872	0.119068
4	0.061217	0.547924	0.653361	0.864192	0.601082

Figure 4.2: Head of the DataFrame

As you can see in *Figure 4.2*, the **head()** method, if used on Jupyter Notebook, shows the first five lines of the DataFrame with its particular formatting seen previously, as follows:

```
In [ ]: dfr.tail()
```

Refer to *Figure 4.3*:

	0	1	2	3	4
15	0.951379	0.987939	0.869214	0.724106	0.805649
16	0.682436	0.949039	0.428778	0.902600	0.735342
17	0.991081	0.664901	0.953110	0.462377	0.017509
18	0.265634	0.609697	0.099757	0.734682	0.730406
19	0.002649	0.706732	0.573928	0.310536	0.536113

Figure 4.3: Tail of the DataFrame

As shown in *Figure 4.3*, we obtain the same result with the *tail()* method.

These two methods allow us to see the first and last five lines of the DataFrame. This default behavior can be changed by passing the number of lines to be displayed as the argument of the two methods. For example, if we want to see only the first three rows of the DataFrame, we will get the results, as shown in *Figure 4.4*:

```
In [ ]: dfr.head(3)
```

	0	1	2	3	4
0	0.713321	0.407743	0.272693	0.591089	0.778127
1	0.033181	0.007454	0.692392	0.383027	0.485039
2	0.323282	0.219315	0.141534	0.701166	0.106942

Figure 4.4: Head delle prime 3 right del DataFrame

Selection

In the previous chapter, during the creation of the DataFrame, we already learned how to select the elements inside it. In this section, we will address the selection in the foreground, deepening this topic which will then be the basis of all the other features present in this and subsequent chapters. It is, therefore, crucial to start with this topic to better understand the concepts, and then to address all the subsequent topics in this book with greater clarity.

Selection by Subsetting

The selection of the elements within a DataFrame is a common operation and is the basis of many subsequent operations. In fact, you can select a single element, but much more often, we will need to select a subset of elements (**Subsetting**) which can be a smaller DataFrame or even a Series.

Therefore, the selection involves the extraction (if it is then assigned to a variable), or the focus (if you will operate directly on it), of a subset of the DataFrame – a part of data of our interest on which we will then perform some operations (manipulating data) to obviate our data analysis.

In principle, the selection can be made by subsetting a DataFrame, that is, by directly explaining one or more rows to be selected (even if they are not adjacent to each other), whose values will then be further chosen, limited to one or more columns (also not adjacent to each other), or vice versa.

Subsetting by index or by position

Structured objects such as DataFrame and Series, have been created specifically to carry out the selection process on them in a simple and efficient way. Within these objects, each dimension is characterized by an Index object, the purpose of which is to label the individual elements on each of them. It is precisely the Index objects that differentiate DataFrame and Series from the n-dimensional arrays (ndarray) of NumPy. On the latter, since they have no index objects, the positions of the elements are specified by means of a sequence of progressive integers from 0 to N-1 (where N is the length of the dimension).

Since the Pandas library is based on the NumPy library, and in its way, extends some of its features, it wanted to keep both the possibility of being able to select the elements of the DataFrame and Series with the numbers of the positions. Both extend this concept through the Indexes and their labels.

Subsetting can then be done via the following:

- **Indexing**: Users can select the data using the labels that distinguish the individual rows and columns, through the Index objects.

- **Integer Positioning**: Users can select data using positions for integers of rows and columns, such as NumPy ndarrays.

When you want to select a single element, things are quite simple – you specify the label corresponding to the row and the corresponding column (indexing) or the position within the DataFrame by means of the pair of integers (integer positioning) – as shown as follows:

```
In [  ]: df = pd.DataFrame(np.random.randint(0,9,16).reshape(4,4),
                           index = ['a','b','c','d'],
                           columns = ['A','B','C','D'])
         print(df)


   A  B  C  D
a  5  1  4  5
b  7  3  1  1
c  6  6  2  0
d  3  7  7  3


In [ ]: print(df.at['a','A']) #indexing
        print(df.iat[0,0])    #integer positioning
```

5

5

But most of the time, we need to select certain subsets of the DataFrame and not a single element. So, we will have to extend the single values (integer or label) with words that somehow express a particular subset on which to make the selection.

Selection operators and indexers accept the following terms in this regard:

- Lists (integer or labels)
- Slices (slicing)

Lists specify all the columns or rows we want to include in the subsetting. As the name implies, they are simple Python lists containing integer values or labels corresponding to the rows or columns to be selected.

Slices, on the other hand, specify ranges of indexes, thus, including in a single wording, a set of contiguous columns or rows, without having to specify them individually. To define the slices, the slicing techniques are used with the ':' operator (the same way as in NumPy with ndarray).

Scalars and Series as return values

When selecting a single element, you get a scalar value as a return value. If, on the other hand, you select on a subset, you get a Series or a DataFrame, as shown as follows:

```
In [ ]: print(df.iloc[2,1])
```

6

If you want to receive a Series or DataFrame as a return value even in the case of a selection on a single element, you must use a list containing a single element to specify both rows and columns, as shown as follows:

```
In [ ]: print(df.iloc[[2],[1]])
```

B

c   6

Indexing Operators and Indexers

From what we have seen in the previous examples and learned in the previous chapter, there are different selection modes with different captions and operators. The variety of these selection methods can easily lead to confusion, and it is, therefore, very important, before going on, to define the concept as best as possible.

First of all, it may be useful to define the following two different types of selection separately, which may appear very similar:

- Selection with indexing operators
- Selection with indexers

The two square brackets that we often find immediately after the name of a DataFrame can be defined as an indexing operator. Its operation is inherited from NumPy arrays and is handled in a similar way to that used with **ndarrays**, as shown as follows:

```
df[ ]
```

Within the square brackets, special terms are made explicit that will express the subset selection methods. Depending on the form of this wording, the indexing operator will interpret how to make this selection.

If you simply enter a string (enclosed in brackets), this will be interpreted as the label corresponding to a column, as shown as follows:

```
In [ ]: print(df['B'])
```

```
a    1

b    3

c    6

d    7

Name: B, dtype: int64
```

And the indexing operator will extract the values contained in that particular column, thus obtaining a Series.

Instead, if you pass a list of strings within the operator, these will be considered the columns to be selected (not adjacent), as shown as follows:

```
In [ ]: print(df[['B','D']])
```

```
     B   D
a    1   5
b    3   1
c    6   0
d    7   3
```

If, on the other hand, we pass a numerical value inside the indexing operator, in the hope of obtaining the corresponding column, we will be disappointed. We will get the following error message:

```
In [ ]: print(df[0])
```

```
...
```

```
raise KeyError(key) from err
```

```
KeyError: 0
```

Another unexpected behavior is when the slicing operator ':' is used. The indexing operator will always interpret strings as row (and not column) labels, as shown as follows:

```
In [ ]: print(df['a':'c'])
```

```
     A   B   C   D
a    5   1   4   5
b    7   3   1   1
c    6   6   2   0
```

The indexing operator will select all the rows covered by the interval indicated by the two labels separated by the slicing operator :. Slicing cannot be used for columns.

We have another asymmetry when using the numerical values corresponding to the positions. We saw that by directly entering a numeric value, you get an error message, but if we insert them in the context of slicing, they are accepted and interpreted as the positions of the corresponding rows.

For example, to select a single row, we will still have to use a slicing, as shown as follows:

```
In [ ]: print(df[0:1])
```

```
   A  B  C  D
a  5  1  4  5
```

Although, it is normal to use it in selecting a set of adjacent rows, as follows:

```
In [ ]: print(df[0:2])
```

```
   A  B  C  D
a  5  1  4  5
b  7  3  1  1
```

What if we wanted to select non-adjacent rows instead? This is actually not the way to go. The indexing operator may be intuitive and comfortable at first, in particular for selecting a single column, but given its ambiguous behavior, it often leads to confusion or the construction of complex wordings.

However, there are particular attributes, which we will refer to as indexers, created and optimized specifically in the Pandas library to perform the selection operations.

Indexer for selecting individual elements are as follows:

- `at[]`
- `iat[]`

Indexer for the selection of subsets are as follows:

- `loc[]`
- `iloc[]`

These indexers are characterized by having two square brackets at the end. In fact, they too are indexing operators. Their peculiarity lies in the fact that they have been created specifically to work with the structured objects of the Pandas library such as DataFrame and Series. These indexers are able to make simultaneous selections of rows and columns, eliminating so many of the features of the previous indexing operator that it only leads to confusion.

It is, therefore, advisable to always use these operators instead of the previous methods. This will result in a more readable and efficient code, making uniform the way to specify the subsets to be selected.

As far as the selection arguments are concerned, the same previous rules are kept – integers or labels for the single elements, lists, and slices for the subsets.

loc[ ] – Selection by Labels

The **loc[]** operator focuses on selection based on the labels contained within the Index objects, as shown as follows:

```
loc[ row labels, column labels]
```

If you want to select a single element within the DataFrame, you will first specify the row label and then that of the column, as shown as follows:

```
In [ ]:  print(df.loc['a','B'])
```

1

A single element as a scalar is obtained as a return value.

Whereas, if you want to select a subset of adjacent elements, you can use the slicing technique with labels, as shown as follows:

```
In [ ]: print(df.loc['b':'d','A':'C'])
```

	A	B	C
b	7	3	1
c	6	6	2
d	3	7	7

In slicing, all the elements included between the extremes expressed by the two labels are selected, including these. A smaller DataFrame is obtained as a return value.

If, on the other hand, you want to select the entire range of columns or rows, just write the slicing operator :, as shown as follows:

```
In [ ]: print(df.loc['a':'c', :])
```

```
   A  B  C  D
a  5  1  4  5
b  7  3  1  1
c  6  6  2  0
```

But the columns and rows may also not be contiguous. In this case, you can use lists containing the labels to be selected, as shown as follows:

```
In [ ]: print(df.loc[['a','c'], ['A','D']])
```

```
   A  D
a  5  5
c  6  0
```

So, where we have selections with contiguous rows and columns, it is advisable to specify the range with slicing, and where instead the rows and columns are isolated, the labels are specified in the form of lists. However, using both words in the same column or row selection gives an error, as shown as follows:

```
df.loc['a':'c', ['A':'B','D']]
```

```
...
```

File "<ipython-input-252-a327202e8297>", line 1

```
    df.loc['a':'c', ['A':'B','D']]
```

                    ^

`SyntaxError: invalid syntax`

To overcome this problem, you can combine two selections using the `join()` method. The union between two different selections or DataFrames will be dealt with in *Chapter 6, Day 4 - Working with two or more DataFrames*. For now, accept it as a solution to obviate the simultaneous use of listing and slicing, that is, the selection of adjacent and non-adjacent indexes, as shown as follows:

```
In [ ]: print(df.loc['a':'c', 'A':'B'].join(df.loc['a':'c', 'D']))
```

```
   A  B  D

a  5  1  5

b  7  3  1

c  6  6  0
```

An alternative way to achieve the same results is by chaining the selections to gradually narrow the field (subsetting of subsetting), until the desired results are obtained, as shown as follows:

```
In [ ]: print(df.loc[:,['A','B','D']].loc['a':'c', :])
```

```
   A  B  D

a  5  1  5

b  7  3  1

c  6  6  0
```

iloc[ ] – Selection by location

The **iloc[]** operator works with the same rules as the selection operator **[ ]** for lists in Python. That is, it focuses on the positions of the elements expressed by sequences of integers from 0 to *N*-1 with *N* as the length of the Index, as shown as follows:

```
iloc[ row number, column number]
```

So, if we want to select a single element, it will be enough to add its numerical coordinates of the corresponding position, as shown as follows:

```
In [ ]: print(df.iloc[1,3])
```

```
1
```

Whereas, if we want to select a subset of the DataFrame, we can use the slicing technique by specifying the ranges of the numerical indices if they are adjacent, as shown as follows:

```
In [ ]: print(df.iloc[0:2,1:3])
```

```
   B  C
```

```
a   1   4
```

```
b   3   1
```

And if the elements are not adjacent, we can replace slices with lists, as shown as follows:

```
In [ ]: print(df.iloc[[1],[0,2]])
```

```
    A   C
```

```
b   7   1
```

If you must select a single row, insert the value within a single element list, to have a DataFrame that preserves the same indexing structure as a return value, as shown as follows:

```
In [ ]: print(type(df.iloc[[1],[0,2]]))
```

```
<class 'pandas.core.frame.DataFrame'>
```

In fact, if you simply specify the number as an argument, you will get a Series as a return value, with the column labels in the index, as shown as follows:

```
In [ ]: print(df.iloc[1,[0,2]])
```

```
A     7
```

```
C     1
```

```
Name: b, dtype: int64
```

```
In [ ]: print(type(df.iloc[1,[0,2]]))
```

```
<class 'pandas.core.series.Series'>
```

Indexer ix[ ]

In addition to those listed in the current section, there is also another indexer **ix[]**. This indexer works in a hybrid way between **iloc[]** and **loc[]**. **ix[]** will accept as input the labels present in the indexers such as **loc[]**, but if that input cannot be interpreted as such, it will be treated as the integer reference to the position as **iloc[]** does. Since the indexers were introduced in Pandas to avoid the confusion generated by the behavior of the other indexing operators, and **ix[]** also has quite ambiguous behavior, it would be better not to take it into account.

at[] and iat[] – Selection by value

There are two indexers that can only be used to select a single element within a DataFrame, and these are **at[]** and **iat[]**.

If we want to use indexing through labels of the single element, then we will use the indexer **at[]**, as shown as follows:

```
In [ ]: print(df.at['b','D'])
```

1

Or, if we want to use the position by means of numerical indices, we will use the indexer **iat[]**, as shown as follows:

```
In [ ]: print(df.iat[2,1])
```

6

These two indexers only work to select a single item. If you try subsetting by slicing or listing, you will get an error message, as shown as follows:

```
In [ ]: print(df.iat[0:2,1:3])
```

. . .

```
ValueError: iAt based indexing can only have integer indexers
```

Selection on dtype

So far, we have seen that the selections can be made by subsetting by exploiting the indexing of the DataFrame. But there are also other selection methods, for instance, based on the values contained in the DataFrame. For example, selections can be made based on the type of data (**dtype**).

To make this type of selection, we do not use an operator, but a method called `select_dtypes()`. This method accepts the following two possible parameters:

- `include`
- `exclude`

A list containing the types of data (**dtype**) to be included or excluded in the selection will be passed on to these parameters. In this regard, we create a DataFrame containing different types of data for each column, as shown as follows:

```
In [ ]: df = pd.DataFrame([[6,0.3,'one', True],
                           [2,5.1,'two', False],
                           [1,4.3,'three', True]],
                          index=['a','b','c'],
                          columns=['A','B','C','D'])

print(df)
```

```
      A    B      C      D
a     6   0.3    one    True
b     2   5.1    two    False
c     1   4.3    three  True
```

To obtain the list of the **dtypes** of each single column of the DataFrame, we can call the dtypes attribute, as shown as follows:

```
In [ ]: df.dtypes
```

```
A        int64
B       float64
C        object
D         bool
dtype: object
```

At this point, based on **dtypes**, we can select by passing, for example, a list containing the dtypes we want in the include parameter, as shown as follows:

```
In [ ]: df2 = df.select_dtypes(include=['bool','int64'])

        print(df2)
```

```
     A    D

a    6    True

b    2    False

c    1    True
```

If, on the other hand, we want to select by exclusion, we use the exclude parameter instead with a list containing the **dtypes** we want to exclude, as shown as follows:

```
In [ ]: df2 = df.select_dtypes(exclude=['bool','int64'])

        print(df2)
```

```
      B       C

a    0.3     one

b    5.1     two

c    4.3    three
```

Filtering

We saw in the previous section how it is possible to select elements within a DataFrame (or even a Series) by specifying appropriate spatial indicators such as labels or numerical position indices. In this section, we will see another very similar operation, which also selects, but is totally focused on the values of the elements – **filtering**. In this case, we will set particular conditions in the selection designed to select only the elements with the values that satisfy them. There is, therefore, filtering of the values of a DataFrame.

The Boolean condition

The Filtering technique is, therefore, based on a particular condition, called a Boolean condition, which is nothing more than a Boolean expression, that is, a mathematical expression that results in **True** and **False** (Boolean values). An example of a Boolean expression could be as follows:

`x > 5 (values greater than 5)`

If this condition is true, it will return **True**, otherwise **False**. These Boolean expressions are characterized by the use of Boolean operators such as (<,>,! =, ==, <=,> =), which are intended to compare two values and set a condition that can either be verified or not.

In the case of DataFrames, this Boolean condition is applied to the values contained in a particular subset of the DataFrame, establishing which part (column or row) will respond to this condition and returning a Series of Boolean values (**True** or **False**). The final result is a filtering that returns us a DataFrame that preserves the same structure as the original but that includes only some rows or columns of the original DataFrame.

Filtering on the lines

The most intuitive filtering is filtering on lines, that is, the one that will pass only a few lines of a DataFrame based on a Boolean condition.

We first create a DataFrame of random values between 0 and 1, distributed over 4 columns, as shown as follows:

```
In [ ]: df = pd.DataFrame(np.random.rand(40).reshape(10,4),
                        columns = ['A','B','C','D'])

print(df)
```

	A	B	C	D
0	0.208446	0.549985	0.508571	0.999901
1	0.510624	0.487230	0.780932	0.262326
2	0.812751	0.201271	0.126839	0.325091
3	0.903366	0.983182	0.483946	0.534748
4	0.904145	0.388162	0.381774	0.891533
5	0.954762	0.294765	0.134748	0.285515
6	0.342220	0.730722	0.520042	0.388452
7	0.191207	0.394109	0.478749	0.013134

```
8   0.487388   0.077178   0.017320   0.770331

9   0.974672   0.641839   0.886975   0.300326
```

Now, we will define a Boolean condition, based on which the selection will be made. For example, we want to filter only those rows of a DataFrame that have the value of column A greater than 0.5. Since these are floating-point numbers, let's add some significant digits, as shown as follows:

```
In [ ]: df['A'] > 0.500000
```

```
0     False

1      True

2      True

3      True

4      True

5      True

6     False

7     False

8     False

9      True

Name: A, dtype: bool
```

As a result, we got a Series of Boolean values. We can easily see that only a few lines meet this condition (**True**). At this point, if we pass the Boolean condition to an indexing operator, we will perform a filtering of the DataFrame, with the passage of only those rows that meet the requirement (**Filtering**).

As an indexing operator, we use the one represented by two square brackets [ ]. This operator will then take care of passing only the rows corresponding to the True values, based on the indices of the Series generated by the Boolean condition, as shown as follows:

```
In [ ]: df2 = df[ df['A'] > 0.500000 ]

        print(df2)
```

	A	B	C	D
1	0.510624	0.487230	0.780932	0.262326
2	0.812751	0.201271	0.126839	0.325091
3	0.903366	0.983182	0.483946	0.534748
4	0.904145	0.388162	0.381774	0.891533
5	0.954762	0.294765	0.134748	0.285515
9	0.974672	0.641839	0.886975	0.300326

But you can also use other indexing operators, such as indexer **loc[]**, as shown as follows:

```
In [ ]: df2 = df.loc[ df['A'] > 0.500000]
        print(df2)
```

	A	B	C	D
1	0.510624	0.487230	0.780932	0.262326
2	0.812751	0.201271	0.126839	0.325091
3	0.903366	0.983182	0.483946	0.534748
4	0.904145	0.388162	0.381774	0.891533
5	0.954762	0.294765	0.134748	0.285515
9	0.974672	0.641839	0.886975	0.300326

The result is pretty much the same.

Filtering on columns

The complementary case to the previous one is filtering on columns. In this case, only those columns of the DataFrame are filtered, whose values meet certain requirements. Again, we will define a Boolean condition. For example, we want to select only those columns whose average of values is greater than 0.5, as shown as follows:

```
In [ ]: df.mean() > 0.500000
```

```
A    False
```

B   True

C   True

D   True

`dtype: bool`

From the Series returned as a result, we can see which columns meet this condition from the elements with the value **True**. We apply this Boolean condition to indexer **loc[]** to filter on columns, as shown as follows:

```
In [ ]: df2 = df.loc[:,df.mean() > 0.500000]

        print(df2)
```

	A
	0.208446
	0.510624
2	0.812751
3	0.903366
4	0.904145
5	0.954762
6	0.342220
7	0.191207
8	0.487388
9	0.974672

As we can see from the result, only the columns that meet the requirements of the Boolean condition will be passed into the new DataFrame (Filtering).

Application of multiple conditions

In Filtering, you can apply several Boolean conditions at the same time. To do this, different conditions can be applied at the same time, thanks to the logical operators AND, OR, and NOT. In the Pandas library, these logical operators are expressed in the following way:

- & (and)
- | (or)
- ~ (not)

So, every single condition is enclosed in square brackets and joined together by the previous logical operators. We can express joint Boolean conditions in the following way:

```
In [ ]: (df['A'] < 0.300000) | (df['A'] > 0.700000)
```

```
0       True

1       True

2       False

3       True

4       False

5       True

6       True

7       False

8       False

9       True

Name: A, dtype: bool
```

Apply it inside an indexing operator or an indexer, as shown as follows:

```
In [ ]: df2 = df[(df['A'] < 0.300000) | (df['A'] > 0.700000)]

        print(df2)
```

```
          A          B          C          D

0   0.208446   0.549985   0.508571   0.999901

2   0.812751   0.201271   0.126839   0.325091

3   0.903366   0.983182   0.483946   0.534748

4   0.904145   0.388162   0.381774   0.891533
```

```
5   0.954762   0.294765   0.134748   0.285515

7   0.191207   0.394109   0.478749   0.013134

9   0.974672   0.641839   0.886975   0.300326
```

If the same Boolean conditions are often used within the code, it would be a good practice to first define them as variables and then use them when necessary. For example, by putting the Boolean conditions used previously, you can write the filtering criteria in a concise and readable way inside the indexing operator, as shown as follows:

```
In [ ]: cond1 = df['A'] < 0.300000

        cond2 = df['A'] > 0.700000

        cond3 = df.mean() > 0.500000
```

```
In [ ]: df2 = df.loc[cond1 | cond2 ,cond3]

        print(df2)
```

```
           A

0   0.208446

2   0.812751

3   0.903366

4   0.904145

5   0.954762

7   0.191207

9   0.974672
```

Boolean reductions

One topic related to the concept of filtering is Boolean reductions. There are a number of methods, called reduction methods, which allow you to obtain a reduced result, as shown as follows:

- any()
- all()

But, let's see some examples to clarify their function. We apply a Boolean condition in which all the elements of the DataFrame are evaluated. For example, we want to know which elements of the DataFrame have a value greater than 0.1, as shown as follows:

```
In [ ]: df2 = df > 0.1

        print(df2)
```

	A	B	C	D
0	True	True	True	True
1	False	False	True	True
2	True	False	True	True
3	True	True	True	True
4	True	True	True	True
5	True	True	True	True
6	True	True	True	True
7	True	True	True	True
8	False	True	True	True
9	True	True	True	True

In this case, we got a DataFrame full of Boolean values. A reduction method can be applied to this DataFrame, such as the **all()** method to know if, within each column, all the values meet these requirements (all on **True**), as shown as follows:

```
In [ ]: df2.all() #(df > 0.1).all()
```

A	False
B	True
C	True

```
D    False
```

dtype: bool

Whereas, the **any()** method has the opposite behavior, that is, it allows us to know if in the context of each single column, there is at least one value that satisfies the condition (only one **True**), as shown as follows:

```
In [ ]: df2.all() # (df > 0.1).any()
```

```
A    True

B    True

C    True

D    True
```

dtype: bool

An interesting thing is when we apply the **any()** method twice. A single Boolean value is obtained by confirming at least the presence in the entire DataFrame of a single element that satisfies the condition, as shown as follows:

```
In [ ]: df2.any().any() # (df > 0.1).any().any()
```

True

Filtering with isin()

Another method of Filtering is **isin()**. This method lets you know if one or more elements are present inside an object such as a DataFrame or a Series. In this regard, we define an example DataFrame, with predefined values, as shown as follows:

```
In [ ]: df = pd.DataFrame(np.arange(9).reshape(3,3),

                columns = ['A','B','C'])

        print(df)
```

```
   A  B  C

0  0  1  2
```

```
1  3  4  5

2  6  7  8
```

Now, let's apply the **isin()** method with some values to search for, as follows:

```
In  [ ]: df2 = df.isin([0,3])

         print(df2)
```

```
        A      B      C

0    True  False  False

1    True  False  False

2   False  False  False
```

As we can see, by passing a list of values as an argument to the **isin()** method applied to the DataFrame, we get a Boolean DataFrame of the same size, where we have **True** if the value belongs to the list, and **False** if it doesn't exist. As we can see, this is also a filtering operation.

Then, passing this Boolean DataFrame to the indexing operator, you get a filtering of the values, in which only those which correspond to True as a value will be passed, while all the others, which correspond to False, will be evaluated as NaN, as shown as follows:

```
In  [ ]: print(df[df2])   #print(df.isin([0,3])
```

```
       A    B    C

0   0.0  NaN  NaN

1   3.0  NaN  NaN

2   NaN  NaN  NaN
```

Then it will be up to us to decide how to handle these NaN values (which we will discuss later in *Chapter 8 – Day 6 – Troubleshooting challenges with real datasets*). For example, we can enhance them with other values, or completely remove them from the DataFrame, leaving only the enhanced elements, as shown as follows:

```
In  [ ]: df2 = df[df.isin([0,3])].dropna(thresh=1).dropna(axis=1)

         print(df2)
```

```
   A

0  0.0

1  3.0
```

Editing

In the previous sections, we saw how to select some parts (subset) of a DataFrame to view them, to extract them as a new object (new Series or DataFrame), or more often, to manipulate them later, operating on their values in some way.

Another basic operation that is carried out is that of editing. That is, once you have created a DataFrame with a constructor (or loaded from other sources as we will see in *Chapter 7 – Day 5 – Working with data sources and real-world datasets*), it will be necessary to make changes to its structure. Sometimes, it will be necessary to add at the end, or even insert inside, new elements (such as rows or columns), and other times, it will be necessary to remove entire rows or columns.

In this section, we will, therefore, deal with the editing of a complex object such as a DataFrame, so that we can then learn how to make all the changes necessary to prepare a DataFrame for analysis.

Adding, inserting, and deleting a column in a DataFrame

You will have understood by now that due to the way the DataFrames are structured within them, you can think of the columns as separate Series, assembled together to form data tables. So the editing operations of a DataFrame working on the columns are somewhat easier.

Let's create an example DataFrame like the following:

```
In [ ]: df = pd.DataFrame([[1,2,3],[4,5,6],[7,8,9]],
                 index=['a','b','c'],
                 columns=['A','B','C'])

        print(df)


   A  B  C

a  1  2  3
```

```
b  4  5  6

c  7  8  9
```

Adding a column at the end is a fairly simple operation. It is sufficient to select a column that does not yet exist, specify a new label within the indexing operator, and enhance it in some way. In this way, a new column will automatically be created which will be added after the last existing column.

For example, if we value a non-existent column with a scalar value, , we will get a column completely valued with that number, as shown as follows:

```
In [ ]: df['D'] = 17

        print(df)
```

```
   A  B  C   D

a  1  2  3  17

b  4  5  6  17

c  7  8  9  17
```

From now on, if you select this column, the behavior will be the normal selection behavior, where the returned value will be a Series, as shown as follows:

```
In [ ]: df['D'] # seleziona Colonna
```

```
a      17

b      17

c      17
```

```
Name: D, dtype: int64
```

If we wanted to create a new column with all different values, instead of a single scalar, we can pass a list containing all the values, as shown as follows:

```
In [ ]: df['E'] = [13,14,15]

        print(df)
```

```
   A  B  C   D   E
```

```
a   1   2   3   17   13

b   4   5   6   17   14

c   7   8   9   17   15
```

The same technique can be used to update the values of an already existing column. For example, passing a list of values to an already existing column will replace those already present, as shown as follows:

```
In [ ]: df['D'] = ['one','two', 'three']
        print(df)
```

```
    A   B   C     D    E

a   1   2   3   one   13

b   4   5   6   two   14

c   7   8   9   three  15
```

To enhance a column, you can use an existing Series instead of a list. In this case, however, you must pay close attention to the correspondence between the labels of the Series and those of the DataFrame, as shown as follows:

```
In [ ]: sr = pd.Series([10,11,12],index=['a','b','c'])
        df['D'] = sr
        print(df)
```

```
    A   B   C   D    E
a   1   2   3   10   13
b   4   5   6   11   14
c   7   8   9   12   15
```

Another very useful operation is the removal of a column from a DataFrame. The **del** keyword exists in Python that can be used for this purpose, as shown as follows:

```
In [ ]: del df['E']
        print(df)
```

```
   A  B  C   D

a  1  2  3  10

b  4  5  6  11

c  7  8  9  12
```

In this case, the column is permanently removed from the DataFrame, but there may be cases where the removed column wants to be preserved in some way. The **pop()** method allows you to remove the column from the DataFrame and return it as Series that can be stored in a new variable, as shown as follows:

```
In [ ]: sr = df.pop('D')

        print(type(sr))

        print(df)
```

```
<class 'pandas.core.series.Series'>

   A  B  C

a  1  2  3

b  4  5  6

c  7  8  9
```

Another useful method for editing a column within a DataFrame is the **insert()** method. This method inserts a new column within a DataFrame in a predetermined position.

For example, we can insert the Series we extracted earlier with the **pop()** method, back into the DataFrame in position 1, calling it as label '**Z**'. All this information is passed as arguments to the **insert()** function, as shown as follows:

```
In [ ]: df.insert(1, 'Z', sr)

        print(df)
```

```
   A   Z  B  C

a  1  10  2  3

b  4  11  5  6

c  7  12  8  9
```

The same **insert()** method can also be used to copy a column within a DataFrame. For example, in the previous case, the column to be copied is passed instead of an external Series, as shown as follows:

```
In [ ]: df.insert(3, 'B2', df['B'])

        print(df)
```

```
   A   Z  B  B2  C

a  1  10  2   2  3

b  4  11  5   5  6

c  7  12  8   8  9
```

Adding, inserting, and deleting a row in a DataFrame

As for the editing of the rows, it is appropriate to make some small considerations to understand how to make these operations very similar to the case of columns.

First, let's start again with a test DataFrame, as follows:

```
In [ ]: df = pd.DataFrame([[1,2,3],[4,5,6],[7,8,9]],

                    index=['a','b','c'],

                    columns=['A','B','C'])

        print(df)
```

```
   A  B  C

a  1  2  3

b  4  5  6

c  7  8  9
```

We saw that in using the columns, we are privileged because we largely exploit the internal structure of the DataFrame, which provides the columns as a Series. So, just call a column with the corresponding label to get a Series, as shown as follows:

```
In [ ]: print(df['A'])
```

```
a    1

b    4

c    7

Name: A, dtype: int64
```

This reality has been pushed into the syntax within the library to the point of considering the columns as real attributes, without even using the indexing operator anymore, as shown as follows:

```
In [ ]: print(df.A)
```

```
a    1
b    4
c    7
Name: A, dtype: int64
```

In both cases, the results are identical, and we get Series as return values. But in the previous sections, we saw that indexers are powerful tools that allow us to work smoothly with rows and columns. Let's use the indexer **loc[]** as follows:

```
In [ ]: t = df.loc['a']

        print(type(t))
```

```
<class 'pandas.core.series.Series'>
```

It allows us to extract the rows of the DataFrame as Series, in a similar way to what can be done with columns. This is useful for editing on rows, making the row approach similar to when that is applied to columns.

You can then add a row in the same way as for columns. For example, by assigning a scalar value to a selection of a non-existing row, a new row is added at the bottom of the DataFrame, whose values are the repetition of that scalar value, and the label is the one passed in the selection operator, as shown as follows:

```
In [ ]: df.loc['d'] = 12
        print(df)
```

```
    A    B    C
a   1    2    3
b   4    5    6
c   7    8    9
d   12   12   12
```

The symmetry with respect to the editing of the columns, thus, remains unchanged and follows the same operations, but using the **loc[]** operator, the same editing results will be obtained.

Then you can change the values of a row with a scalar, as shown as follows:

```
In [ ]: df.loc['d'] = 10

        print(df)
```

```
    A    B    C
a   1    2    3
b   4    5    6
c   7    8    9
d   10   10   10
```

Or, you can change it by using a list of values, as shown as follows:

```
In [ ]: df.loc['d'] = [10, 11, 12]

        print(df)
```

```
    A    B    C
a   1    2    3
b   4    5    6
c   7    8    9
d   10   11   12
```

Or, instead of a list, you can change it by using an already existing Series, as shown as follows:

```
In [ ]: sr = pd.Series([13,14,15], index=['A','B','C'], name="e")

        df.loc['d'] = sr

        print(df)
```

	A	B	C
a	1	2	3
b	4	5	6
c	7	8	9
d	13	14	15

On the other hand, a completely different speech occurs with the insertion of a line in a specific position. This is not that simple since the **insert()** method only works for columns, and there is no corresponding method for rows.

A similar argument applies to the removal of a line. In fact, if we try to remove a row from the DataFrame with **del**, we get an error message, as shown as follows:

```
In [ ]: del df.loc['d']
```

...

```
AttributeError: __delitem__
```

But in this case, it can be easily remedied by reasoning in another way. In fact, you can use the **drop()** method which returns a new DataFrame eliminating both columns and rows. This method accepts the axis parameter as an argument, which works differently depending on how it is set. If axis = 0, then it will delete the rows, if instead axis = 1, it will delete the columns. To select the row or column to delete, specify the label within a list as the first argument.

This method does not act directly on the calling object but returns the modified object which must then be inserted into a variable.

Then, to delete a row, use the following:

```
In [ ]: df2 = df.drop(['a'],axis=0)

        print(df2)
```

```
   A  B  C

b  4  5  6

c  7  8  9
```

Whereas, use the following to delete a column:

```
In [ ]: df3 = df.drop(['A'],axis=1)

        print(df3)
```

```
   B  C

a  2  3

b  5  6

c  8  9
```

If we want to delete multiple rows or columns at the same time, just add the corresponding labels in the passed list as an argument, as shown as follows:

```
In [ ]: df2 = df.drop(['a','c'],axis=0)

        print(df2)
```

```
   A   B   C

b  4   5   6

d  13  14  15
```

In the previous results, it can be seen that the original DataFrame is not changed (passing by copy). If, on the other hand, we want the removal to be permanent and on the calling object, we must assign the returned value to the object itself, as shown as follows:

```
In [ ]: df = df.drop(['a'],axis=0)

        print(df)
```

```
   A  B  C

b  4  5  6
```

```
c   7    8    9

d   13   14   15
```

Adding new columns with assign()

Among the methods applicable to DataFrames that have editing functions, there is the **assign()** method that allows you to create new columns to be added easily, deriving them from those already present. For example, we can add a new column to the DataFrame starting from the values of an already existing column by multiplying it by 2, as shown as follows:

```
In [ ]: df = pd.DataFrame(np.random.randint(1,10,9).reshape(3,3),

                index=['a','b','c'],

                columns=['A','B','C'])

    print(df)


    A   B   C

a   2   8   1

b   8   4   9

c   2   5   7


In [ ]: df2 = df.assign(D = df['A']*2)

        print(df2)


    A   B   C   D

a   2   8   1   4

b   8   4   9   16

c   2   5   7   4
```

The **assign ()** method does not modify the original DataFrame but creates a new copy of it as a return value. So, the result can be assigned to a new variable, as we have just done, or reassigned to the original DataFrame, modifying it. The choice of what to do is therefore up to the user, as shown as follows:

```
In [ ]: df = df.assign(D = df['A']*2)

        print(df)
```

```
   A  B  C   D

a  2  8  1   4

b  8  4  9  16

c  2  5  7   4
```

But the **assign()** method can also be used to overwrite an existing column, which is often very useful for correcting or modifying the data within the DataFrame, as shown as follows:

```
In [ ]: df = df.assign(D = np.sqrt(df['A']))

        print(df)
```

```
   A  B  C          D

a  2  8  1   1.414214

b  8  4  9   2.828427

c  2  5  7   1.414214
```

As you can see, in addition to arithmetic operations, functions can also be used to modify the values of a column. Another useful application of the **assign()** method is to create new columns containing values generated by special functions. For example, we often need to generate columns containing the same numeric value, as shown as follows:

```
In [ ]: df2 = df.assign(D = np.repeat(1,3))

        print(df2)
```

```
   A  B  C  D

a  2  8  1  1

b  8  4  9  1

c  2  5  7  1
```

Descriptive Statistics

Pandas is a library designed for data analysis, and the DataFrames are the basic objects on which all the related activities are carried out. So having an idea of their contents and their structure at the outset is important in order to better target the operations to be carried out. Among the basic activities, there is, therefore, the calculation of general statistics that can somehow give an idea of the values contained within the DataFrame under analysis. In this section, we will see many basic features that the Pandas library offers to obtain this type of descriptive data.

The describe() method

Inside the Pandas library, there is a **describe()** method that calculates a whole series of descriptive statistics of the reference DataFrame, as shown as follows:

```
In [ ]: df = pd.DataFrame(np.random.rand(40).reshape(10,4))

        print(df)
```

```
           0         1         2         3
0   0.849185  0.620823  0.189868  0.565580
1   0.406432  0.137276  0.795648  0.334122
2   0.986831  0.258703  0.446036  0.105455
3   0.689956  0.876793  0.107509  0.623454
4   0.880415  0.357991  0.671395  0.010990
5   0.602713  0.092022  0.418403  0.436085
6   0.891531  0.918529  0.340645  0.832337
7   0.025438  0.141173  0.361074  0.462877
8   0.021278  0.271381  0.846825  0.896003
9   0.593093  0.121741  0.446063  0.522072
```

It is launched directly on the DataFrame to be analyzed, and the result is a table of descriptive statistics carried out at the column level and reported in the structure of a DataFrame, as shown in *Figure 4.5*:

```
In [ ]: df.describe()
```

	0	1	2	3
count	10.000000	10.000000	10.000000	10.000000
mean	0.594687	0.379643	0.462347	0.478897
std	0.347328	0.314004	0.242739	0.280994
min	0.021278	0.092022	0.107509	0.010990
25%	0.453097	0.138250	0.345752	0.359613
50%	0.646335	0.265042	0.432220	0.492474
75%	0.872608	0.555115	0.615062	0.608985
max	0.986831	0.918529	0.846825	0.896003

Figure 4.5: Descriptive statistics

The statistics processed are also returned in the form of DataFrame, each of which is processed by a single column. Among the reported values, we see the element count, the mean and its standard deviation, the maximum and minimum value, and 3 percentiles. This information will be reported only for the columns of the DataFrame that contain numeric values, as shown in *Figure 4.6*:

```
In [ ]: df2 = pd.DataFrame([[1,'one', True],[2,'two',False],
                            [3,'three',True],[4,'four',False],
                            [5,'five', False]],
                            columns=['numb','word','bool'])

        df2.describe()
```

	numb
count	5.000000
mean	3.000000
std	1.581139
min	1.000000
25%	2.000000
50%	3.000000
75%	4.000000
max	5.000000

Figure 4.6: Descriptive statistics only on numeric columns

If, on the other hand, there are no columns with numerical values to be calculated, it will present in addition to the number of elements present, other statistics such as the number of unique elements, and the most frequent value for every single column with its frequency, as shown in *Figure 4.7*:

```
In [ ]: df2[['word','bool']].describe()
```

	word	bool
count	5	5
unique	5	2
top	one	False
freq	1	3

Figure 4.7: Descriptive statistics on no-numeric columns

So in a DataFrame with many columns, it would be a good practice to be able to select only a few columns (or exclude the ones that don't interest us) without having to first make a selection of subsettings and then applying **describe()** as done before. In this regard, there are two parameters, **include** and **exclude**, which allow us to explicitly specify which columns should be included or excluded in the calculation of descriptive statistics. The peculiarity is that you do not pass lists containing labels, but **dtypes**. That is, the selection is made by the type of data. See the result in *Figure 4.8*:

```
In [ ]: df2.describe(include=['int'])
```

	numb
count	5.000000
mean	3.000000
std	1.581139
min	1.000000
25%	2.000000
50%	3.000000
75%	4.000000
max	5.000000

Figure 4.8: Descriptive statistics only on columns of integers

Calculation of individual statistics

There are several methods to calculate descriptive statistics and other related operations on Series and DataFrames. Those mainly taken into consideration are a whole series of methods taken from the NumPy library that are also applicable on the DataFrame. Many of these methods produce aggregations, that is, they produce a smaller result by agglomerating a group of values (rows or columns) under a single result. Aggregating functions are, for example, `sum()`, `mean()`, `quantile()` which, if applied to a DataFrame, aggregate its values returning a Series. Other methods of this type produce results of the same size, and are, for example, functions like `cumsum()`, and `cumprod()`. Generally, these methods take an axis parameter passed as an argument to determine whether the calculation should be evaluated by column (*axis = 0*) or by row (*axis = 1*).

The statistical evaluation by column is the default one and you can also omit to insert the axis parameter. For example, if you want to calculate the mean of values in each column, you can easily use the `mean()` method, as shown as follows:

```
In [ ]: df.mean(0)    #df.mean(axis=0)  or df.mean()
```

```
0    0.517778

1    0.267020

2    0.374945

3    0.524760

dtype: float64
```

In fact, as many results are obtained as there are columns in the DataFrame. Whereas, if we want to carry out the statistical evaluation by row, the value 1 must be specified (both with and without axis), as shown as follows:

```
In [ ]: df.mean(1) #df.mean(axis=1)
```

```
0    0.184021

1    0.267213

2    0.449525

3    0.380613
```

```
4    0.694051

5    0.376302

6    0.449975

7    0.463459

8    0.448033

9    0.498063

dtype: float64
```

The Skipna option

All these methods have the **skipna** option to set whether the method should exclude the missing data (**True** by default) or not.

A statistical value related to the calculation of the mean is the standard deviation, expressed by the **std()** method, as shown as follows:

In [ ]: df.std()

```
0    0.243282

1    0.254994

2    0.272401

3    0.289059

dtype: float64
```

For this type of statistical calculation, there are, therefore, many methods that can be used directly on the DataFrame. *Table 4.1* shows the most common and used ones:

count	Number of observations (excluding NaNs)
sum	Sum of values
mean	Mean of values
mad	Mean absolute deviation
median	Median
min	Minimum value
max	Maximum value
mode	Mode

abs	Absolute value
prod	Product of a sequence
std	Standard deviation
var	Unbiased variance
sem	Standard error of the mean
skew	skewness
kurt	kurtosis
quantile	Quantile in percent
cumsum	Cumulative sum
cumprod	Cumulative product
cummax	Cumulative maximum
cummin	Cumulative minimum

Table 4.1: *Statistical methods*

The standardization of data

To conclude this section, let's add data standardization. This technique is widely used in statistics and data analysis to make the different data series better comparable to each other, making them "standard". These data groups are somehow "aligned" statistically in order to be able to compare them more easily and highlight the differences. In a practical way, standardization consists of making the mean of this group of values equal to 0 and the standard deviation unitary.

This can be done simply on a DataFrame (but also a Series), as follows:

```
In [ ]: std = ( df - df.mean())/ df.std()

        print(std.mean())

        print(std.std())
```

```
0    -1.087672e-16

1    -5.551115e-17

2     2.858824e-16

3     8.326673e-17

dtype: float64
```

```
0    1.0

1    1.0

2    1.0

3    1.0

dtype: float64
```

Transposition, Sorting, and Reindexing

In this final section, we will see some of the techniques that somehow rearrange the internal structure of the DataFrame by acting at the index level. In fact, the order of the labels within a DataFrame is not immutable but can be changed during the analysis. There are, therefore, some techniques that act at this level including transposition, sorting, and reindexing.

Transposition

The transposition of a DataFrame is equivalent to the mathematical operation of the transposition of a matrix. In this operation, the rows become the columns and vice versa. Applying a transposition to a DataFrame will, therefore, have the exchange of labels between index and columns, with the consequent reordering of the values related to them, as shown as follows:

```
In [ ]: df = pd.DataFrame([[1,2,3],[4,5,6],[7,8,9]],
                    index=['a','b','c'],
                    columns=['A','B','C'])
        print(df)


   A  B  C
a  1  2  3
b  4  5  6
c  7  8  9
```

To carry out the transposition of a DataFrame, it is sufficient to recall the attribute T, as shown as follows:

```
In [ ]: print(df.T)
```

```
    a  b  c

A   1  4  7

B   2  5  8

C   3  6  9
```

We, thus, obtain the transposed DataFrame.

Sorting

Often, when loading a DataFrame from a data source, it happens that the order of the rows or columns is not the desired one. Or during the various analysis phases, we may wish to sort the values of a specific column in the ascending or descending order. All these sorting operations can be summarized in the following three types:

- Sorting by labels
- Sorting by values
- Sorting by a combination of both

All of these sorting types are feasible with the Panda library. For this purpose, we will create a DataFrame with the inside of the index and columns labels arranged in an unordered way (this is practically the case for almost all real DataFrames), as shown as follows:

```
In [ ]: df = pd.DataFrame(np.random.randint(10, size=16).reshape(4,4),

               index=['b','d','c','a'],

               columns=['C','D','A','B'])

        print(df)


    C  D  A  B

b   3  1  8  6

d   0  6  0  6

c   2  8  3  8

a   6  1  7  8
```

Sorting by label

Sorting by labels, or **sorting by index**, is based on sorting the labels in axis or columns based on their value (numeric or string), and it is performed efficiently by the **sort_index()** method. By default, this method puts the labels on the index in the DataFrame in the ascending order. Matching the values on each row will also follow the same order, as shown as follows:

```
In [ ]: df2 = df.sort_index()

        print(df2)
```

	C	D	A	B
a	6	1	7	8
b	3	1	8	6
c	2	8	3	8
d	0	6	0	6

As we can see from the result, the rows of the DataFrame have been reordered following the ascending order of the index labels. We, therefore, had a sort order by row, while the order of the columns remained unchanged. If, on the other hand, we need to sort the labels in descending order, simply add the ascending parameter and set it to **False** (by default, **ascending = True**), as shown as follows:

```
In [ ]: df2 = df.sort_index(ascending=False)

        print(df2)
```

	C	D	A	B
d	0	6	0	6
c	2	8	3	8
b	3	1	8	6
a	6	1	7	8

If we want to sort the labels in columns in ascending order, it will be necessary to explicitly define the parameter **axis = 1** (by default **axis = 0**), as shown as follows:

```
In [ ]: df2 = df.sort_index(axis=1)

        print(df2)
```

	A	B	C	D
b	8	6	3	1
d	0	6	0	6
c	3	8	2	8
a	7	8	6	1

As you can see from the result, this time, it will be the column labels that will be sorted in the ascending order. The same thing will be done for the corresponding values on the columns. Also in this case, if we want to sort in the descending order, we explicitly set **ascending = False**, as shown as follows:

```
In [ ]: df2 = df.sort_index(axis=1, ascending=False)

        print(df2)
```

	D	C	B	A
b	1	3	6	8
d	6	0	6	0
c	8	2	8	3
a	1	6	8	7

If we want to sort by both row labels and column labels, we can do it safely by chaining the methods. We sort the DataFrame first by row, and then later by column, or vice versa, as shown as follows:

```
In [ ]: df2 = df.sort_index(axis=0).sort_index(axis=1)

        print(df2)
```

	A	B	C	D
a	7	8	6	1
b	8	6	3	1

```
c  3  8  2  8

d  0  6  0  6
```

Sorting by values

Another way to sort a DataFrame is to sort the rows or columns according to their contained values. Sorting by values is done by the **sort_values()** method. In order to work, this method needs a mandatory parameter that must be explicitly set. The 'by parameter' must be labeled columns, according to which, the values within the column will be sorted in the ascending order, as shown as follows:

```
In [ ]: df2 = df.sort_values(by='A')

        print(df2)
```

```
   C  D  A  B

d  0  6  0  6

c  2  8  3  8

a  6  1  7  8

b  3  1  8  6
```

As can be seen from the result, the DataFrame has the values of column A in the ascending order. Consequently, the order of the corresponding rows of the DataFrame has also changed to follow that order.

The by parameter can also accept a list of column labels. The **sort_values()** method will first sort the column values corresponding to the first label in the list. Then, in the context of the equal values present in this column, it will sort on the column corresponding to the second label in the list, and so on, as shown as follows:

```
In [ ]: df['A'] = [0,0,2,2]

        df2 = df.sort_values(by=['A','B'])

        print(df2)
```

```
   C  D  A  B

b  3  1  0  6
```

```
d  0  6  0  6

c  2  8  2  8

a  6  1  2  8
```

As we can see from the result, the values of column B will be ordered limited to the range of identical values present in column A. Although, in this simple example, it may be trivial, this combined sorting will be very useful in DataFrame, where there are many rows with data on some columns whose values repeat noticeably.

Finally, both the **sort_index()** method and the **sort_values()** method will not modify the original DataFrame but will return an ordered copy of it. Any changes made to the latter will not affect the original DataFrame in the least, as shown as follows:

```
In [ ]: df2 = df.sort_values(axis=0)

        df2.loc['a','A'] = 0

        print(df)

        print(df2)
```

```
    C  D  A  B

b   4  7  0  6

d   8  9  0  5

c   2  1  2  4

a   8  7  2  8

    C  D  A  B

a   8  7  0  8

b   4  7  0  6

c   2  1  2  4

d   8  9  0  5
```

So, if we want our changes to be final, it will be necessary to assign the DataFrame returned by the function to the starting DataFrame, as shown as follows:

```
In [ ]: df = df.sort_values(by='A')

        print(df)
```

```
   C  D  A  B

b  4  7  0  6

d  8  9  0  5

c  2  1  2  4

a  8  7  2  8
```

Reindexing

Reindexing is the fundamental method of aligning data in Pandas. Reindexing means conforming the data to match a given set of labels along a particular axis. This involves a set of things, which are as follows:

- Reordering of existing data to respond to the new set of labels
- The insertion of NaN in the positions where there is no correspondence
- Possibility of filling in cases of missing data (NaN) with special data following appropriate rules

Refer to the following:

```
In [ ]: df = pd.DataFrame(np.random.randint(10, size=16).reshape(4,4),

                    index=['b','d','c','a'],

                    columns=['C','D','A','B'])

        print(df)
```

```
   C  D  A  B

b  3  9  2  7

d  6  2  5  3

c  4  0  1  3

a  3  6  7  9
```

To reindex, use the **reindex()** method specifying the new order of the labels that the DataFrame must have. The method will not operate on the reference DataFrame, but will return a copy of the DataFrame that will follow the new indexing rules. To select which particular Index object will be reindexed, we will add the axis parameter with its specific value as the function argument, as shown as follows:

- **axis = 0** to edit rows (index)
- **axis = 1** to edit columns (columns)

```
In [ ]: df2 = df.reindex(['a','b','c','d'],axis=0)

        print(df2)
```

```
   C  D  A  B

a  6  3  2  4

b  1  6  9  3

c  8  1  5  2

d  1  8  2  9
```

As you can see, the order of the rows of the DataFrame has been completely changed, following the order in the list of labels specified as an argument of the method.

The new DataFrame will be a completely independent copy, and any changes made to it will not affect the original one in the least, as shown as follows:

```
In [ ]: df2.iloc[1,1] = 0

        print(df2)

        print(df)
```

```
   C  D  A  B

a  6  3  2  4

b  1  0  9  3

c  8  1  5  2

d  1  8  2  9

   C  D  A  B
```

```
b  1  6  9  3

d  1  8  2  9

c  8  1  5  2

a  6  3  2  4
```

The same goes for the columns, as shown as follows:

```
In [ ]: df2 = df.reindex(['A','B','C','D'],axis=1)

        print(df2)
```

```
   A  B  C  D

b  9  3  1  6

d  2  9  1  8

c  5  2  8  1

a  2  4  6  3
```

But what happens if we insert labels that are not present in our DataFrame? Or, if we omit some present label? Refer to the following:

```
In [ ]: df2 = df.reindex(['A','E','C','D',],axis=1)

        print(df2)
```

```
   A   E   C  D

b  9  NaN  1  6

d  2  NaN  1  8

c  5  NaN  8  1

a  2  NaN  6  3
```

As we can see, if a new label is inserted in the reindexing, the method will create a new column (or row) containing NaN (missing values) as values. While if you do not report an existing label in the reindexing, the column (or row) will be removed in the new returned DataFrame.

Reindexing using another DataFrame as a reference

There is also the possibility of using a reference DataFrame from which to take the order of the indexes (both by row and by column) and apply it to our DataFrame. This is possible with the **reindex_like()** method. This method will also not change the object that it is called on but will return a copy of the DataFrame as a result.

In this regard, we create a reference DataFrame, as shown as follows:

```
In [ ]: dfo = pd.DataFrame(np.zeros(16).reshape(4,4),
                    index=['a','b','c','d'],
                    columns=['A','B','C','D'])

        print(dfo)
```

	A	B	C	D
a	0.0	0.0	0.0	0.0
b	0.0	0.0	0.0	0.0
c	0.0	0.0	0.0	0.0
d	0.0	0.0	0.0	0.0

We will apply the **reindex_like()** method on our DataFrame on which we want to reindex, as shown as follows:

```
In [ ]: df2 = df.reindex_like(dfo)

        print(df2)
```

	A	B	C	D
a	2	4	6	3
b	9	3	1	6
c	5	2	8	1
d	2	9	1	8

Also in this case, if in the reference DataFrame, there are labels that do not exist in our DataFrame on which to index, these rows or columns will be added to the new DataFrame returned with all the NaN values (missing values) inside. Whereas, if in the reference DataFrame, some labels are not present, the corresponding rows or columns will be removed from the new DataFrame returned, as shown as follows:

```
In [ ]: dfo = pd.DataFrame(np.zeros(16).reshape(4,4),

                    index=['a','b','c','e'],

                    columns=['A','B','W','Z'])

        print(dfo)
```

	A	B	W	Z
a	0.0	0.0	0.0	0.0
b	0.0	0.0	0.0	0.0
c	0.0	0.0	0.0	0.0
e	0.0	0.0	0.0	0.0

```
In [ ]: df2 = df.reindex_like(dfo)

        print(df2)
```

	A	B	W	Z
a	2.0	4.0	NaN	NaN
b	9.0	3.0	NaN	NaN
c	5.0	2.0	NaN	NaN
e	NaN	NaN	NaN	NaN

Conclusion

In this chapter, we dealt with a whole series of basic operations that apply to DataFrame (and also to Series) and which greatly help in understanding this type of object and how they work. The concept of selection is very important because it allows us to focus our attention on a subset of the DataFrame. This type of object often has dimensions that are too large to be considered in their entirety, and in addition to the often-insufficient selection, a filtering system that allows us to select only what meets particular requirements that come to our aid.

Moreover, in this chapter, thanks to the various editing operations, it was possible to better understand the functioning of the internal structure of a DataFrame and how to manipulate it to modify, extend, or remove the useless parts. Finally, although complex, the index and label structure within the DataFrame is not immutable but can be varied, rearranged, and transposed according to our needs, thus, showing how the Pandas library is really a powerful tool already with these basic operations. In the next chapter, we will move on to more complex operations to apply to a DataFrame, which will involve the manipulation of internal values. More in detail, we will see how to apply calculations on numeric values using functions, and a series of common operations that will modify the structure of the DataFrame such as aggregation and grouping.

Questions

1. What are the reasons that the indexing operator [] generates ambiguous behavior during the selection of elements within the DataFrame?

2. How can it be useful to have a descriptive statistic on the columns of a DataFrame?

3. Can filtration be considered a form of selection?

MCQs

1. Which of these three selections produces an error message?

   A. `df.loc['a':'a', ['A','A','A']]`

   B. `df.loc[:'b', ['D']]`

   C. `df.loc[['a':'c',d] , 'D']`

2. Which of these selections with the iloc [] indexer produces an error message?

   A. `df.iloc[1,4]`

   B. `dfo.iloc['a':'c',3]`

   C. `df.iloc[[1,2,4]]`

3. From the following commands, how do you remove a 'd' line in a DataFrame?

   A. `df.drop( ['d'], axis=1)`

   B. `del df.loc['d']`

C. `df.drop( ['d'], axis=0)`

4. What does the df.sort_index (axis = 1) method do?

   A. Sort the columns in ascending order

   B. Sort the columns in descending order

   C. Sort the rows in ascending order

5. Which of the three rows of a DataFrame do not satisfy this Boolean condition (df['A'] < 0.300000) | (df['C'] > 0.700000)?

   A. In one row, the value of A is 0.1

   B. In a row, the value of A is 0.3 and the value of C is 0.7

   C. In a row, the value of A is 0.23 and the value of C is 0.5

Solution:

1: C; 2: B; 3: C; 4: A; 5: B

Key Terms

Selection, Subsetting, Filtering, Indexing, Reindex, Transposition, Sorting.

References/Further Readings

- *Python for Data Analysis. Data Wrangling with Pandas, NumPy, and IPython, McKinney, OReilly*
- *Python Data Analytics With Pandas, NumPy, and Matplotlib, Fabio Nelli, Apress*
- https://pandas.pydata.org/docs/user_guide/index.html

.

## Chapter 5

Day 3 - Working within a DataFrame, Advanced Functionalities

For better or for worse, we have reached the third day of our course week. In the previous chapters, we became familiar with the structured data of Pandas, especially the DataFrame. The creation of these objects and the use of most of the basic operations should be familiar to us by now. Once this knowledge is consolidated, it is time to go to the heart of the analysis of these objects. In this chapter, we will see many of the advanced features of the Pandas library that will allow us to manipulate this type of object in many ways – all in order to obtain information from the results.

Structure

In this chapter, we will cover the following topics:

- Shifting

- Reshape

- Iteration

- Functions application

- Transform

- Aggregation

- Grouping
- Categorization

Objective

After studying this chapter, you will learn how to operate on any DataFrame in maximum autonomy, having understood most of the functionalities that underlie it. In this chapter, again thanks to simple and schematic examples, you will be gradually introduced to the heart of data analysis in tabular form – data manipulation to obtain information from the results. The application of calculation functions taken from other libraries will allow us to actually carry out the re-processing of the data, and the complementary concepts of transformation and aggregation will open the doors to two different types of data processing. These techniques will then be resumed in grouping, a real conceptual jewel applicable to the Pandas bookcase.

Shifting

The DataFrame is a structured tabular object and some operations can be performed on it to manipulate the values inside. Among the simplest is **shifting**, which essentially consists of moving the internal values of a DataFrame (or even of a Series) by one position, while maintaining the position of the labels on both the index and the columns unchanged.

The shift() method

The shifting on objects such as DataFrame is essentially done with the **shift()** method. Let's first create an example DataFrame, as follows:

```
In [ ]: df = pd.DataFrame(np.arange(1,10).reshape(3,3),
                index=['a','b','c'],
                columns=['A','B','C'])

        print(df)


   A  B  C
a  1  2  3
b  4  5  6
c  7  8  9
```

If we want to move the values within each row by one position, we will pass the value 1 as an argument to the **shift()** method, as shown as follows:

```
In [ ]: df2 = df.shift(1)

        print(df2)
```

```
     A    B    C
a   NaN  NaN  NaN
b   1.0  2.0  3.0
c   4.0  5.0  6.0
```

As we can see, all the values have been translated vertically by one row. The first row has remained empty and has NaN (missing values), while the values that were present in the last row have been lost. There are several ways to manage these valuations or item losses. One, for example, is to fill the missing values (NaN) with a value decided by us. To do this, add the optional **fill_value** parameter to which the desired value is assigned, as shown as follows:

```
In [ ]: df2 = df.shift(1, fill_value=0)

        print(df2)
```

```
   A  B  C
a  0  0  0
b  1  2  3
c  4  5  6
```

As you can see from the result, now the elements left empty due to shifting are set to 0. However, even in this way, the values of the last row are lost. It may be what we want, but it can be an efficient way to move the values of the last row to the first row, as shown as follows:

```
In [ ]: df2 = df.shift(1)

        df2.iloc[0] = df.iloc[2]

        print(df2)
```

```
      A    B    C
a   7.0  8.0  9.0
b   1.0  2.0  3.0
c   4.0  5.0  6.0
```

Yet another approach (this depending on the user's needs) is to permanently delete the row with the NaN values, as shown as follows:

```
In [ ]: df2 = df.shift(1)

        df2 = df2.drop(['a'])

        print(df2)
```

```
      A    B    C
b   1.0  2.0  3.0
c   4.0  5.0  6.0
```

The **shift()** method as default behavior shifts element values vertically down and by a single position (unless otherwise specified). But the direction and the number of positions of the displacement can be decided according to the passed parameters. For example, we can move the elements still vertically (by row) but in the opposite direction, that is, upwards. This can be accomplished by passing negative integers as an argument. If, for example, we want to shift all the values two lines up, we will pass -2 as the method argument, as shown as follows:

```
In [ ]: df2 = df.shift(-2)

print(df2)
      A    B    C
a   7.0  8.0  9.0
b   NaN  NaN  NaN
c   NaN  NaN  NaN
```

Or, if we want to move the values of the elements horizontally, that is, from column to column, we will add the optional parameter **axis = 1 (default axis = 0)**, as shown as follows:

```
In [ ]: df2 = df.shift(1, axis=1)

        print(df2)
```

```
   A   B   C
a NaN  1   2
b NaN  4   5
c NaN  7   8
```

As we can see from the result, the values have shifted to the right, leaving the first column with NaN values. To get the reverse movement, negative integers are also entered here, as shown as follows:

```
In [ ]: df2 = df.shift(-1, axis=1)

        print(df2)

   A   B   C
a  2   3  NaN
b  5   6  NaN
c  8   9  NaN
```

Here, too, the management methods for columns without values are the same as for the vertical shifting on rows.

Reshape

Another way to modify the internal structure of a DataFrame is to modify its size; this technique is called reshape. That is, after this operation, the DataFrame will present a different number of columns and rows, largely due to the transposition of some rows or columns. That is, the operation will convert some column indexes into row indexes and vice versa. The values within the DataFrame being related to these indices will move following the new position of the indices.

The stack() and unstack() methods

One of the ways to reshape a DataFrame is to reorder the internal elements, moving the indexing levels from column to row and vice versa. There are the following two methods in the Pandas library that perform this kind operations, one the inverse of the other:

- **stack():** The **stack()** method reshapes the DataFrame by passing a level of indexing from columns to rows. As a result, we will have a DataFrame with an additional indexing level in the rows and one less than in the columns.
- **unstack():** The **unstack()** method does exactly the reverse – reshaping the DataFrame by transferring a level of indexing from rows to columns.

To better understand this operation, let's start with a simple DataFrame with a single indexing level, both on row and on the column, as shown as follows:

```
In [ ]: df = pd.DataFrame(np.arange(1,10).reshape(3,3),
                 index=['a','b','c'],
                 columns=['A','B','C'])
            print(df)
```

```
   A  B  C
a  1  2  3
b  4  5  6
c  7  8  9
```

Let's see how these two methods work, for example, by applying the **stack()** method to this DataFrame, as shown as follows:

```
In [ ]: dfs = df.stack()
            print(dfs)
```

```
a  A    1
   B    2
   C    3
b  A    4
   B    5
   C    6
c  A    7
   B    8
   C    9
dtype: int32
```

As we can see from the result, now the indexing levels on the rows are 2, while there are no indexes on the columns. In fact, the DataFrame has been reduced in size to a Series with two indexing levels. The columns Index has been nested for each label present in the lowest level of index. Now we have under the label **a,** the labels A, B and C, and the same for the labels **b** and **c**. In this way, a series of 9 elements is obtained with all the values that keep the labels of the starting DataFrame as indices, without having any loss of information.

This reshape operation undergone by the DataFrame is perfectly reversible. Applying the **unstack()** method which does the reverse operation, we get back the starting DataFrame as a result, as shown as follows:

```
In [ ]: print(dfs.unstack())
```

```
   A  B  C
a  1  2  3
b  4  5  6
c  7  8  9
```

This is because the **unstack()** method works exactly the other way around, taking the last row indexing level and transferring it to columns. In this case, since this level is not present, the Series is converted back into a DataFrame, acquiring, in fact, an indexing level on columns.

Let's now consider a MultiIndex DataFrame, for example, with two indexing levels per row and two per column, as shown as follows:

```
In [ ]: index = pd.MultiIndex.from_tuples([('x','a'),
                                            ('x','b'),
                                            ('y','a'),
                                            ('y','b')])

        columns = pd.MultiIndex.from_tuples([('X','A'),
                                             ('X','B'),
                                             ('Y','A'),
                                             ('Y','B')])

        dfm = pd.DataFrame(np.arange(1,17).reshape(4,4),
                  index=index,
                  columns=columns)

        print(dfm)
```

		X		Y	
		A	B	A	B
x	a	1	2	3	4
	b	5	6	7	8
y	a	9	10	11	12
	b	13	14	15	16

So far, we have seen that the methods **stack()** and **unstack()** convert the last indexing level (lowest level) present on both row and column. But, this default behavior can also be changed. In fact, the level to be converted can be passed as an argument. For example, we can convert the highest level of Index of columns (with **level = 0**) to Index of rows. The optional level parameter can also be omitted and the integer value can directly be passed to the method, as shown as follows:

```
In [ ]: print(dfm.stack(0)) # print(dfm.stack(level=0))
```

			A	B
x	a	X	1	2
		Y	3	4
	b	X	5	6
		Y	7	8
y	a	X	9	10
		Y	11	12
	b	X	13	14
		Y	15	16

As you can see from the result, this time, it is the Index of columns at the highest level (level 0) to be converted into Index of rows and put at the last level. The same goes for **unstack()**, as shown as follows:

```
In [ ]: print(dfm.unstack(0)) #print(dfm.stack(level=0))
```

	X				Y			
	A		B		A		B	
	x	y	x	y	x	y	x	y
a	1	9	2	10	3	11	4	12
b	5	13	6	14	7	15	8	16

Pivoting

One of the possible ways to reshape a DataFrame is pivoting. This process restructures the DataFrame in a complex way by simultaneously applying the reindex of the indexes and the aggregation of the internal elements, as shown as follows:

```
In [ ]: df = pd.DataFrame([['red','x',1,1],
                           ['red','x',0,1],
                           ['black','y',0,2],
                           ['red','y',1,0],
                           ['red','y',2,0],
                           ['black','x',2,1]],
                          columns=['A','B','C','D'])
        print(df)


       A  B  C  D
0    red  x  1  1
1    red  x  0  1
2  black  y  0  2
3    red  y  1  0
4    red  y  2  0
5  black  x  2  1
```

The pivoting operation is performed in Pandas through the **pivot_table()** method. This method accepts several optional parameters such as columns which converts the values present in the column to indexes for the columns of the pivot (aggregations of common types). The index parameter converts the values in the column to indexes for the rows of the pivot (aggregation of common types). The index labels of the original DataFrame are not considered. For each label aggregation, the corresponding values in the starting DataFrame are aggregated using the function specified with the optional **aggfunc** parameter, as shown as follows:

```
In [ ]: table = pd.pivot_table(df, values=['C','D'],
                               index=['A'],
                               columns=['B'],
```

```
                                aggfunc=np.sum)
          print(table)
```

	C		D	
B	x	y	x	y
A				
black	2	0	1	2
red	1	3	2	0

You can extend the pivot table by applying different aggregating functions for each column of values. The **aggfunc** parameter can, in fact, accept a **dict**, in which the keys are the columns while the values are the aggregating functions. If we want to apply more functions to the same column, we can insert a list as a value, as shown as follows:

```
In [ ]: table = pd.pivot_table(df, values=['C','D'],
                      index=['A'],
                      columns=['B'],
                      aggfunc={'C': np.sum,
                            'D': [min, max, np.mean]})
          print(table)
```

	C		D					
	sum		max		mean		min	
B	x	y	x	y	x	y	x	y
A								
black	2	0	1.0	2.0	1.0	2.0	1.0	2.0
red	1	3	1.0	0.0	1.0	0.0	1.0	0.0

The result gives as many columns as there are aggregation functions called.

Iteration

DataFrames are structured data, as **dict** or, more simply, lists and **ndarrays** are in Python. All structured objects, regardless of their shape, are often involved in implementations that require an iteration that allows access to the elements within them. For the DataFrame, we have seen that there are selection techniques that allow us to overcome this system in the most common operations. But sometimes, particularly if we need to implement methods that work in some way on this type of object, it is necessary to iterate. However, Pandas helps us in this regard through a number of solutions.

Iteration with for loops

The iteration on the structured objects of the Pandas library varies depending on whether we are dealing with a Series or a DataFrame. In the case of the Series, the iteration will follow an array-like trend, while in the case of the DataFrames, we will have a **dict**-like trend.

So, iterating through a Series will behave the same way as iterating through an array (elementwise). It will directly scan the elements inside, on which you can operate directly, for example, by applying a function to its value.

Thus, let's define an example Series as follows:

```
In [ ]: ser = pd.Series(np.arange(1,12))
        print(ser)
```

```
0        1
1        2
2        3
3        4
4        5
5        6
6        7
7        8
8        9
9        10
10       11
dtype: int32
```

You can loop through one level only using the **for** construct, as shown as follows:

```
In [ ]: for i in ser:
```

```
            print(i, ' ', np.sqrt(i))
```

1   1.0

2   1.4142135623730951

3   1.7320508075688772

4   2.0

5   2.23606797749979

6   2.449489742783178

7   2.6457513110645907

8   2.8284271247461903

9   3.0

10   3.1622776601683795

11   3.3166247903554

In this case, for simplicity, we have calculated the square roots of the individual elements.

The iteration on the DataFrame instead works in the same way as the iterations on the dictionaries. It will scan the columns labels (like the keys in the **dict**) and then operate on them (column wise), thus defining a test DataFrame, as shown as follows:

```
In [ ]: df = pd.DataFrame(np.arange(1,10).reshape(3,3),
                index=['a','b','c'],
                columns=['A','B','C'])
        print(df)
```

```
   A  B  C
a  1  2  3
b  4  5  6
c  7  8  9
```

If we perform a **for** loop in the DataFrame, this time, we will only get the list of columns labels, as shown as follows:

```
In [ ]: for i in df:

            print(i)
```

A

B

C

In order to access the elements contained in the DataFrame at the lowest level, we should apply, within the **for** loop, selections that exploit the iterator **i**. For example, knowing from the previous example that **i** corresponds to the column labels, it can be entered directly in the selection operator, as shown as follows:

```
In [ ]: for i in df:

            print(df[i])
```

a   1

b   4

c   7

Name: A, dtype: int32

a   2

b   5

c   8

Name: B, dtype: int32

a   3

b   6

c   9

Name: C, dtype: int32

In this way, in each **for** loop, we get a Series corresponding to the column selected by the iterator **i**.

If, on the other hand, you want to iterate over the elements inside the columns, you will have to add another level of iteration, so there will be two nested **for** loops, as shown as follows:

```
In [ ]: for i in df:
```

```
for j in df[i]:
    print(j)
```

1

4

7

2

5

8

3

6

9

Methods of iteration

We have seen how it is possible to iterate between elements within a DataFrame by means of the **for** loop. The Pandas library, however, provides methods specifically designed to iterate with the DataFrame, more efficiently.

The **items()** method allows you to iterate within a DataFrame at the level of key-value pairs, as shown as follows:

```
In [ ]: df = pd.DataFrame(np.arange(1,10).reshape(3,3),
            index=['a','b','c'],
            columns=['A','B','C'])
    print(df)
```

```
   A  B  C
a  1  2  3
b  4  5  6
c  7  8  9
```

In the for construct, two different iteration indices are entered, one for the key and one for the value, which in the case of the DataFrame, are respectively the label of the single column, and the corresponding Series. These two indexes will be handled by the **items()** method, as shown as follows:

```
for label, ser in df.items():

    print(label)

    print(ser)

A

a    1

b    4

c    7

Name: A, dtype: int32

B

a    2

b    5

c    8

Name: B, dtype: int32

C

a    3

b    6

c    9

Name: C, dtype: int32
```

This form of iteration allows us to iterate by column, using only one for loop. If, on the other hand, you want to iterate line by line within a DataFrame, the **pandas** library provides the following methods:

- **iterrows()**
- **itertuples()**

The **iterrows()** method works in a similar way to items, with the pair of key-value iteration indices, where this time, however, the column label is a key and the values of each single row are used for value, converting them into a Series. So, this method allows us to iterate row by row through the index-Series pairs. Let's see an example of returning each row as a Series, as follows:

```
In [ ]: for index, row in df.iterrows():
            print(index)
            print(row)
a
A    1
B    2
C    3
Name: a, dtype: int32
b
A    4
B    5
C    6
Name: b, dtype: int32
c
A    7
B    8
C    9
Name: c, dtype: int32
```

The `itertuples()` method allows you to iterate line by line, similar to the previous example, but consider them as `namedtuples`. This iteration method is more efficient than `iterrows()`. The elements of every single column will be directly accessible, calling the corresponding label as an attribute, while the index label will be accessible via the `Index` attribute, as shown as follows:

```
In [ ]: for row in df.itertuples():
            print(row)
            print(row.A)
```

```
        print(row.B)

        print(row.C)

        print(row.Index)
```

```
Pandas(Index='a', A=1, B=2, C=3)

1

2

3

a

Pandas(Index='b', A=4, B=5, C=6)

4

5

6

b

Pandas(Index='c', A=7, B=8, C=9)

7

8

9

c
```

They are obtained from the iteration of **namedtuples**, whose internal values can be easily accessed as attributes.

Row iterations in DataFrames

Iterating by row within a DataFrame is a slow and not very efficient operation due to how a DataFrame is structured internally (Series correspond to columns and not rows). So, if it is possible, it would be better to avoid this type of iteration, and use other ways such as indexing, built-in methods, or the **apply()** method.

Application of Functions on a Dataframe

In the previous sections, we saw how to manipulate the DataFrame in their internal structure. In this section, we will deal with a different type of manipulation, which consists of carrying out operations essentially on the values contained within them.

In Python, as in all other programming languages, values can be processed through the use of functions. This applies to any type of data, whether they are numbers, times, character strings, or complex objects. In the case of numbers, we have functions that allow you to perform any mathematical calculation on them; in the case of strings, many functions perform alphanumeric transformations on the various characters. But there are endless possibilities.

It is clear that applying functions to a DataFrame involves a transformation of its internal values, all aimed at obtaining a result. It is clear, at this point, that the application of functions on a DataFrame is very often the heart of data analysis.

The levels of operability of the functions

Before starting to work on applying functions to complex objects such as a DataFrame, we should first ask ourselves at what level the function will operate within our DataFrame. In fact, with regard to a DataFrame, we can divide the functions into the following different levels of operability:

- By aggregation
  - table wise
  - row wise or column wise
- By element
  - elementwise

By aggregation functions take a set of values as input, such as a list to return a single value. For example, the `np.mean()` function calculates the average from a list of incoming numeric values. In this case, since we are dealing with DataFrames, such a function could work at different levels. For example, we might want to calculate the average of all values in a column or row, and then we would have a function that operates at the row-wise or column-wise level. Or, we might want to calculate the average of all the values contained in a DataFrame, then the function will operate at the table-wise level.

By element functions operate on a single value to get another. So applied to a DataFrame, we would have as many results as there are elements in the DataFrame. One such function could be the exponentiation of a value, such as `np.exp()`. In this case, we are dealing with elementwise functions as they work at the single element level.

Applying NumPy functions directly on DataFrame

The Pandas library relies heavily on its calculations and building objects such as DataFrames on the NumPy library. There is, therefore, considerable compatibility between objects such as DataFrame and Series and NumPy functions. Many NumPy functions can be used directly on Series and DataFrame, with the limitation, however, to the fact that values within them are numeric.

To begin with, let's define a DataFrame with random values between 0 and 1, as shown as follows:

```
In [ ]: df = pd.DataFrame(np.random.rand(16).reshape(4,4),
                index=['a','b','c','d'],
                columns=['A','B','C','D'])
        print(df)
```

	A	B	C	D
a	0.043123	0.571331	0.540262	0.535363
b	0.963704	0.952495	0.306369	0.529315
c	0.388860	0.417357	0.610182	0.765126
d	0.965486	0.876697	0.910901	0.179562

Any NumPy computation function can be applied to it, for example, in the case of an elementwise function such as **np.exp()**, as shown as follows:

```
In [ ]: df2 = np.exp(df)
        print(df2)
```

	A	B	C	D
a	1.044066	1.770621	1.716456	1.708069
b	2.621387	2.592169	1.358483	1.697768
c	1.475298	1.517944	1.840766	2.149266

```
d   2.626062   2.402950   2.486562   1.196693
```

As a result of the function, you still get a DataFrame object where even the row and column labels remain unchanged, as shown as follows:

```
In [ ]: type(df2)
```

```
pandas.core.frame.DataFrame
```

If instead, you want to convert the result into a NumPy ndarray, you can also use a NumPy function in this case, as shown as follows:

```
In [ ]: np.asarray(df2)
```

```
array([[0.04312318, 0.5713306 , 0.54026152, 0.53536327],
       [0.96370368, 0.95249482, 0.30636858, 0.52931453],
       [0.38886004, 0.4173568 , 0.61018159, 0.76512622],
       [0.96548556, 0.87669694, 0.9109011 , 0.17956181]])
```

Other than that, you can use aggregative NumPy functions such as **np.max()**, as shown as follows:

```
In [ ]: np.max(df)
```

```
A    0.965486

B    0.952495

C    0.910901

D    0.765126

dtype: float64
```

In this case, the DataFrame is reduced to a Series, in which each element corresponds to the maximum value of each column. So, the application of a NumPy by aggregation function on a DataFrame is column wise.

Applying functions with the apply () method

The Pandas library provides the possibility to apply any function (not just NumPy ones) on objects such as DataFrame and Series. To do this, the library provides several methods, including the **apply()** method.

The **apply()** method takes a function and, by default, applies it to the DataFrame column by column, considering their values as input. The result will then depend on what the function is programmed to do. If the function used is aggregating, that is, it takes an input list and returns a single value, as a result, we will get a Series, with each element corresponding to a column. Otherwise, it will operate element by element, and in this case, we will obtain as a result a DataFrame of the same size as the original one.

For example, **np.sum()** is an aggregating function. That is, it adds up a list of values and returns the result. So, if applied to a DataFrame, we will have a Series, with each element equivalent to the sum of every single column, as shown as follows:

```
In [ ]: df = pd.DataFrame([[1,2,3],[4,5,6],[7,8,9]],
                    index=['a','b','c'],
                    columns=['A','B','C'])

        print(df)


   A  B  C

a  1  2  3

b  4  5  6

c  7  8  9


In [ ]: df.apply(np.sum)


A     12

B     15

C     18

dtype: int64
```

If instead, we wanted to apply this function line by line, it would be sufficient to explicitly specify the axis parameter as an argument and set it to 1 (by default this **axis = 0**), as shown as follows:

```
In [ ]: df.apply(np.sum, axis=1)


a      6

b      15

c      24

dtype: int64
```

Now, if we use a function such as **np.sqrt()** which evaluates each element in an input list and returns as many results (elementwise function), we will obtain a DataFrame having the same dimensions and labels as the original, as shown as follows:

```
In [ ]: df2 = df.apply(np.sqrt)

        print(df2)

          A         B         C

a   1.000000  1.414214  1.732051

b   2.000000  2.236068  2.449490

c   2.645751  2.828427  3.000000
```

Although we have used NumPy functions to explain how the **apply()** method works, this is especially useful for applying custom functions to our DataFrame. These can be functions previously defined in the same Python code, or via the lambda construct.

Being able to use functions external to the Pandas library (and NumPy), often defined for other purposes, can be useful in our calculations. To give an example, we could use in our DataFrame a function created to double the values previously defined within the same Python code. This function can be applied to our DataFrame by passing its name as an argument to **apply()**, as shown as follows:

```
In [ ]: def dubble_up(x):

            return x * 2


In [ ]: df2 = df.apply(dubble_up)

        print(df2)
```

	A	B	C
a	2	4	6
b	8	10	12
c	14	16	18

As you can see, the elementwise behavior of the external function has been taken into consideration, applying it to the DataFrame element by element. A new DataFrame was obtained with doubled values.

Another method of defining a function is to use the **lambda** operator. This allows us to specifically insert a function in a concise and direct way (inline function), without having to define any function in the code, as shown as follows:

```
In [ ]: df.apply(lambda x: x.max() - x.min())
```

```
A    6

B    6

C    6

dtype: int64
```

Also, in this case, the aggregation nature of this function is respected. The inline function is evaluated column by column, resulting in a Series as the result. This can also be done per line, by explicitly setting the parameter **axis = 1**, as shown as follows:

```
In [ ]: df.apply(lambda x: x.max() - x.min(), axis=1)
```

```
a    2
b    2
c    2
dtype: int64
```

Applications of functions with the pipe() method

In addition to the **apply()** method, the Pandas library provides another important method, the **pipe()** method that allows you to apply functions on the DataFrame. It is used often in cases where the apply() method is unable to do this.

For example, although very rare, there may be functions that operate at the level of table wise by aggregation. A simple example could be that of having to calculate the maximum value of all the values within a DataFrame containing all numeric values, as shown as follows:

```
In [ ]: df = pd.DataFrame([[1,2,3],[4,5,6],[7,8,9]],
                  index=['a','b','c'],
                  columns=['A','B','C'])
        print(df)
    A  B  C
a   1  2  3
b   4  5  6
c   7  8  9
```

In this case, we may have an already defined external function available to perform this task. In our case, it could be the following:

```
In [ ]: def maximus(x):
            return np.max(np.max(x))
```

To apply it to our DataFrame, just pass it as an argument to the **pipe()** method, as shown as follows:

```
In [ ]: df.pipe(maximus)
```

```
9
```

As we can see, we have a single value as a result, which is the maximum value present within the DataFrame. But couldn't we have done the same with the **apply()** method? Well, if we apply these kinds of functions to the **apply()** method, we get unexpected results, as shown as follows:

```
In [ ]: df.apply(maximus)
```

```
A    7
```

```
B    8

C    9
```

dtype: int32

As we can see from the result, **apply()** works at the level of row wise or column wise, and even though it is very adaptable (it also manages to work at the elementwise level), it cannot move up to the level of operability (table wise). In these cases, we are, therefore, forced to use the **pipe()** method.

Chaining pipe() and apply() methods

Another peculiarity of the **pipe()** and **apply()** methods is their ability to operate in chaining. Several calls to the method are chained, so that in each of them, a different function will be applied to the incoming object (DataFrame or Series), and the result obtained (DataFrame or Series) will be passed on to the next method call. During these steps, the starting DataFrame will be processed until the desired result is obtained.

Take for example, the table wise **maximus()** function used earlier. The same result can be obtained by combining two applications of the **np.max()** function placed in a chain, as shown as follows:

```
In [ ]: df.pipe(np.max).pipe(np.max)
```

9

We have applied two column wise functions. In the first **pipe()**, the maximum values for a single column were calculated; in the second **pipe()**, the maximum value among all the maximums of the columns were calculated. This can be clearly seen if we break down the steps, as follows:

```
In [ ]: step1 = df.pipe(np.max)

        print(step1)

        step2 = step1.pipe(np.max)

        print(step2)
```

```
A    7
```

```
B    8

C    9

dtype: int64
```

```
9
```

Thanks to the chaining of the **pipe()** method, it is possible to apply all the combinations of functions necessary to obtain the desired result, whether they are external functions, inline functions, or NumPy functions. It is only necessary to take into account that at each step-in chaining, elementwise functions will return objects of the same size (Series remain Series, and DataFrame remain DataFrame), while if there are functions by aggregation, the dimensions will decrease (Series will become single values, DataFrame will become Series), as shown as follows:

```
In [ ]: def dubble_up(x):

            return x * 2
```

```
In [ ]: df.pipe(dubble_up).pipe(np.mean).pipe(lambda x: x-2)
```

```
A     6.0

B     8.0

C    10.0

dtype: float64
```

In this case, we would have achieved the same result using the **apply()** method, as shown as follows:

```
In [ ]: df.apply(dubble_up).apply(np.mean).apply(lambda x: x-2)
```

```
A     6.0

B     8.0

C    10.0

dtype: float64
```

Applying functions with arguments with the pipe() method

So far, we saw all functions that take no arguments being applied. But this does not always happen; sometimes to carry out the calculation implemented by the function, it may be necessary to specify one or more values useful for the calculation. For this purpose, the **pipe()** method helps us, which is able to accept as arguments, in addition to the name of the function to be applied, the values to be passed.

For example, we specify an external function that does the addition between two objects, as shown as follows:

```
In [ ]: def adder(a, b):
            return a + b
```

This function will need two operands to work. So far, we saw that the first operand gives the DataFrame calling the **pipe()** method, while the second operand must be passed to the applied function. So, you just need to add a second argument to the **pipe()** method containing the value to pass, as shown as follows:

```
In [ ]: df2 = df.pipe(adder, 2)

print(df2)
```

	A	B	C
a	3	4	5
b	6	7	8
c	9	10	11

In this case, we passed a scalar value to add to our DataFrame, element by element. But you can go further and go directly to a Series or DataFrame. The rules then applied within the function will respond to the arithmetic rules between the structured data of the Pandas library (see *Chapter 6, Day 4 - Working with two or more DataFrames*), as shown as follows:

```
In [ ]: print(df)
        df2 = pd.DataFrame(np.repeat(1,9).reshape(3,3),
                    index=['a','b','c'],
                    columns=['A','B','C'])
```

```
        print(df2)
        df3 = df.pipe(adder, df2)
        print(df3)
```

```
   A  B  C
a  1  2  3
b  4  5  6
c  7  8  9
```

```
   A  B  C
a  1  1  1
b  1  1  1
c  1  1  1
```

```
   A  B   C
a  2  3   4
b  5  6   7
c  8  9  10
```

The applymap() and map() methods

In addition to **pipe()** and **apply()**, there are the following two methods that allow the application of functions on structured data Pandas:

- **applymap()** for DataFrames
- **map()** for Series

However, these methods work differently, accepting only elementwise functions. In fact, while the **apply()** method lets the function work according to its programming (by aggregation or elementwise), the **applymap()** or **map()** methods will force the function to evaluate element by element. This will result in a DataFrame or a Series with the same number of elements as the original one. If the applied function is aggregation and is not able to do this, we will not get any variation in the values inside the DataFrame or even an error message, as shown as follows:

```
In [ ]: df2 = df.applymap(dubble_up)

        print(df2)
```

```
     A   B   C

a    2   4   6

b    8   10  12

c    14  16  18
```

```
In [ ]: ser = pd.Series([1,3,5,7,9,11])

        ser.map(dubble_up)
```

```
0       2

1       6

2       10

3       14

4       18

5       22

dtype: int64
```

Transforming

Let's go on with the concept of manipulating the values of a DataFrame through the use of functions. We have said that applying functions to a DataFrame has the purpose of "transforming" it in some way, to obtain results that bring us closer to the information we need in the data analysis process. Well, in this section, we will cover the core of the Transforming concept, through the use of the **transform()** method.

The transform() method

The **transform()** method applies transformations on the starting DataFrame, by applying functions. Apparently, it would appear as identical behavior to the **apply()** method, as shown as follows:

```
In [ ]: df = pd.DataFrame(np.arange(1,10).reshape(3,3),

                index=['a','b','c'],

                columns=['A','B','C'])
```

```
        print(df)
```

```
    A  B  C
a   1  2  3
b   4  5  6
c   7  8  9
```

```
In [ ]: def double(x):
            return x*2
```

```
In [ ]: df2 = df.transform(double)
        print(df2)
```

```
    A    B    C
a   2    4    6
b   8    10   12
c   14   16   18
```

```
In [ ]: df2 = df.apply(double)
        print(df2)
```

```
    A    B    C
a   2    4    6
b   8    10   12
c   14   16   18
```

From what we've just seen, the results are much the same. Both use the **double()** function and apply it to elements within the DataFrame. So, it would seem like two redundant methods apparently. But the differences are there and appear in more complex cases, where the peculiarities of the **transform()** method are highlighted with respect to **apply()**.

The **transform()** method can work with multiple functions at the same time. These can be passed either as a list or as a **dict**, which the **apply()** method cannot do, as shown as follows:

```
In [ ]: multidf = df.transform([np.sqrt, double])

        print(multidf)
```

	A		B		C	
	sqrt	double	sqrt	double	sqrt	double
a	1.000000	2	1.414214	4	1.732051	6
b	2.000000	8	2.236068	10	2.449490	12
c	2.645751	14	2.828427	16	3.000000	18

By passing a list of methods, the MultiIndex of the DataFrame is obtained with the formation of the second level of labels in the produced DataFrame. For each column of the original DataFrame, as many columns are generated as there are passed methods. Within each of them, there will be listed the results obtained by applying these methods.

Reducing a MultiIndex DataFrame to a DataFrame

As a result of passing a list of functions to the **transform()** method, you always get a MultiIndex DataFrame. From these complex objects, it is possible to extract the DataFrame related to each single function. For example, if we want the DataFrame related to the transformation for the **double()** function, we can operate as follows:

```
In [ ]: idx = pd.IndexSlice

        dfn = multidf.loc[idx[:], idx[:, 'double']]

        dfn.columns = dfn.columns.droplevel(1)

        print(dfn)
```

	A	B	C
a	2	4	6

```
b   8  10  12

c  14  16  18
```

For this kind of operation concerning the MultiIndex DataFrame, we use objects such as the **IndexSlice**, necessary to make the selections on several levels, and the **droplevel()** method, necessary to eliminate the level of indexes from the columns. For further information on these issues, it is advisable to consult the official documentation.

Instead, passing a **dict** with the column label as key and the function to be applied as values, you will get a new DataFrame with the structure specified in the **dict**, as shown as follows:

```
In [ ]: df2 = df.transform({

               'A': np.sqrt,

               'B': np.double,

          })

        print(df2)



              A    B

a   1.000000  2.0

b   2.000000  5.0

c   2.645751  8.0
```

Transform() does not aggregate elements

On the other hand, the **transform()** method is unable to do some things that the **apply()** method does correctly. The **transform()** method cannot work with functions that work by aggregation.

In fact, if you pass a function like **np.sum()** to the **transform()** method, you will get a "Function did not transform" error message, meaning that this function is not intended as a transformation of one DataFrame into another, as shown as follows:

```
In [ ]: df.transform(np.sum)

ValueError: Function did not transform
```

While, as we have seen before, the **apply()** method manages to do it without problems, as shown as follows:

```
In [ ]: df.apply(sum)
```

```
A      12

B      15

C      18
```

```
dtype: int64
```

Transform() works with a single column at a time

Another difference with the **apply()** method is that the **transform()** method does not have access to other columns while it "transforms" one (single Series). However, the **apply()** method has no such limitations.

For example, we specify a method that takes two specific columns of the DataFrame by adding their values together, as shown as follows:

```
In [ ]: def adding(x):
            return x[0] + x[1]
```

```
In [ ]: df.apply(adding, axis=1)
```

```
a      3
b      9
```

```
c      15
```

```
dtype: int32
```

As we can see from the result, the **apply()** method works without any problem on two columns at the same time. If instead, we apply the same function in the **transform()** method, we will get an error message, again with the message **Function did not transform**, as shown as follows:

```
In [ ]: df.transform(subtract_two, axis=1)
```

```
ValueError: Function did not transform
```

In fact, if we check the result of this function with **apply()**, we certainly get a result, but it is not a DataFrame.

All these limitations on the **transform()** method are set specifically to give a semantic meaning to the concept of Transforming specific to the Pandas library – **Transforming** means *transforming* one DataFrame into another, manipulating the data, making it evolve into something different. They are imposed to avoid that; sometimes even unconsciously, the structure of the DataFrame being analyzed can be varied in some way.

Aggregation

A completely opposite concept to transforming is **Aggregation**. It is no coincidence that those who designed the Pandas library wanted to create two complementary *poles* as regards the manipulation of the values of a DataFrame. Aggregation carries out precisely the operation that is not allowed for transforming, that is, summarizing a set of values through a function into a single result; therefore, the values are aggregated. The DataFrame, in this case, reduces its size and changes structurally.

The agg() method

Aggregation allows you to express many operations simultaneously in a concise way and is expressed using the **agg()** method.

We define, if not yet, a DataFrame, as follows:

```
In [ ]: df = pd.DataFrame(np.arange(1,10).reshape(3,3),
                index=['a','b','c'],
                columns=['A','B','C'])

        print(df)


   A  B  C

a  1  2  3

b  4  5  6

c  7  8  9
```

```
In [ ]: df.agg(np.sum)
```

```
A    12

B    15

C    18

dtype: int64
```

Even **agg()** like the **transform()** method can receive multiple functions simultaneously, either as elements of a list or as values in a **dict**, as shown as follows:

```
In [ ]: multidf = df.agg([np.sqrt, double])

        print(multidf)
```

	A		B		C	
	sqrt	double	sqrt	double	sqrt	double
a	1.000000	2	1.414214	4	1.732051	6
b	2.000000	8	2.236068	10	2.449490	12
c	2.645751	14	2.828427	16	3.000000	18

```
In [ ]: df2 = df.agg({

            'A': np.sqrt,

            'B': np.double,

        })

        print(df2)        A    B
```

	A	B
a	1.000000	2.0
b	2.000000	5.0
c	2.645751	8.0

So far, it would seem that there is no difference whatsoever with the **transform()** method. Actually, **agg()** handles the by aggregation functions perfectly, which **transform()** cannot.

In fact, if we pass the NumPy **np.sum()** function, we get a Series as a result, instead of an error message, as shown as follows:

```
In [ ]: df.agg(np.sum)
```

```
A    12

B    15

C    18

dtype: int64
```

So, by inserting functions by aggregation, you get very different results from the **transform()** method. For example, passing a list of these functions, we obtain a two-dimensional DataFrame, where this time, the names of the functions are passed as labels to the index of the lines, as shown as follows:

```
In [ ]: df = df.agg([np.mean, np.sum])

        print(multidf)
```

```
         A      B      C

mean    4.0    5.0    6.0

sum    12.0   15.0   18.0
```

Whereas, we get a series as a result, if we pass the functions as values of a **dict**, as shown as follows:

```
In [ ]: df2 = df.agg({

            'A': np.mean,

            'B': np.sum,

        })

        print(df2)
```

A   4.0

B   15.0

dtype: float64

It is, therefore, clear that the purpose of the **agg()** method is complementary to that of **transform()**, where the former should work exclusively with functions by aggregation, and the latter with functions by element.

In fact, if we pass both types of functions or only those element by element, we get an error with the message – **cannot combine transform and aggregation operations**.

We get a Series as a result, as shown as follows:

```
In [ ]: df = df.agg([np.mean, np.sum, np.sqrt])

        print(multidf)
```

```
ValueError: cannot combine transform and aggregation operations
```

Grouping

Grouping is a particular process in which one or more of the following steps are involved:

- splitting
- applying
- combining

The first step, that of splitting, is based on dividing the DataFrame into groups, based on a particular criterion. The second step, instead, involves the application of one or more functions, transformations or aggregations, on each individual group independently. Finally, the third step involves the reunification of all the results of the second step to regain a new DataFrame.

The groupby() method

The **groupby()** method divides the DataFrame into different groups, based on different selection criteria passed as an argument. A DataFrame can be grouped by either of the following:

- columns
- index

In both cases, the **groupby()** method groups together, based on the selection, all the elements with the same value, as shown as follows:

```
In [ ]: df = pd.DataFrame(np.random.randint(1,5,18).reshape(6,3),
                index=['a','b','c','a','b','c'],
                columns=['A','B','C'])
        print(df.sort_values(by=['A']))
```

	A	B	C
a	1	2	3
c	1	4	2
b	2	4	4
a	3	1	1
b	3	1	4
c	4	3	4

The first step of grouping is to divide the rows of the DataFrame into groups (splitting) based on the values contained within a given column. To do this, we use the optional by parameter to which the label of the reference column is passed, in our case, A. All the rows that have the same value in this column will be grouped together. It is clear that, in the end, we will have as many groups as the possible values present in A, as shown as follows:

```
In [ ]: df.groupby(by='A')
```

```
<pandas.core.groupby.generic.DataFrameGroupBy object at 0x00000215EAC58700>
```

Splitting into groups produces a **DataFrameGroupBy** object that is not printable (it does not show the contents using the **print()** function). One way to see all the groups the DataFrame has been split into and the elements within them is by writing the following iteration:

```
In [ ]: for name, group in df.groupby(by='A'):
            print(name)
            print(group)
```

1

	A	B	C
a	1	2	3
c	1	4	2

2

	A	B	C
b	2	4	4

3

	A	B	C
a	3	1	1
b	3	1	4

4

	A	B	C
c	4	3	4

The situation of splitting can be well represented in *Figure 5.1*:

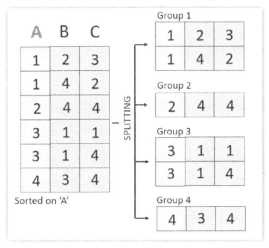

Figure 5.1: Splitting step in grouping

The non-visibility of the result of the operation of the division into groups is due to the fact that this is not the result that is expected from this operation. In fact, grouping requires that a function is subsequently applied to each group, implicitly defined by the **groupby()** function. In our example, we can use the **np.max()** function, as shown as follows:

```
In [ ]: dfg = df.groupby(by='A').max()
        print(dfg)
```

```
      B  C

A

1     4  3

2     4  4

3     1  4

4     3  4
```

The result is in fact what we would have expected, as shown in *Figure 5.2*:

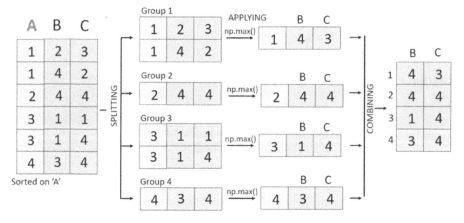

Figure 5.2: Grouping schema: splitting, applying and combining

As you can see, a smaller DataFrame is obtained, in which column A is no longer present. The column label A has become the name of the DataFrame index, and the labels inside correspond to the values into which the various groups have been divided. The **np.max** function (but this is valid for any other function) is applied to all the values belonging to the same group and in each of them, the result is given for each column (the maximum value of the group for column B and the maximum group value for column C).

Let's see the operations in more detail. The maximum value on column B of the group having value 1 in column A is 1, while the maximum value on column C is

3. Now, let's move on to the second row. The maximum value on column B of the group having value 2 in column A is 4, while the one on column C is 3, and so on.

The groupby() method for indexes

The grouping as well as by column and by row, can also be obtained at the index level, by specifying the indexing level using the optional level parameter. This type of grouping is particularly useful in the case of MultiIndex, where there are levels in which some labels are repeated many times, and which can be used to divide the data into groups.

We then define a MultiIndex DataFrame with some repeating labels, as shown as follows:

```
In [ ]: tuples = [('x', 'a'), ('x', 'b'), ('y', 'a'), ('y', 'b')]

        index = pd.MultiIndex.from_tuples(tuples,

                names=['first','second'])

        tuples = [('X', 'A'), ('X', 'B'), ('Y', 'A'), ('Y', 'B')]

        columns = pd.MultiIndex.from_tuples(tuples,

                names=['high','low'])

        dfm = pd.DataFrame(np.arange(1,17).reshape(4,4),

                index = index, columns = columns)

        print(dfm)
```

high		X		Y	
low		A	B	A	B
first	second				
x	a	1	2	3	4
	b	5	6	7	8
y	a	9	10	11	12
	b	13	14	15	16

And then we apply a level 0 grouping, as shown as follows:

```
In [ ]: df2 = dfm.groupby(level=0).max()

        print(df2)
```

high	X		Y	
low	A	B	A	B
first				
x	5	6	7	8
y	13	14	15	16

In this case, the rows with the same label at level 0 of the Index of row (that is, **x** and **y**) are grouped, and within the group, the greater value is chosen for each column. Information regarding the second-level labels of the index is lost.

Instead, we can apply a grouping at level 1, as shown as follows:

```
In [ ]: df2 = dfm.groupby(level=1).max()

        print(df2)
```

high	X		Y	
low	A	B	A	B
second				
a	9	10	11	12
b	13	14	15	16

In this case, the same operation will happen, but with regards to the labels of the second level of the index. Information regarding top-level labels is lost.

It is interesting to note that in this case, by grouping according to the levels of the indexes, it is possible to group by column. In fact, by also adding the optional parameter **axis = 1**, more columns with the same label are grouped together.

The following is the case for level 0:

```
In [ ]: df2 = dfm.groupby(level=0, axis=1).max()

print(df2)
```

high		X	Y
first	second		
x	a	2	4
	b	6	8
y	a	10	12
	b	14	16

And the following is the case for level 1:

```
In [ ]: df2 = dfm.groupby(level=1, axis=1).max()

        print(df2)
```

low		A	B
first	second		
x	a	3	4
	b	7	8
y	a	11	12
	b	15	16

In our example, we have directly used the **np.sum** function of the NumPy library to make it easier to understand how grouping works, in particular for the splitting phase. In general, however, any type of function can be applied to grouping. Therefore, techniques such as the transformations and aggregations that we have seen previously enter into this regard. These are operations that can be used in conjunction with Grouping. In fact, the methods **apply()**, **transform()** and **agg()** can be used in conjunction with **groupby()**, and depending on which technique is used, you will get very different results.

Grouping with Transformation

By applying the **transform()** method in conjunction with grouping, we get a DataFrame that has the same number of rows as the original DataFrame. While as far as the columns are concerned, they will be one less, as shown as follows:

```
In [ ]: gdf = df.groupby('A').transform(np.sum)

        print(gdf)
```

	B	C
a	6	5
b	4	4
c	6	5
a	2	5
b	2	5
c	3	4

With the transformation, the values contained in column A have been lost. They only served to subdivide into computational groups. The results obtained by the group were then assigned to every single row according to their belonging group. In fact, there are lines with identical results.

Grouping with Aggregation

Applying the **agg()** method in conjunction with the **groupby()** method results in one row for each group. While with regards to the columns, there will be one less (column A has become the index of the new DataFrame), as shown as follows:

```
In [ ]: gdf = df.groupby('A').agg(np.sum)

        print(gdf)
```

	B	C
A		
1	6	5
2	4	4
3	2	5
4	3	4

Although the same **np.sum()** function has been applied, the results obtained are significantly different between transformation and aggregation. In fact, the aggregation necessarily produces a smaller result. The number of rows will now correspond to the existing groups, while for the other columns, the aggregating function replaces the different values with a single value that is the result.

Inversely, from the case of the transformation, it is the index labels of the original DataFrame that are no longer present, since in the new system, they have lost their meaning, while the values of column A have become the new labels.

Apply() with groupby()

As far as the grouping is concerned, a method can be applied outside the system of aggregation and transformation. With **apply()** in conjunction with the **groupby()** method, you get one row for each group as a result, as shown as follows:

```
In [ ]: gdf = df.groupby('A').apply(np.sum)

        print(gdf)
```

	A	B	C
A			
1	2	6	5
2	2	4	4
3	6	2	5
4	4	3	4

In this case, the result is still different. As far as column A is concerned, we have the same behaviour as the aggregation, with the conversion of its values into index labels. We, therefore, have an aggregation that has led to the reduction of the DataFrame to only 4 lines, each for each group. But at the same time, there are some differences, such as column A which still remained as such in the DataFrame, and whose values are the result of the aggregation (sum) such as columns B and C.

Categorization

An operation that may come in handy during the analysis of a DataFrame is to categorize the rows within it, dividing them into different categories of belonging (classes). The categorization is explicitly implemented in the Pandas library, which provides a series of objects and methods that perform it in an extremely controlled manner by the user.

Specifying a category column

Let's create a simple DataFrame to better understand the categorization, as follows:

```
In [ ]: df = pd.DataFrame(np.arange(1,10).reshape(3,3),
                index=['a','b','c'],
                columns=['A','B','C'])

    print(df)
```

```
    A  B  C

a   1  2  3

b   4  5  6

c   7  8  9
```

One way to implement them in a DataFrame is to choose a column with a series of values (repeated over and over again between the various rows) that can somehow express the different categories of belonging. If this column does not exist, a new one can still be created with the elements appropriately valued. In the example case, having no columns in the DataFrame with information that helps us identify the categories of belonging of the rows, we can provide a new column with values of belonging categories that we have somehow evaluated externally.

To create a category column, we use the **Categorical()** constructor. As input data, a list (or even a Series) is inserted in which there are the values of the categories corresponding to the various lines. Then two more optional parameters are added. The categories in the list may not be all possible, and also often the categories have an order or a hierarchy. So, in the categories parameter, we insert a list with all possible categories (in the right order). And if these categories have a hierarchy or a precise order, then we will set the ordered parameter to **True** (by default it is **False**) , as shown as follows:

```
In [ ]: cat = pd.Categorical(['IV','I','IV'],
                categories=['I','II','III','IV','V'],
                ordered=True)
```

The newly created **Categorical** object is then assigned to a column with a non-existent label to create a new one, as shown as follows:

```
In [ ]: df['cat'] = cat

        print(df)
```

```
   A  B  C  cat

a  1  2  3  IV

b  4  5  6   I

c  7  8  9  IV
```

To check if the column belongs to a category, and what its order is, we first specify the cat attribute, and then we call the **as_ordered()** method, as shown as follows:

```
In [ ]: print(df['cat'].cat.as_ordered())
```

```
a    IV

b     I

c    IV
```

```
Name: cat, dtype: category
```

```
Categories (5, object): ['I' < 'II' < 'III' < 'IV' < 'V']
```

As we can see, the **dtype** of the column is category, and then the correct order of all possible categories is shown (even if they are not present in the DataFrame).

At this point, having consolidated the fact that the DataFrame has a column of categories, you can sort its values within it according to the hierarchical scale of the categories. We then use the **sort_values()** method, as shown as follows:

```
In [ ]: print(df.sort_values(by='cat'))
```

```
   A  B  C  cat

b  4  5  6   I

a  1  2  3  IV

c  7  8  9  IV
```

Grouping can also be used in the case of categories. A useful application in categorization is knowing how many rows in a DataFrame belong to each category, as shown as follows:

```
In [ ]: print(df.groupby('cat').size())
```

```
cat

I       1

II      0

III     0

IV      2

V       0

dtype: int64
```

So far, we have created a new column to specify categories in a DataFrame. But as mentioned earlier, there may already be a column that has suitable values to express a categorization. In this case, we proceed in this way.

Let's modify the example DataFrame, assuming it already has a fourth column in which there are values suitable for expressing categories, as shown as follows:

```
In [ ]: df['cat'] = ['IV','I','III']

print(df)
```

```
   A  B  C  cat

a  1  2  3   IV

b  4  5  6    I

c  7  8  9  III
```

In this case, we, therefore, have a **cat** column that contains the categories to which each row belongs. First, we need to change the **dtype** of the column, turning it into **category**, as shown as follows:

```
In [ ]: df['cat'] = df['cat'].astype('category')
```

Then if, as in the previous case, the categories have an order, you can specify the series of categories with their order using the **set_categories()** method, launching it from the **cat** attribute. The first argument of the method will be the list containing the ordered sequence of the categories, and the second argument will be **ordered = True**, as shown as follows:

```
In [ ]: df['cat'] = df['cat'].cat.set_categories(['I','II','III','IV','V'],
ordered=True)

        print(df)
```

```
   A  B  C  cat

a  1  2  3   IV

b  4  5  6    I

c  7  8  9  III
```

Again, you can sort the rows by category using the **sort_values()** method in the same way, as shown as follows:

```
In [ ]: print(df.sort_values(by='cat'))
```

```
   A  B  C  cat

b  4  5  6    I

c  7  8  9  III

a  1  2  3   IV
```

Conclusion

In this chapter, we acquired all the necessary knowledge to be able to fully use the features provided by Pandas to operate on its tabular structured data, the DataFrames. In particular, in this chapter, we understood what the manipulation of data in tabular form consists of – modifying the entire structure of the DataFrame or performing calculations on the values inside.

Shifting, reshaping, and pivoting are very common practices for those who work on spreadsheets and these are now familiar concepts even for those who only work with Pandas. While with regard to data processing, the ability to apply a generic function, coming from any Python library, extends the ability to perform data analysis with Pandas even in fields of application far from each other. Furthermore, by now, you must have understood the difference between the operations of transformation or aggregation of data in a DataFrame, concepts that are very useful even in the case of grouping operations.

In the next chapter, we will complete the discussion of operations on DataFrame, considering the case of working with two or more of them. We will see how to use arithmetic operations using DataFrame as operators and how to align the structure of one DataFrame with that of another used as a reference.

Questions

1. What can be the practical utility of reshaping a DataFrame?
2. What are the substantial differences between aggregation and transformation?
3. The applying and combining steps are included in the grouping procedure of a DataFrame. Could you explain why?

MCQs

1. Which of the following statements about shifting a DataFrame is false?
   A. After shifting is complete, all row values in the DataFrame are in different locations.
   B. All row values in the DataFrame move out of position.
   C. Shifting can be applied in any direction in the DataFrame.
2. Which of the following statements about stacking is true?
   A. Stacking on a DataFrame causes information loss.
   B. The stacking operation on a DataFrame is reversible.
   C. Stacking on a DataFrame always produces a MultiIndex Series.
3. What does df.apply(lambda x: x.max() - x.min()) return?
   A. A DataFrame of the same size as df
   B. A Series with as many elements as there are columns of df
   C. A Series with as many elements as there are lines of df
4. What are the steps of the Grouping process?
   A. Reshape, Applying, Combine
   B. Splitting, Transforming, Combine
   C. Splitting, Applying, Combine
5. Which of the statements on the categorization is false?
   A. For categorization, a category column must necessarily be added to the DataFrame
   B. The categorization is specified based on the labels of a DataFrame

C. The categorization is based on a set of values which may or may not have a predetermined order.

Solution:

1: A; 2: B; 3: B; 4: C; 5: C

Key Terms

Stacking, Reshape, Shifting, Pivoting, Aggregation, Transforming, Grouping, Data Manipulation.

References/Further Readings

- *Python for Data Analysis. Data Wrangling with Pandas, NumPy, and IPython, McKinney, OReilly*
- *Python Data Analytics With Pandas, NumPy, and Matplotlib, Fabio Nelli, Apress*
- *https://pandas.pydata.org/docs/user_guide/index.html*
- *https://towardsdatascience.com/difference-between-apply-and-transform-in-pandas-242e5cf32705*

CHAPTER 6

Day 4 - Working with Two or More DataFrames

Once we have acquired the many features that allow us to create, transform, subject the DataFrame to calculations, and, in some way, interpret the data within them, we must face the final part. In fact, in this chapter, we will see some possible operations between two or more Pandas objects, whether they are DataFrames or simple Series.

Structure

In this chapter, we will cover the following topics:

- Adding data to a DataFrame
- Joining between two DataFrames
- Arithmetic with DataFrames
- Flexible binary arithmetic methods
- Flexible Boolean binary methods
- Aligning on DataFrames

Objective

After studying this chapter, you will complete the first part of the book that deals with the functionality provided by the Pandas library to operate on DataFrame and Series. By now, you should be perfectly familiar with many operations that allow you to operate within a DataFrame, and with this chapter, you will address the tools that the library offers you for working with two or more objects of this type. The possibility of being able to join two different DataFrames together, or that of adding Series to an already existing DataFrame are simple and fast methods to add data to a DataFrame. Subsequently, flexible binary operations will be introduced, which will allow you to perform real calculations between two different DataFrames like any other type of data. Finally, this chapter will end with Aligning two DataFrames, an operation widely used in data analysis.

Add data to a DataFrame

A fast and common method to add data to a DataFrame is to insert values from another DataFrame or other Series into them. The Pandas library provides us with the following two different methods for this:

- append()
- concat()

In this section, we will see that each of these two methods will allow you to add data separately. In fact, **append()** is suitable for adding new data as new rows of a starting DataFrame, while **concat()** is suitable for adding new data as new columns of a DataFrame.

Let's create two sample DataFrames that we will use to make examples with these methods, as follows:

```
In []: df1 = pd.DataFrame(np.random.randint(10, size=16).reshape(4,4),
                    index=['a','b','c','d'],
                    columns=['A','B','C','D'])

        print(df1)


    A  B  C  D
a   0  8  5  0
b   3  4  1  7
c   7  8  2  8
d   6  7  1  4
In [ ]: df2 = pd.DataFrame(np.zeros(16).reshape(4,4),
                    index=['e','f','g','h'],
```

```
                        columns=['A','B','C','D'])
          print(df2)
```

```
     A    B    C    D
e   0.0  0.0  0.0  0.0
f   0.0  0.0  0.0  0.0
g   0.0  0.0  0.0  0.0
h   0.0  0.0  0.0  0.0
```

The append() method

The **append()** method called on a DataFrame allows the addition of the data of a second DataFrame starting from the last row. If the two DataFrames have a consistent structure, that is, same labels on the columns, we will have, as a result, a new DataFrame containing the values of both the source DataFrames, without any NaN (missing value) added, as shown as follows:

In [ ]: df = df1.append(df2)
**   print(df)**

```
     A    B    C    D
a   0.0  8.0  5.0  0.0
b   3.0  4.0  1.0  7.0
c   7.0  8.0  2.0  8.0
d   6.0  7.0  1.0  4.0
e   0.0  0.0  0.0  0.0
f   0.0  0.0  0.0  0.0
g   0.0  0.0  0.0  0.0
h   0.0  0.0  0.0  0.0
```

It is also possible to add a single Series to a DataFrame. In this case, using the **append()** method is like adding a row to the DataFrame, and it is, in fact, a great way to do it.

We then define a Series with the elements to be inserted in a row and specify the labels as those of the columns of our DataFrame, as shown as follows:

In [ ]: ser = pd.Series([7,7,7,7], index=['A','B','C','D'])
**   print(ser)**

```
A    7
B    7
C    7
D    7
dtype: int64
```

Everything would seem simple and linear, but if we add a Series like the one just created to the DataFrame, an error is generated, as shown as follows:

```
In [ ]: df1.append(ser)
```

```
TypeError: Can only append a Series if ignore_index=True or if the Series
has a name
```

As we can see from the error message, if we want to add a Series to a DataFrame, we will have to add the optional **ignore_index** parameter set to **True**, among the arguments passed to the **append()** method, or have a previously assigned name (name **attribute**) to the Series. If we ignore the indices, setting **ignore_index = True**, we will have the addition of the Series at the bottom of the DataFrame, as shown as follows:

```
In [ ]: df2 = df1.append(ser,ignore_index=True)
print(df2)
```

```
   A  B  C  D
0  0  8  5  0
1  3  4  1  7
2  7  8  2  8
3  6  7  1  4
4  7  7  7  7
```

As we can see, the Series has been added at the bottom of the DataFrame, but the index labels have been lost, which are replaced by a sequence of integers generated by default. Therefore, ignoring the indexes is certainly not an optimal operation. A better method will be to define the name of the Series during its creation (if it is not already defined), and then add it to the DataFrame. Note that the Series name will become the index label of the corresponding row. So, if you create a new Series, specifically name it with the desired label name, as shown as follows:

```
In [ ]: ser = pd.Series([7,7,7,7], index=['A','B','C','D'], name='e')
print(ser)
```

```
A    7
B    7
C    7
D    7
Name: e, dtype: int64
```

```
In [ ]: df2 = df1.append(ser)    # df1.append(ser,ignore_index=False)
        print(df2)
```

```
   A  B  C  D
a  0  8  5  0
b  3  4  1  7
c  7  8  2  8
d  6  7  1  4
e  7  7  7  7
```

We have finally achieved the desired result. Very often you will use the existing and defined series elsewhere. If you don't want to use the current name, you can always rename it as you like, as shown as follows:

```
In [ ]: ser.name = 'z'
        df2 = df1.append(ser)
        print(df2)
```

```
   A  B  C  D
a  0  8  5  0
b  3  4  1  7
c  7  8  2  8
d  6  7  1  4
z  7  7  7  7
```

Appending multiple Series

Extending the concept further, the **append()** method allows you to add several Series at the same time. In fact, you can pass a list of Series as an argument. These will be added as rows to the DataFrame in the same sequence as the inserted list.

In our example, we could insert three new rows to the DataFrame, adding an existing Series and another two obtained by applying a simple arithmetic operation on the first, as shown as follows:

```
In [ ]: df2 = df1.append([ser,ser+1,ser+2])
        print(df2)
```

	A	B	C	D
a	0	8	5	0
b	3	4	1	7
c	7	8	2	8
d	6	7	1	4
z	7	7	7	7
z	8	8	8	8
z	9	9	9	9

The concat() function

As for **concat()**, the situation is different. In fact, it is not a method, but a real function of Pandas. **Concat()** has no reference DataFrame from which to be called, but it is done directly from the library, and accepts a list of the objects to be concatenated as an argument.

So, if in our case, we want to concatenate the two example DataFrames, we can write the following:

```
In [ ]: df = pd.concat([df1,df2])
        print(df)
```

	A	B	C	D
a	0	8	5	0

```
b   3   4   1   7

c   7   8   2   8

d   6   7   1   4

a   0   8   5   0

b   3   4   1   7

c   7   8   2   8

d   6   7   1   4

z   7   7   7   7

z   8   8   8   8

z   9   9   9   9
```

Also, in this case we will have an identical result to that obtained with the **append()** method. Except that in this case, it is possible to concatenate several DataFrames at the same time, and not just two, by inserting them in sequence in a list passed as argument of the function, as shown as follows:

```
In [ ]: df = pd.concat([df1,df2,df1])
        print(df)
```

```
    A   B   C   D

a   0   8   5   0

b   3   4   1   7

c   7   8   2   8

d   6   7   1   4

a   0   8   5   0

b   3   4   1   7

c   7   8   2   8

d   6   7   1   4

z   7   7   7   7

z   8   8   8   8

z   9   9   9   9

a   0   8   5   0

b   3   4   1   7
```

```
c  7  8  2  8
d  6  7  1  4
```

With **concat()**, it is also possible to concatenate together a DataFrame with a Series, but following a different behavior compared to **append()**. In this case, the Series will become a new column of the DataFrame. The name of the Series will become the label of the column, and if the labels of the Series correspond perfectly to those of the rows of the DataFrame, we will have a perfect concatenation horizontally, as shown as follows:

```
In [ ]: ser = pd.Series([7,7,7,7], index=['a','b','c','d'], name='E')
        print(ser)
```

```
a    7
b    7
c    7
d    7
Name: E, dtype: int64
```

```
In [ ]: df = pd.concat([df1,ser],axis=1)
        print(df)
```

```
   A  B  C  D  E
a  0  8  5  0  7
b  3  4  1  7  7
c  7  8  2  8  7
d  6  7  1  4  7
```

Concatenations between DataFrame and Series that are not homogeneous

Also, with regards to **concat()**, if there is no perfect consistency between the row indexes of the DataFrame and those of the Series, new rows will be generated with NaN values added where there was no correspondence, as shown as follows:

```
In [ ]: ser = pd.Series([7,7,7,7,7], index=['a','c','d','e','f'], name='E')
        df = pd.concat([df1,ser],axis=1)
```

```
print(df)
```

	A	B	C	D	E
a	0.0	8.0	5.0	0.0	7.0
b	3.0	4.0	1.0	7.0	NaN
c	7.0	8.0	2.0	8.0	7.0
d	6.0	7.0	1.0	4.0	7.0
e	NaN	NaN	NaN	NaN	7.0
f	NaN	NaN	NaN	NaN	7.0

So in this case, a new column corresponding to the Series is added. Its values are aligned with the corresponding labels if present, otherwise NaN values are added. Furthermore, if there are new labels in the Series compared to those of the DataFrame, new rows are created in the DataFrame which are also valued with NaN values. The best way to manage them will then be up to the user.

A better way to handle these inconsistent concatenations is to change the insert mode by setting the optional join parameter to inner. In this way, only the elements that have a concrete indexing correspondence between the DataFrame and the added Series will be concatenated, as shown as follows:

```
In [ ]: ser = pd.Series([7,7,7,7,7],
                    index=['a','c','d','e','f'], name='E')
        df = pd.concat([df1,ser],axis=1,join='inner')
        print(df)
```

	A	B	C	D	E
a	0	8	5	0	7
c	7	8	2	8	7
d	6	7	1	4	7

Multiple concatenations

However, if the DataFrame and Series have corresponding indexing, they can be chained together, even alternatively, by extending the DataFrame horizontally, as shown as follows:

```
In [ ]: ser = pd.Series([7,7,7,7], index=['a','b','c','d'], name='E')
        ser2 = ser + 1
        ser3 = ser + 2
        df = pd.concat([df1,ser,ser2,ser3,df1],axis=1)
        print(df)
```

	A	B	C	D	E	E	E	A	B	C	D
a	0	8	5	0	7	8	9	0	8	5	0
b	3	4	1	7	7	8	9	3	4	1	7
c	7	8	2	8	7	8	9	7	8	2	8
d	6	7	1	4	7	8	9	6	7	1	4

Joining between two DataFrames

In the previous section, we saw how the **append()** and **concat()** methods allow us to join together different objects such as DataFrame and Series, both horizontally and vertically, in a sequential way. But if, on the other hand, our purpose of union is to *merge* them together, rather than join them, the Merging technique is the most suitable.

The merge() method

Merge(), like **concat()**, is also applied directly from the library and not on an instance of an object. Similarly, this function also accepts, as arguments, the two objects to be merged, or rather on which to join, which is nothing more than the SQL JOIN. Anyone familiar with SQL and databases will find the same logic applied to JOINs between SQL tables in the merge() method. The following are the four JOIN logics applicable in Pandas as well:

- **left** (LEFT OUTER JOIN in SQL)
- **right** (RIGHT OUTER JOIN in SQL)
- **outer** (FULL OUTER JOIN in SQL)
- **inner** (INNER JOIN in SQL)

These values are passed to the **how** parameter to set the joining logic. Another parameter, **on**, is used to indicate **on** which table it should be based.

We define two DataFrames containing random integer values and with both row and column labels that are inconsistent with each other, as shown as follows:

```
In [ ]: df1 = pd.DataFrame(np.random.randint(10, size=16).reshape(4,4),
                   index=['a','b','c','d'],
                   columns=['A','B','C','D'])
        df2 = pd.DataFrame(np.random.randint(10, size=16).reshape(4,4),
                   index=['b','c','d','e'],
                   columns=['B','C','D','E'])
        print(df1)
        print(df2)
```

```
    A   B   C   D
a   1   7   9   4
b   2   5   8   8
c   5   2   6   2
d   5   0   1   6


    B   C   D   E
b   7   9   4   1
c   2   2   5   8
d   6   8   7   2
e   2   3   6   0
```

The LEFT Join

So, let's first apply the Joining between these two DataFrames by applying the LEFT logic, as shown as follows:

```
In [ ]: df = pd.merge(df1,df2, on = 'B', how='left')
        print(df)
```

```
    A   B   C_x   D_x   C_y   D_y    E
0   1   7    9     4    9.0   4.0   1.0
1   2   5    8     8    NaN   NaN   NaN
2   5   2    6     2    2.0   5.0   8.0
3   5   2    6     2    3.0   6.0   0.0
4   5   0    1     6    NaN   NaN   NaN
```

From the result, you can see the following things:

The row labels (**index**) of the two DataFrames are not considered during the joining operation, and are lost as information in the new DataFrame, replaced by progressive numeric labels. And this will apply to all joining operations performed with the **merge()** method.

Furthermore:

- Column A (column present only in the left DataFrame) remains unchanged.
- Column B (column on which joining is based) is identical to that of the left DataFrame.
- Columns **C_x**, **D_x**, **C_y**, **D_y** are four new columns derived from joining the columns C, D of the two DataFrames. **C_x** and **D_x** have remained identical to those of the left DataFrame. **C_y** and **D_y** are instead valued only in the indexes that have the same value on B in both DataFrames. The values shown are those of the right DataFrame. For all the others, it is enhanced with NaN.
- Column E (column present only in the DataFrame on the right) has the value only in the indexes that have the same value on B in both DataFrames. All other values are enhanced with NaN.

The RIGHT Join

Using a RIGHT logic on joining, the result is perfectly opposite to the previous one, as shown as follows:

```
In [ ]: df = pd.merge(df1,df2, on = 'B', how='right')
        print(df)
```

```
     A   B  C_x  D_x  C_y  D_y  E
0  1.0   7  9.0  4.0    9    4  1
1  5.0   2  6.0  2.0    2    5  8
2  NaN   6  NaN  NaN    8    7  2
3  5.0   2  6.0  2.0    3    6  0
```

From the result, you can see the following things:

- Column A (column present only in the left DataFrame) has the value only in the indexes that have the same value on B in both DataFrames. All other values are enhanced with NaN.

- Column B (column on which the join is based) is identical to that of the right DataFrame

- Columns C_x, D_x, C_y, D_y are four new columns derived from joining the columns C, D of the two DataFrames. C_y and D_y remained identical to those of the right DataFrame. C_x and D_x are instead valued only in the indexes that have the same value on B in both DataFrames. The values shown are those of the left DataFrame. For all the others, it is enhanced with NaN.

- Column E (column present only in the right DataFrame) remains unchanged.

The OUTER Join

Another different behavior is when we join with the OUTER logic, as shown as follows:

```
In [ ]: df = pd.merge(df1,df2, on = 'B', how='outer')
        print(df)
```

	A	B	C_x	D_x	C_y	D_y	E
0	1.0	7	9.0	4.0	9.0	4.0	1.0
1	2.0	5	8.0	8.0	NaN	NaN	NaN
2	5.0	2	6.0	2.0	2.0	5.0	8.0
3	5.0	2	6.0	2.0	3.0	6.0	0.0
4	5.0	0	1.0	6.0	NaN	NaN	NaN
5	NaN	6	NaN	NaN	8.0	7.0	2.0

In this case, all the values present in the two starting DataFrames are reported in the new DataFrame. The only fully valued rows are those that have the same value in column B, in which all the values of the two DataFrames are shown on the same row. We have A, C_x and D_x with the values of the left DataFrame, and C_y, D_y, and E with the values of the right DataFrame. Where there is no correspondence between the two DataFrames in column B, the NaN values are reported.

The INNER Join

Finally, by applying the INNER logic in the join of the two DataFrames, we obtain only the row, or rows, in which there was a correspondence between the two DataFrames on column B. All other information is excluded, as shown as follows:

```
In [ ]: df = pd.merge(df1,df2, on = 'B', how='inner')
        print(df)
```

```
   A  B  C_x  D_x  C_y  D_y  E
0  1  7   9    4    9    4   1
1  5  2   6    2    2    5   8
2  5  2   6    2    3    6   0
```

The INNER logic is the default of the merge method and may not even be explicitly expressed with the how parameter, as shown as follows:

```
In [ ]: df = pd.merge(df1,df2, on = 'B')
        print(df)
```

```
   A  B  C_x  D_x  C_y  D_y  E
0  1  7   9    4    9    4   1
1  5  2   6    2    2    5   8
2  5  2   6    2    3    6   0
```

Arithmetic with DataFrames

DataFrames, like Series, can be used as operands in normal arithmetic operations. However, when these two types of structured data are operated on each other, being equipped with indexing, this characteristic must always be kept in mind during these operations.

Two homogeneous DataFrames as operands

We define two numeric DataFrames having the same structure, that is, same index and columns labels, as shown as follows:

```
In [ ]: df1 = pd.DataFrame(np.random.randint(10, size=16).reshape(4,4),
                    index=['a','b','c','d'],
                    columns=['A','B','C','D'])
        print(df1)
```

```
   A  B  C  D
a  0  1  7  3
```

```
b  4  4  5  0
c  5  2  7  2
d  9  9  7  1
```

```
In [ ]: df2 = pd.DataFrame(np.random.randint(10, size=16).reshape(4,4),
                    index=['a','b','c','d'],
                    columns=['A','B','C','D'])
        print(df2)
```

```
   A  B  C  D
a  4  5  2  1
b  2  2  3  9
c  9  9  8  2
d  6  5  4  4
```

With these two objects, it is possible to perform any arithmetic operation. For example, they can simply be added together, as shown as follows:

```
In [ ]: print(df1 + df2)
```

```
    A   B   C  D
a   4   6   9  4
b   6   6   8  9
c  14  11  15  4
d  15  14  11  5
```

Or, put them in an arithmetic expression, as shown as follows:

```
In [ ]: print(df1 - 2*df2)
```

```
     A    B   C   D
a   -8   -9   3   1
b    0    0  -1 -18
c  -13  -16  -9  -2
d   -3   -1  -1  -7
```

The same goes for the Boolean arithmetic operations, as follows:

```
In [ ]: print(df1 > df2)
```

```
       A      B       C       D
a   False   False   True    True
b    True    True   True    False
c   False   False   False   False
d    True    True   True    False
```

In all cases, we observe the same behavior – whether we are dealing with arithmetic operations or Boolean expressions, the calculations are applied by taking a single element of the first DataFrame and the corresponding (for labels) in the second DataFrame. The elements are calculated one at a time, gradually up to the last element present in both. That is, the operations are performed element by element. In the end, the result is a DataFrame with the same dimensions and the same structure (labels) of the two operands.

Two non-homogeneous DataFrames as operands

So far, we saw two DataFrames with the same structure operate between them. The elements correspond to each other and are used in arithmetic or Boolean expressions individually and then reported in the new result DataFrame. But, what if the DataFrames didn't have an equivalent structure?

Let's take for example the case that between the first DataFrame and the second, there are only some columns in common, as shown as follows:

```
In [ ]: df1 = pd.DataFrame(np.random.randint(10, size=16).reshape(4,4),
                  index=['a','b','c','d'],
                  columns=['A','B','C','D'])
        df2 = pd.DataFrame(np.random.randint(10, size=16).reshape(4,4),
                  index=['a','b','c','d'],
                  columns=['B','C','D','E'])
        print(df1)
        print(df2)
```

```
     A  B  C  D
a    7  8  8  8
```

```
b  8  7  5  1
c  8  4  8  5
d  6  7  7  9


   B  C  D  E
a  4  1  4  1
b  2  9  0  0
c  2  0  0  6
d  7  5  4  7
```

If we perform an arithmetic operation between the two this time, the following will happen:

```
In [ ]: print(df1 + df2)


     A   B   C   D    E
a  NaN  12   9  12  NaN
b  NaN   9  14   1  NaN
c  NaN   6   8   5  NaN
d  NaN  14  12  13  NaN
```

We can see from the result that the calculations are made only for the columns in common between the two DataFrames. The columns that do not have a counterpart in the other DataFrame are in any case added to the result but are valued with the NaN value (missing value).

Same goes for the lines. If we perform some arithmetic operations between two DataFrames that have only some labels in common, the following will happen:

```
In [ ]: df1 = pd.DataFrame(np.random.randint(10, size=16).reshape(4,4),
                  index=['a','b','c','d'],
                  columns=['A','B','C','D'])
        df2 = pd.DataFrame(np.random.randint(10, size=16).reshape(4,4),
                  index=['b','c','d','e'],
                  columns=['A','B','C','D'])
        print(df1)
        print(df2)
```

```
   A  B  C  D
a  2  7  6  9
b  7  0  7  6
c  2  6  4  8
d  3  6  2  7


   A  B  C  D
b  1  2  6  8
c  3  4  1  6
d  2  5  5  1
e  0  1  5  2


In [ ]: print(df1 + df2)


     A     B     C     D
a  NaN   NaN   NaN   NaN
b  8.0   2.0  13.0  14.0
c  5.0  10.0   5.0  14.0
d  5.0  11.0   7.0   8.0
e  NaN   NaN   NaN   NaN
```

Here too, only the rows that have a common label between the two DataFrames are taken into consideration for the calculation. Whereas, the unmatched rows in the other DataFrame are added to the result but valued with the NaN (missing value) values.

Operations between a DataFrame and a Series

If instead, we take into consideration the arithmetic operations between a DataFrame and a Series, the elements of the Series will be calculated with the corresponding elements of each single row of the DataFrame, as shown as follows:

```
In [ ]: df1 = pd.DataFrame(np.random.randint(10, size=16).reshape(4,4),
                index=['a','b','c','d'],
                columns=['A','B','C','D'])
```

```
ser = pd.Series(np.random.randint(10, size=4),
                index=['A','B','C','D'])

print(df1)

print(ser)
```

```
   A  B  C  D
a  4  7  9  6
b  1  3  1  2
c  8  9  4  3
d  5  0  2  1
```

```
A    2
B    0
C    8
D    2
dtype: int32
```

```
In [ ]: print(df1 + ser)
```

```
    A  B   C  D
a   6  7  17  8
b   3  3   9  4
c  10  9  12  5
d   7  0  10  3
```

As we can see from the result, the four elements of the Series are calculated for each row of the DataFrame. Here too, the labels of the index of the Series will have to correspond with the labels of the columns of the DataFrame; otherwise, they will be added in the result with the value NaN, as shown as follows:

```
In [ ]: df1 = pd.DataFrame(np.random.randint(10, size=16).reshape(4,4),
                           index=['a','b','c','d'],
                           columns=['A','B','C','D'])

        ser = pd.Series(np.random.randint(10, size=4),
                        index=['B','C','D','E'])
```

```
        print(df1)

        print(ser)
```

```
      A   B   C   D
a     0   3   2   3
b     6   0   1   8
c     8   2   2   3
d     5   1   8   9


B     3
C     4
D     0
E     5
dtype: int32
```

```
In [ ]: print(df1 + ser)
```

```
      A     B      C     D    E
a   NaN   6.0    6.0   3.0  NaN
b   NaN   3.0    5.0   8.0  NaN
c   NaN   5.0    6.0   3.0  NaN
d   NaN   4.0   12.0   9.0  NaN
```

Flexible binary arithmetic methods

In addition to the classic arithmetic operators that are expressed in Python using the symbols (+, -, * and /), the Pandas library provides a set of relative methods to be applied to DataFrames to perform binary operations, as follows:

- add()
- sub()
- mul()
- div()

By using these methods, you can somehow manage the behavior of these operations, which is not possible with the corresponding arithmetic operators.

In fact, using these methods, you can choose whether to use the match on the labels of index or on those of columns, through the optional **axis** parameter.

To see how these functions work, let's first create two DataFrames containing random integer values. The two DataFrames do not have all corresponding index labels, while they will have the same column labels, as shown as follows:

```
In [ ]: df1 = pd.DataFrame(np.random.randint(10, size=16).reshape(4,4),
                    index=['a','b','c','d'],
                    columns=['A','B','C','D'])
        df2 = pd.DataFrame(np.random.randint(10, size=16).reshape(4,4),
                    index=['b','c','d','e'],
                    columns=['A','B','C','D'])
        print(df1)
        print(df2)
```

```
   A  B  C  D
a  5  9  5  4
b  9  5  8  6
c  8  7  7  1
d  9  2  4  0
   A  B  C  D
b  2  4  3  7
c  2  1  8  8
d  6  1  9  3
e  7  0  0  9
```

Flexible binary methods and arithmetic operators

As we have seen, the functions of binary operations correspond to the four arithmetic operators. For example, if we want to add two DataFrames together, we can use the **add()** method, as shown as follows:

```
In [ ]: df = df1.add(df2)
        print(df)
```

```
      A     B     C     D
a    NaN   NaN   NaN   NaN
b    11.0  9.0   11.0  13.0
c    10.0  8.0   15.0  9.0
d    15.0  3.0   13.0  3.0
e    NaN   NaN   NaN   NaN
```

This **add()** method is exactly equivalent to the arithmetic sum between the two DataFrames, as shown as follows:

```
In [ ]: df = df1 + df2
        print(df)
```

```
      A     B     C     D
a    NaN   NaN   NaN   NaN
b    11.0  9.0   11.0  13.0
c    10.0  8.0   15.0  9.0
d    15.0  3.0   13.0  3.0
e    NaN   NaN   NaN   NaN
```

The same goes for operations between a DataFrame and a Series. In this case, however, we will have a consistent result only if the labels of the Series correspond to the labels of columns of the DataFrame to some extent, as shown as follows:

```
In [ ]:  ser = pd.Series([1,1,1,1],index=['A','B','C','D'])
         print(ser)
```

```
A    1
B    1
C    1
D    1
dtype: int64
```

For example, if we add the DataFrame **df1** with the Series, the following will happen:

```
In [ ]: data = [
[ 5,  9,  5,  4, 3],
[ 9,  5,  8,  6, 3],
```

```
[ 8,   7,   7,   1, 1],
[ 9,   2,   4,   0, 2]
]
df1 = pd.DataFrame(data,
    index=['a','b','c','d'],
    columns=['A','B','C','D','E'])
print(df1)


In [ ]: df = df1.add(ser)
        print(df)


     A     B    C    D   E
a   6.0  10.0  6.0  5.0 NaN
b  10.0   6.0  9.0  7.0 NaN
c   9.0   8.0  8.0  2.0 NaN
d  10.0   3.0  5.0  1.0 NaN
```

The result is perfectly identical to the one we will have obtained using the arithmetic operator **+**, as shown as follows :

```
In [ ]: df = df1 + ser
        print(df)


     A     B    C    D   E
a   6.0  10.0  6.0  5.0 NaN
b  10.0   6.0  9.0  7.0 NaN
c   9.0   8.0  8.0  2.0 NaN
d  10.0   3.0  5.0  1.0 NaN
```

Differences between arithmetic operators and flexible binary methods

As we saw in the previous examples, the behavior between arithmetic operators and the corresponding methods is identical – the values of the Series are summed with the corresponding elements on each row of the DataFrame.

So, why use these methods when there are arithmetic operators that could do the same thing?

Using the methods for binary operations, you can vary their behavior, depending on the optional parameters specified. For example, thanks to the optional axis parameter (whose default value is **axis = 1**), you can vary the application of the operator by column or by row.

In fact, inserting the parameter **axis = 0**, and specifying a Series with labels in a manner consistent with those in the index of the DataFrame, the following will happen:

```
In [ ]: ser = pd.Series([1,2,3,4], index=['a','b','c','d'])
        df = df1.add(ser, axis=0) # df.add(df2, axis='index')
        print(df)
```

	A	B	C	D
a	6	10	6	5
b	11	7	10	8
c	11	10	10	4
d	13	6	8	4

The values present within the Series will be summed with the corresponding elements present in each column. This is a different behavior from the one seen previously, which differs significantly from that of the corresponding arithmetic operator, as shown as follows:

```
In [ ]: df = df1 + ser
        print(df)
```

	A	B	C	D	a	b	c	d
a	NaN	NaN	NaN	NaN	NaN	NaN	NaN	NaN
b	NaN	NaN	NaN	NaN	NaN	NaN	NaN	NaN
c	NaN	NaN	NaN	NaN	NaN	NaN	NaN	NaN
d	NaN	NaN	NaN	NaN	NaN	NaN	NaN	NaN

Another optional operator that can be used with this type of function is level, which will be very useful in the case of MultiIndex DataFrames. In this regard, we define a MultiIndex DataFrame, with two levels for each dimension, that is, two for the columns and two for the rows. In addition, we will assign names to the various levels of indexing during construction, as shown as follows:

```
In [ ]: tuples = [('x', 'a'), ('x', 'b'), ('y', 'a'), ('y', 'b')]
            index = pd.MultiIndex.from_tuples(tuples,
                names=['first','second'])
        tuples = [('X', 'A'), ('X', 'B'), ('Y', 'A'), ('Y', 'B')]
        columns = pd.MultiIndex.from_tuples(tuples, names=['high','low'])
        dfm = pd.DataFrame(np.arange(1,17).reshape(4,4) ,
            index = index, columns = columns)
        print(dfm)
```

high		X		Y	
low		A	B	A	B
first	second				
x	a	1	2	3	4
	b	5	6	7	8
y	a	9	10	11	12
	b	13	14	15	16

In this case, we can choose the indexing level in which to operate the operation, adding the name of the indexing level to the optional level parameter. For example, we can subtract the values of a Series from the indices corresponding to the second indexing level of the columns, in this case, with the name **low**, as shown as follows:

```
In [ ]: ser = pd.Series([10,20], index=['A','B'])
        df = dfm.sub(ser, level='low')
        print(df)
```

high		X		Y	
low		A	B	A	B
first	second				
x	a	-9	-18	-7	-16
	b	-5	-14	-3	-12
y	a	-1	-10	1	-8
	b	3	-6	5	-4

As we can see, the elements of the series are 2 and correspond to the labels of the low level of the columns. Therefore, for each row of the DataFrame, the elements of the Series will operate twice, once for the group labeled X, and once for the group labeled Y.

If instead we want to apply the operation on the first level, the following will happen:

```
In [ ]: ser = pd.Series([10,20], index=['X','Y'])
        df = dfm.sub(ser, level='high')
        print(df)
```

high		X		Y	
low		A	B	A	B
first	second				
x	a	-9	-8	-17	-16
	b	-5	-4	-13	-12
y	a	-1	0	-9	-8
	b	3	4	-5	-4

In this case, the subtraction behavior is quite different. Both values under the X label are subtracted from the first value in the Series, while those from the Y label are subtracted from the second value. The result is, therefore, different.

By combining the optional parameter level with axis, this time you can work on the row indices, acting at the 'second' level, as in the following case:

```
In [ ]: ser = pd.Series([10,20], index=['a','b'])
        df = dfm.sub(ser, level='second',axis=0)
        print(df)
```

high		X		Y	
low		A	B	A	B
first	second				
x	a	-9	-8	-7	-6
	b	-15	-14	-13	-12
y	a	-1	0	1	2
	b	-7	-6	-5	-4

Or, you can act at the first level, and get the following result:

```
In [ ] ser = pd.Series([10,20], index=['x','y'])
        df = dfm.sub(ser, level='first',axis=0)
        print(df)
```

high		X		Y	
low		A	B	A	B
first	second				
x	a	-9	-8	-7	-6
	b	-5	-4	-3	-2
y	a	-11	-10	-9	-8
	b	-7	-6	-5	-4

Things get more complex when we perform the previous operations between two DataFrames. For example, we use a DataFrame instead of the series containing, in addition to the column and row indexes of the MultiIndex DataFrame, other further indexes, as shown as follows:

```
In [ ]: df3 = pd.DataFrame(np.random.randint(10, size=4).reshape(2,2),
                        index=['a','b'],
                        columns=['A','B'])
        print(df3)
```

	A	B
a	5	0
b	4	1

In this case, we will consider a DataFrame that is in any case consistent with the labels used at the various indexing levels, as shown as follows:

```
In [ ]: df= dfm.add(df3, axis=1, level=1)
        print(df)
```

high		X		Y	
low		A	B	A	B
first	second				
x	a	6	2	8	4

		9	7	11	9
	b	9	7	11	9
y	a	14	10	16	12
	b	17	15	19	17

In this case, the DataFrame used as the second operator corresponds to a subset of the MultiIndex DataFrame, whose values are added four times, as many as there are the corresponding subsets in the MultiIndex: (x, X), (x, Y), (y, X) and (y, Y).

Arithmetic operations between subsets of the same DataFrame

Always remaining in the context of binary methods, a common operation is to use a subset of the original DataFrame as an operand to be applied in the calculation. In fact, columns and rows of the DataFrame are often used as operators to be used for arithmetic calculations.

For example, let's extract a row and a column from a DataFrame, as shown as follows:

```
In [ ]: row = df1.iloc[0]
        print(row)
        column = df1['A']
        print(column)
```

```
A    8
B    7
C    1
D    4
Name: a, dtype: int32
```

```
a    8
b    1
c    0
d    4
Name: A, dtype: int32
```

These subsets can be used as operands in operations on the same DataFrame, as shown as follows:

```
In [ ]: df = df1.mul(column, axis=0)
        print(df)
```

```
    A   B   C   D
a   25  45  25  20
b   81  45  72  54
c   64  56  56  8
d   81  18  36  0
```

```
In [ ]: df = df1.mul(row, axis=1)
        print(df)
```

```
    A   B   C   D
a   25  81  25  16
b   45  45  40  24
c   40  63  35  4
d   45  18  20  0
```

Arithmetic operations between subsets of different DataFrames

A more general case is to apply these binary methods corresponding to the mathematical operators not between two integer DataFrames, but by selecting particular subsets in them, as needed.

In this regard, we define two example DataFrames, as shown as follows:

```
In [ ]: df1 = pd.DataFrame(np.random.randint(10, size=16).reshape(4,4),
                   index=['a','b','c','d'],
                   columns=['A','B','C','D'])

        df2 = pd.DataFrame(np.random.randint(10, size=16).reshape(4,4),
                   index=['b','c','d','e'],
                   columns=['A','B','C','D'])

        print(df1)
```

```
        print(df2)
```

```
   A  B  C  D
a  0  6  8  0
b  2  1  6  5
c  7  2  7  0
d  3  5  3  2
```

```
   A  B  C  D
b  7  0  5  4
c  1  8  3  2
d  2  5  2  1
e  9  6  6  2
```

```
In [ ]: column = df2['A']
        print(column)
```

```
b    7
c    1
d    2
e    9
Name: A, dtype: int32
```

```
In [ ]: df = df1.loc['b':'d',['A','B']]
        print(df)
```

```
   A  B
b  2  1
c  7  2
d  3  5
```

```
In [ ]: df = df2.loc['b':'d',['A','B']].mul(column, axis=0)
```

```
        print(df)
```

```
       A      B
b   49.0    0.0
c    1.0    8.0
d    4.0   10.0
e    NaN    NaN
```

Depending on the labels present in the subset indices, if there is no correspondence between the two operators, rows or columns may appear valued with NaN.

The relative binary methods

To complete the picture of methods that replace mathematical operators, there are relative operators, as follows:

- radd()
- rsub()
- rmul()
- rdiv()

These operators are useful when a different value is produced depending on the order of the operands. In fact, for example, according to the **div()** method, it is possible to express the following division operation with the numerator DataFrame:

```
In [ ]: print(df / 1)
        print(df.div(1))
```

```
       A      B
b   49.0    0.0
c    1.0    8.0
d    4.0   10.0
e    NaN    NaN
```

```
       A      B
b   49.0    0.0
c    1.0    8.0
```

```
d    4.0   10.0
e    NaN    NaN
```

But if the DataFrame must be placed in the denominator, it will be possible to transcribe the mathematical operation in the form of methods, only using **rdiv()**, in which the order of the operands is inverse, compared to the previous case, as shown as follows:

```
In [ ]: print(1 / df)
        print(df.rdiv(1))
```

```
            A       B
b    0.020408     inf
c    1.000000   0.125
d    0.250000   0.100
e         NaN     NaN
            A       B
b    0.020408     inf
c    1.000000   0.125
d    0.250000   0.100
e         NaN     NaN
```

Boolean operations

Regarding the DataFrame, as for the arithmetic operators, the same speech can be done with the Boolean operators. Boolean operators like (<,>, ==, and so on) are applicable between two DataFrame objects, as shown as follows:

```
In [ ]: df1 = pd.DataFrame(np.random.randint(10, size=16).reshape(4,4),
                   index=['a','b','c','d'],
                   columns=['A','B','C','D'])
        df2 = pd.DataFrame(np.random.randint(10, size=16).reshape(4,4),
                   index=['a','b','c','d'],
                   columns=['A','B','C','D'])
        print(df1)
        print(df2)
```

```
    A  B  C  D
a   1  9  2  8
b   2  4  7  8
c   1  3  4  7
d   1  4  5  1


    A  B  C  D
a   0  8  1  5
b   3  7  1  8
c   1  5  7  2
d   7  0  3  1
```

Boolean operations between two DataFrames

By making a comparison between two DataFrames having the same structure, we expect, as a result, a DataFrame of Boolean values, in which for each element, we have the **True** value when the Boolean condition is satisfied, **False** when it is not, as shown as follows:

```
In [ ]: print(df1 > df2)


       A      B      C      D
a   True   True   True   True
b  False  False   True  False
c  False  False  False   True
d  False   True   True  False
```

As we saw in the previous chapters, these Boolean conditions are great for particular selections. For example, if we want to select only the elements that meet that condition, the following will happen:

```
In [ ]: df = df1[df1 > df2]
        print(df)


     A    B    C    D
a  1.0  9.0  2.0  8.0
b  NaN  NaN  7.0  NaN
```

```
c  NaN  NaN  NaN  7.0
d  NaN  4.0  5.0  NaN
```

Flexible Boolean binary methods

Like the arithmetic operators that have a corresponding binary method, for the Boolean operators, there are a whole series of corresponding methods, as follows:

- `eq()` corresponds to `==`
- `ne()` corresponds to `!=`
- `lt()` corresponds to `<`
- `gt()` corresponds to `>`
- `le()` corresponds to `<=`
- `ge()` corresponds to `>=`

These are applied in the same way as Boolean operators, as shown as follows:

```
In [ ]: df = df1.lt(df2) # df1 > df2
        print(df)
```

```
       A      B      C      D
a  False  False  False  False
b   True   True  False  False
c  False   True   True  False
d   True  False  False  False
```

As we can see, by applying the **lt()** method, we get the same result as the corresponding `>` operator.

Here too, however, we find ourselves with more flexible methods than the corresponding Boolean operators, and their behavior can, therefore, be refined to work with complex objects such as DataFrame and Series. Here too, the same rules explained in the previous sections apply with the use of the optional **axis** and **level** parameters, particularly useful with MultiIndex DataFrame and between a DataFrame and a Series, as shown as follows:

```
In [ ]: df = df1.lt(df2['A'], axis=0)
        print(df)
```

	A	B	C	D
a	False	False	False	False
b	True	False	False	False
c	False	False	False	False
d	True	True	True	True

Aligning on DataFrames

One of the common operations that are carried out when there are two DataFrames under examination is that of **Aligning**. In fact, after having collected our data in the form of DataFrames, it often happens that these have a similar internal structure, but not exactly the same. It, therefore, becomes necessary to align the different DataFrames with each other in order to continue with the analysis.

The align() method

The Pandas library provides the **align()** method to perform an alignment between two different DataFrames. Aligning mutually integrates the DataFrames with the row and column labels present in the other DataFrames, but not in them. In the end, you will get all the DataFrames with identical internal structure (same row and column labels), as shown as follows:

```
In [ ]: df1 = pd.DataFrame(np.random.randint(10, size=16).reshape(4,4),
                    index=['a','b','c','d'],
                    columns=['A','B','D','E'])

        df2 = pd.DataFrame(np.random.randint(10, size=16).reshape(4,4),
                    index=['b','c','d','e'],
                    columns=['A','C','D','E'])

        print(df1)
        print(df2)
```

	A	B	D	E
a	2	3	6	3
b	9	3	2	9
c	1	2	1	4
d	5	3	9	7

	A	C	D	E
b	5	0	9	9
c	6	4	2	4
d	8	0	3	5
e	6	0	7	4

The **align()** method involves two different DataFrames and returns two new ones (step by copy), which must be specifically assigned to two new instances, as shown as follows:

```
In [ ]: df1n, df2n = df1.align(df2)
        print(df1n)
        print(df2n)
```

	A	B	C	D	E
a	2.0	3.0	NaN	6.0	3.0
b	9.0	3.0	NaN	2.0	9.0
c	1.0	2.0	NaN	1.0	4.0
d	5.0	3.0	NaN	9.0	7.0
e	NaN	NaN	NaN	NaN	NaN

	A	B	C	D	E
a	NaN	NaN	NaN	NaN	NaN
b	5.0	NaN	0.0	9.0	9.0
c	6.0	NaN	4.0	2.0	4.0
d	8.0	NaN	0.0	3.0	5.0
e	6.0	NaN	0.0	7.0	4.0

As can be seen from the results, after the alignment, we have two DataFrames with the same internal structure. The new integrated columns and rows will be valued with NaN (missing values). It will then be up to the analyst to determine how they should be managed or valued.

Aligning with the Join modalities

The **align()** method allows you to align two DataFrames following different possible alignment modes. The **join** parameter is specified, which can be enhanced with the following four alignment modes:

- outer (default)
- inner
- left
- right

The **outer** mode is the default and does not need to be explicitly specified in the argument passed to the function. As we have seen, the alignment in this case is based on the union of all the labels present in the two DataFrame which are then assigned to both.

The **inner** mode instead performs the intersection between the indices present in the two DataFrames. In this case, only the labels present in both DataFrames will be kept in both DataFrames, as shown as follows:

```
In [ ]: df1n, df2n = df1.align(df2, join='inner')
        print(df1n)
        print(df2n)
```

	A	D	E
b	9	2	9
c	1	1	4
d	5	9	7

	A	D	E
b	5	9	9
c	6	2	4
d	8	3	5

As we can see from the result, the two DataFrames will have the same internal structure, but the columns and rows that have labels present in only one of the two DataFrames have been eliminated.

The **left** mode aligns the second DataFrame to the structure of the first DataFrame by eliminating all the labels (rows and columns) that are not present in the latter, and adding those that are missing, as shown as follows:

```
In [ ]: df1n , df2n = df1.align(df2, join='left')
        print(df1n)
        print(df2n)
```

	A	B	D	E
a	2	3	6	3
b	9	3	2	9
c	1	2	1	4
d	5	3	9	7

	A	B	D	E
a	NaN	NaN	NaN	NaN
b	5.0	NaN	9.0	9.0
c	6.0	NaN	2.0	4.0
d	8.0	NaN	3.0	5.0

In this case, the alignment is carried out only on the second DataFrame. The first DataFrame remains unchanged. As you can see, column C and row **e** have been deleted because they are not present in the first DataFrame. Whereas, column B and row **a** have been added because they are not present.

The **right** mode behaves in the opposite way to the previous one. In this case, it will be the first DataFrame to be aligned with the structure of the second DataFrame, as shown as follows:

```
In [ ]: df1n , df2n = df1.align(df2, join='right')
        print(df1n)
        print(df2n)
```

	A	C	D	E
b	9.0	NaN	2.0	9.0
c	1.0	NaN	1.0	4.0
d	5.0	NaN	9.0	7.0
e	NaN	NaN	NaN	NaN

	A	C	D	E
b	5	0	9	9
c	6	4	2	4
d	8	0	3	5
e	6	0	7	4

In this case, the second DataFrame returned is practically identical to the original. Whereas, the first DataFrame shows the new column C and the new row **e** that were not present in it, while the column B and row **a** have been deleted.

Conclusion

With this chapter, we concluded the first part of the book. Most of the features of the Pandas library are known to you by now, and thanks to these last notions, you can operate on multiple DataFrames at the same time. When you are dealing with DataFrames with similar but not perfectly identical structures, you now know how to align them (aligning) with each other and then eventually merge them into a single structure (merging, concatenation, and append). Furthermore, you acquired important notions on how to use DataFrames or their subsets as operands in arithmetic or Boolean expressions.

Questions

1. Why is it better to use flexible binary methods than the corresponding operators?

2. What could be the practical benefits in aligning two DataFrames with each other?

3. In which practical cases could it be useful to insert DataFrames in arithmetic or Boolean expressions?

Multiple choice questions

1. Which of the following statements about the concat () method is false?

   A,. A DataFrame is concatenated to another DataFrame by adding after the last row.

   B. A Series is concatenated to a DataFrame as its new column.

   C. A DataFrame is concatenated to another DataFrame by joining the columns in common and discarding the others.

2. Which of the following commands corresponds to the 1/df operation?

   A. `df.T`

   B. `df.div(1)`

   C. `df.rdiv(1)`

3. Which of the Join modes in Aligning corresponds to the intersection between the two DataFrames?

A. Outer

B. Inner

C. Left

4. What information is lost in the DataFrame resulting from merging two DataFrames?

A. The index labels of the two DataFrames

B. The columns labels of the two DataFrames

C. The values of the elements of one of the two DataFrames

5. Which flexible Boolean binary method corresponds to '>='?

A. `ge()`

B. `gt()`

C. `le()`

Solution

1: C; 2: C; 3: B; 4: A; 5: A

Key Terms

Aligning, Merging, Concatenation, Append, Flexible binary methods, Join.

References/Further Readings

- *Python for Data Analysis. Data Wrangling with Pandas, NumPy, and IPython, McKinney, OReilly*

- *Python Data Analytics With Pandas, NumPy, and Matplotlib, Fabio Nelli, Apress*

- *https://pandas.pydata.org/docs/user_guide/index.html*

CHAPTER 7

Day 5 - Working with Data Sources and Real-World Datasets

Let's start the second part of the book with this chapter. In the previous chapters, the data we used was nothing more than simple numbers, and the labels of the columns and rows were the letters of the alphabet. This extreme simplification was made to allow the readers to focus primarily on Pandas' methods and their functionality without worrying too much about the type of data they were working on. It goes without saying that the world of real data is something else entirely.

In this second part of the book, we will deal with all aspects related to data. In fact, in addition to being numerical values, data, in reality, can also be something more complex and less malleable. You will often have to deal with strings of characters, dates, and times, or as we have seen in some cases, wrong or missing values (or NaN). In the previous chapters, we saw how easy it was to work with numbers using the classic mathematical and arithmetic functions, and how these work in a simple and efficient way. But to work with words or with dates or times – it is not quite so intuitive. In this chapter, we will, therefore, learn how to manipulate and manage these kind of values.

Furthermore, about data – not only is their nature important, but also their management. In the previous chapters, we saw, thanks to the `DataFrame ()` and `Series ()` constructors, how to create structured data by directly entering the values or generating them automatically. Again, this is a significant simplification, often useful for working with examples. In concrete cases, the data that is useful to us are present in the surrounding world in different forms – text files, spreadsheets, database tables, and so on. In this chapter, we will, therefore, learn how to read and write the data present in these types of formats.

This chapter covers the management of real data and is a fundamental part if you want to work with Pandas to carry out data analysis.

Structure

In this chapter, we will cover the following topics:

- Data from external files (CSV, Excel)
- Data from web (XML, HTML, JSON)
- Data from databases (SQL queries)
- Time Data
- Text Data

Objective

After studying this chapter, you will have a clear understanding of all the ways to obtain data from the outside world. Thanks to the great flexibility of some import methods provided by the Pandas library, you will be able to import the necessary data from many different file formats. You will also have developed the basic knowledge to connect to any database and extract data from tables for analysis purposes. Finally, with a series of examples at the end of this chapter, you will be able to discern with better clarity the types of data present in the imported files, such as dates, times, and text, as well as the numbers seen in the previous chapters. You will also have a clear overview of a series of techniques and methods to be able to manipulate them more safely.

Files as external data sources

First, let's start this chapter by learning how to import data from the most common formats to date. In fact, outside of Pandas, it is common to collect and save data on text files. Typically, these files are available in different formats, depending on the applications used when collecting them. In this section, we will learn how to manage the most common formats, and thanks to a series of efficient methods made available by the Pandas library, it will be possible to import the data into them and convert them into DataFrame.

Python boasts a particular propensity to work on text files, thanks to its partial nature of scripting and the ability to work interactively by entering commands on the shell. Therefore, Pandas can be a valuable tool for reading and writing data to files. The library provides a large number of functions in this regard, often specific to each type of file format (HTML, CSV, Excel, and so on).

The following are some of the most used reading methods:

- `read_table()`
- `read_csv()`
- `read_excel()`
- `read_html()`
- `read_xml()`
- `read_json()`

The following are the corresponding writing methods:

- `to_csv()`
- `to_excel()`
- `to_html()`
- `to_xml()`
- `to_json()`

The purpose of these methods is to read the data inside the files, according to the different formats, interpret them, and convert them into a DataFrame. This operation may be simple at first glance, but in reality, it requires a lot of attention on the interpretation of what data is in the text file and the large number of exceptions to be handled.

The methods listed earlier have a very large number of optional parameters (over 50) as common characteristics, that have been gradually implemented to efficiently handle all possible exceptions. An exhaustive discussion of these methods is out of the scope of this book, and therefore, it is suggested to consult the official documentation. However, we will not shy away from the possibility of analyzing some of these selected parameters that are considered essential to proceed optimally in most cases.

Read and write data from files in CSV format

Let's start with the most commonly used method of importing external files, **read_csv()**. As the name clearly says, this method is specialized for importing **CSV** (**comma-separated values**) files which is the simplest and most commonly used type of text format for collecting tabular data.

Let's take, for example, a CSV file called **books.csv** containing the data of some books with other information such as author, title, code, and date of publication. If we open this file with a text editor, we will be able to see its contents, as shown in *Figure 7.1*:

```
,ID,Title,Author,PublicationDate
0,001276A,The Rise of the Falcon,John Admiral,25-Apr-2018
1,023125B,Controlled mind,Robert Greens,28-Aug-2016
2,005556E,Only love remains,Greta Blooming,17-Feb-2015
```

Figure 7.1: Textual content of books.csv

As we can see from the preceding figure, the data is in tabular form with rows and columns. The first row shows the headings of each column, separated from each other by commas. Then, there are a few lines, each of which refers to a particular book.

This type of file is easily imported, thanks to its already tabular nature of the data, using the **read_csv()** function, as shown as follows:

```
In [ ]: df = pd.read_csv('books.csv')
        print(df)
Out[ ]:
        ID                Title          Author PublicationDate
0  001276A  The Rise of the Falcon    John Admiral     25-Apr-2018
1  023125B         Controlled mind   Robert Greens     28-Aug-2016
2  005556E       Only love remains  Greta Blooming     17-Feb-2015
```

Generally, the individual values within the CSV files are separated by the comma character (as the name implies), but this is not always true. Sometimes, this type of file can use (for language conventions or some applications used to create them) other separator characters.

Let's take, for example, the **books2.csv** file, which is always a CSV file but uses a semicolon instead of a comma as a separator character, as shown in *Figure 7.2*:

```
ID;Title;Author;PublicationDate
001276A;The Rise of the Falcon;John Admiral;25-Apr-2018
023125B;Controlled mind;Robert Greens;28-Aug-2016
005556E;Only love remains;Greta Blooming;17-Feb-2015
```

Figure 7.2: CSV file with semicolon as separator

In this case, we will use another more generic function than **read_csv()** and which is perfectly suited to read and write any text file format.

The **read_table()** function works the same way as **read_csv()** but has a more general use as it is not limited to CSV files, where data is comma delimited from each other, but extends to any separate data tables from a character or a sequence of characters, which can be defined using the optional **sep** parameter.

We then use this method to import the **books2.csv** file, as shown as follows:

```
In[ ]:  df = pd.read_table('books2.csv', sep=';')
        print(df)
Out[ ]:
```

	ID	Title	Author	PublicationDate
0	001276A	The Rise of the Falcon	John Admiral	25-Apr-2018
1	023125B	Controlled mind	Robert Greens	28-Aug-2016
2	005556E	Only love remains	Greta Blooming	17-Feb-2015

As we can see, the result is practically the same as in the previous example.

These example files are very simple because they only contain a few lines. In the most real cases, the tables contained in the CSV files (and also in the other formats) contain multiple rows. Before importing these files, it may sometimes be necessary to take a look inside them to see their internal structure and the type of values they contain. In this regard, the **read_csv()** function has the optional **nrows** parameter that allows us to define the number of rows to import.

For example, if we wanted to look at the first two rows of the table contained in the CSV file, we would assign the value **2** to the optional **nrows** parameter, as shown as follows:

```
In [ ]: pd.read_csv('books.csv', nrows=2)
```

We will have the result in graphic form (if you are using Jupyter Notebook), as shown in *Figure 7.3*:

	ID	Title	Author	PublicationDate
0	001276A	The Rise of the Falcon	John Admiral	25-Apr-2018
1	023125B	Controlled mind	Robert Greens	28-Aug-2016

Figure 7.3: First 2 rows in books2.csv

In this example, we looked at the contents of the CSV file by reading only the first two lines (**nrows = 2**). We didn't pass the result to any DataFrame as our purpose was to have a look at the content. On Jupyter Notebook, if you don't pass the return value (which is a DataFrame object), it will be displayed in graphical form.

Graphical display of DataFrames in Jupyter Notebook

From this chapter onwards, as far as DataFrames are concerned, we will no longer use the print() function to have a textual representation. Instead, we will take advantage of the Jupyter feature of displaying the DataFrames in graphic format. This will allow us to view the data in the table in a more readable and collected format.

Now that we have seen how to import the data in a CSV file, let's see the opposite operation.

Let's assume that we have carried out a series of operations on some DataFrame we have processed, and once we have finished our work, we want to save the data in some way. Just as we load the data from textual files to convert them into a DataFrame, it is possible to save our DataFrame on textual files. There are various methods for this, depending on the file formats for saving. For example, the most common format is CSV, and the **to_csv()** method allows us to save them.

We then save our DataFrame as a CSV file, calling it **books_saved.csv**, as shown as follows:

```
In [ ]: df.to_csv('books_saved.csv')
```

To see the contents of the saved file, we will obtain the textual data, as represented in *Figure 7.4*:

```
,ID,Title,Author,PublicationDate
0,001276A,The Rise of the Falcon,John Admiral,25-Apr-2018
1,023125B,Controlled mind,Robert Greens,28-Aug-2016
2,005556E,Only love remains,Greta Blooming,17-Feb-2015
```

Figure 7.4: Content of books_saved.csv

As we can see, the content is perfectly identical to that of the **books.csv** file.

Preview of the content being written to file

We have just seen how to save DataFrames in a CSV file. But when writing tests on files are carried out, to avoid having to write and read the contents of the files every time, there is the possibility to generate the textual format directly on the layout without having to save it to a file.

The standard out of Python **sys.stdout** can be exploited by directing the stream of data to be written by the **to_csv()** method. Import the standard **sys** module and then pass **sys.stdout** as an argument in place of the file name, as shown as follows:

```
In [ ]: import sys
        df.to_csv(sys.stdout)
Out[ ]:
,ID,Title,Author,PublicationDate
0,001276A,The Rise of the Falcon,John Admiral,25-Apr-2018
1,023125B,Controlled mind,Robert Greens,28-Aug-2016
2,005556E,Only love remains,Greta Blooming,17-Feb-2015
```

As you can see, the result is the same, and it saves you from writing and opening the file every time to read the result inside.

Some optional to_csv() parameters

The **to_csv()** method and other methods of writing to files also have a large number of optional parameters that allow us to better manage all our needs. For example, we might want to save our values in the DataFrame, without having to write the labels (both column and row).

In this case, we add two optional parameters, **index** and **header**, set to **False** (by default, they are set to **True** and, therefore, omitted), as shown as follows:

```
In [ ]: df.to_csv(sys.stdout, index=False, header=False)
Out[ ]:
001276A,The Rise of the Falcon,John Admiral,25-Apr-2018
023125B,Controlled mind,Robert Greens,28-Aug-2016
005556E,Only love remains,Greta Blooming,17-Feb-2015
```

As can be seen from the result in the standard out, the row indexes and column labels have been omitted, and will not be saved to the CSV file.

Another example is when you are dealing with very large DataFrames, where there are several columns, but only some of them are of interest to us. In this case we would like to save only some of them. Well, it is possible to directly specify the columns of our interest by inserting the labels in a list and passing it to the optional **columns** parameter.

In our case, if we want to save only the contents of the **Title** and **Author** columns to file, we will specify it in the list passed to the **columns** parameter, as shown as follows:

```
In [ ]: df.to_csv(sys.stdout, columns=['Title','Author'],index=False)
Out[ ]:
Title,Author
The Rise of the Falcon,John Admiral
Controlled mind,Robert Greens
Only love remains,Greta Blooming
```

As we can see from the standard out result, the saved CSV file would be limited only to the contents of the two specified columns, eliminating everything else.

However, if you want to perform this kind of operation, a more efficient way to work is to first select the part of the DataFrame that we are interested in saving, and then save it directly to the file.

For example, if we want to save only two lines of our DataFrame, we will write the following code:

```
In [ ]: df[1:].to_csv(sys.stdout)
Out[ ]:
,ID,Title,Author,PublicationDate
1,023125B,Controlled mind,Robert Greens,28-Aug-2016
2,005556E,Only love remains,Greta Blooming,17-Feb-2015
```

Read and Write Microsoft Excel File

-Until now, we saw how DataFrames originally refer to spreadsheets as a form of structured data. And in fact, today a lot of data are available in this format, among which the best known is that of Microsoft Excel, recognizable by the extension **.xls** and **.xlsx**. Given the importance of these files, the Pandas library has methods for reading and writing this kind of file – **read_excel()**. The implementation of this method is based on external Python packages such as **xlrd** (for the **.xls** format) and **openpyxl** (for the **.xlsx** format). When calling the **read_excel()** method for the first time in our examples, in some development environments, you may receive an error message, as shown as follows:

Out [ ]: Missing optional dependency 'openpyxl'. Use pip or conda to install openpyxl.

If so, you may need to install these packages before operating. If you are using the Anaconda environment, it is recommended to open Anaconda Navigator, and after selecting the environment you are working on, search for non-installed packages. At this point, look for the openpyxl package and press the **Apply** button at the bottom right to start installing it, as shown in *Figure 7.5*:

Figure 7.5: Installing openpyxl package in Anaconda Navigator

Anaconda Navigator will download the package and then show you the dependencies of this package in a window. Press the `Apply` button to complete the installation, as shown in *Figure 7.6*:

Figure 7.6: Dependencies of the openlynx package

If you do not use Anaconda as an environment management system, or you do not want to use the graphical system, open a session on your environment and install the library directly using the **conda** command (always for those who use Anaconda), as shown as follows:

```
conda install openpyxl
```

Otherwise, you can use **pip**, as shown as follows:

```
pip install openpyxl
```

Within an Excel file, there are several spreadsheets, so as arguments of the **read_excel()** function you specify both the Excel file and the single spreadsheet from which to read the data.

Figure 7.7 shows the **Sheet1** spreadsheet in the Excel **books.xlsx** file that we will use for our examples:

	A	B	C	D
1	ID	Title	Author	PublicationDate
2	001276A	The Rise of the Falcon	John Admiral	25/04/2018
3	023125B	Controlled mind	Robert Greens	28/08/2016
4	005556E	Only love remains	Greta Blooming	17/02/2015

Figure 7.7: *Spreadsheet Sheet1 in the books.xlsx file*

To import the data contained in an Excel spreadsheet, the source file is first defined by creating an instance of the **ExcelFile** class with the constructor of the same name, using as argument the name of the Excel file to be read. Then, you use the **read_excel()** function to import the data into it, specifying as arguments, the Excel source and the name of the Spreadsheet from which to read the data, as shown as follows:

```
In [ ]: xlssource = pd.ExcelFile('books.xlsx')
        df = pd.read_excel(xlssource, 'Sheet1')
        df
```

The result will correspond to what is represented in *Figure 7.8*:

	ID	Title	Author	PublicationDate
0	001276A	The Rise of the Falcon	John Admiral	2018-04-25
1	023125B	Controlled mind	Robert Greens	2016-08-28
2	005556E	Only love remains	Greta Blooming	2015-02-17

Figure 7.8: *DataFrame imported from books.xlsx file*

Similarly, the opposite operation is performed. Having a DataFrame available on which we have performed some processing, we want to save it in the form of a spreadsheet in an Excel file. For this, we use the **to_excel()** function. But before using this method, it is necessary to first create an **ExcelWriter** object that hooks to an Excel file (already existing or to be generated), for example **newbooks.xlsx**, as shown as follows:

```
In [ ]: XLSWriter = pd.ExcelWriter('newbooks.xlsx')
```

After launching this command, Pandas will point to an XLS file that has the name specified in the argument (the path corresponds to the root of the workspace). If it doesn't exist, it will create a new one. The system is now waiting to be able to write data to this file. We can use the **to_excel()** function to be specified directly on the DataFrame to be saved. As arguments, you specify the newly created **ExcelWriter** object and the name of the spreadsheet within the Excel file in which to insert the data, as shown as follows:

```
In [ ]: df.to_excel(XLSWriter, 'Sheet1')
```

At this point, to conclude, we need to save the Excel file. For this operation, we still use the **Writer** object from which we call the **save()** method, as shown as follows:

```
In [ ]: XLSWriter.save()
```

If we look at the content within the new **newbooks** file, we will observe a spreadsheet like the one shown in *Figure 7.9*:

	A	B	C	D	E
1		ID	Title	Author	PublicationDate
2	0	001276A	The Rise of the Falcon	John Admiral	2018-04-25 00:00:00
3	1	023125B	Controlled mind	Robert Greens	2016-08-28 00:00:00
4	2	005556E	Only love remains	Greta Blooming	2015-02-17 00:00:00
5					

Figure 7.9: Spreadsheet Sheet1 in the new newbooks.xlsx file

As you can see, all the information of our DataFrame has been saved correctly on the Excel spreadsheet.

Read data from HTML pages on the web

Another interesting possibility that the Pandas library gives us is to consider the world of the Web as a direct source of data. In fact, thanks to the **read_html()** method, by inserting a series of links to HTML pages, these pages will be scanned, looking for tables, which will be automatically converted into DataFrame.

This option truly opens the door to a world full of data and opportunities. The only flaw is that it will be necessary to know in advance what to look for.

We then define a link of pages to be scanned such as the Wikipedia page of Rome, the capital of Italy. On this page, we are particularly interested in the table containing the climatic data. We then write the URL of the page and pass it as an argument to the **read_html()** function, as shown as follows:

```
In [ ]: url = 'https://en.wikipedia.org/wiki/Rome'

        dfs = pd.read_html(url)
```

The **read_html()** function returns a list of DataFrames obtained by converting the data read from the HTML page. Let's see, in our case, how many DataFrame has been imported. In this regard, we use the **len()** function, which will tell us the number of elements in the list, as shown as follows:

```
In [ ]: len(dfs)
```

```
Out[ ]: 48
```

As we can see, the **read_html()** method still extracted 48 DataFrames from the HTML page. It must always be borne in mind that in this type of data import, we will always carry a lot of things that do not interest us. We will have to perform a data clean-up afterwards. In fact, we got 48 DataFrames, because in the HTML code of the web page we scanned, there are 48 tags in the HTML code and not always all of them are used to contain data, because they are often also used to adjust the formatting of a page. So, it is necessary to find a solution to avoid scanning the contents of each of the 48 DataFrames obtained.

A helpful technique is to visit the page and check a line of text that can uniquely identify the table of our interest. In our case, as we can see in *Figure 7.10*, the header of the table we are interested in contains the words **Climate data**:

Figure 7.10: Climate data table present on an HTML page

We will pass these words to the optional match parameter inside the **read_html()** function, which will take care of importing only the tables that have these character strings inside them, as shown as follows:

```
In [ ]: dfs = pd.read_html(url, match='Climate data')
        len(dfs)
```

```
Out[ ]: 1
```

This time, the DataFrame extracted from the HTML page is only one. So, let's go and see its contents. We must consider that even if we only have one DataFrame, the value returned by the **read_html()** function is always a list of DataFrames. So, to access the first item, you will need to specify the index, as shown as follows:

```
In [ ]: dfs[0]
```

We will get the DataFrame as represented in *Figure 7.11*:

	Climate data for Rome Urbe Airport (altitude: 24 m sl, 7 km north from Colosseum satellite view)								
	Month	Jan	Feb	Mar	Apr	May	Jun	Jul	Aug
0	Record high °C (°F)	20.2(68.4)	23.6(74.5)	27.0(80.6)	28.3(82.9)	33.1(91.6)	36.8(98.2)	40.0(104.0)	39.6(103.3)
1	Average high °C (°F)	12.6(54.7)	14.0(57.2)	16.5(61.7)	18.9(66.0)	23.9(75.0)	28.1(82.6)	31.5(88.7)	31.7(89.1)
2	Daily mean °C (°F)	7.4(45.3)	8.4(47.1)	10.4(50.7)	12.9(55.2)	17.3(63.1)	21.2(70.2)	24.2(75.6)	24.5(76.1)
3	Average low °C (°F)	2.1(35.8)	2.7(36.9)	4.3(39.7)	6.8(44.2)	10.8(51.4)	14.3(57.7)	16.9(62.4)	17.3(63.1)
4	Record low °C (°F)	-9.8(14.4)	-6.0(21.2)	-9.0(15.8)	-2.5(27.5)	3.7(38.7)	6.2(43.2)	9.8(49.6)	8.6(47.5)
5	Average precipitation mm (inches)	69.5(2.74)	75.8(2.98)	59.0(2.32)	76.2(3.00)	49.1(1.93)	40.7(1.60)	21.0(0.83)	34.1(1.34)
6	Average precipitation days (≥ 1 mm)	7.6	7.4	7.8	8.8	5.6	4.1	2.3	3.2
7	Mean monthly sunshine hours	120.9	132.8	167.4	201.0	263.5	285.0	331.7	297.6
8	Source: Servizio Meteorologico[79] (1971–2000)	Source: Servizio Meteorologico[79] (1971–2000)	Source: Servizio Meteorologico[79] (1971–2000)	Source: Servizio Meteorologico[79] (1971–2000)	Source: Servizio Meteorologico[79] (1971–2000)	Source: Servizio Meteorologico[79] (1971–2000)	Source: Servizio Meteorologico[79] (1971–2000)	Source: Servizio Meteorologico[79] (1971–2000)	Source: Servizio Meteorologico[79] (1971–2000)

Figure 7.11: *DataFrame obtained from the Climate Data Table present on an HTML page*

As we can see from the result, we have extracted the data on the table of our interest. We can then extract the DataFrame from the list and start working on it for our analyses, as shown as follows:

```
In [ ]: df = dfs[0]
```

As there is a function of reading and extracting data from HTML pages, there is a method that converts a DataFrame defined by us into an HTML table. This method is precisely **to_html()**. We then create an example DataFrame by importing it from a CSV file, as shown as follows:

```
In [ ]: df = pd.read_csv('books.csv')

        df
```

As a result, we will get the DataFrame, as shown in *Figure 7.12*:

	ID	Title	Author	PublicationDate
0	001276A	The Rise of the Falcon	John Admiral	25-Apr-2018
1	023125B	Controlled mind	Robert Greens	28-Aug-2016
2	005556E	Only love remains	Greta Blooming	17-Feb-2015

Figure 7.12: Sample DataFrame

Let's convert it to an HTML table, saving it as a **books.html** file, as shown as follows:

```
In [ ]: df.to_html('books.html')
```

A new HTML file will have been created in the workspace. When we open it with any browser, we will obtain the table similar to the one represented in *Figure 7.13*:

	ID	Title	Author	PublicationDate
0	001276A	The Rise of the Falcon	John Admiral	25-Apr-2018
1	023125B	Controlled mind	Robert Greens	28-Aug-2016
2	005556E	Only love remains	Greta Blooming	17-Feb-2015

Figure 7.13: Table in an HTML page

Read and write data from XML files

One file format containing the data that is often found on the Web is XML. This file format contains data in a highly hierarchical form and is recognizable by the use of tags. The tags are recognizable for having a structure similar to the following:

```
<tag_name>Value</tag_name>
```

These tags are the basic elements, which nested one inside the other, form a tree structure, where each tag corresponds to a node.

For working with XML files, Pandas provides some reading and writing methods for this particular file format. Python makes use of the **lxml** library to handle XML files, and so does Pandas. So, you need to make sure you have installed this library in your environment. Try importing the module using Python, as shown as follows:

```
In [ ]: import lxml
```

If you get the following error message, then it means that the library is not present in the environment:

...

ModuleNotFoundError Traceback (most recent call last) in ----> 1 import lxml

ModuleNotFoundError: No module named 'lxml'

You will need to install the **lxml** package. As with previous packages, you can log into Anaconda and install it using the following **conda** command:

conda install lxml

Or, more easily using the Anaconda Navigator graphical interface. You can select the package from those not installed, and then pressing the **Apply** button starts the installation, as shown in *Figure 7.14*:

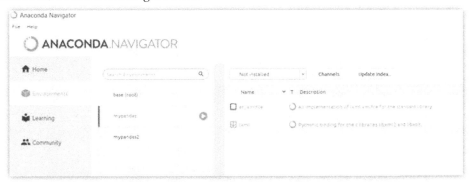

Figure 7.14: Installing the lxml package with Anaconda Navigator

If you are not using Anaconda, you can still use **pip** to install the package, as shown as follows:

pip install lxml

Now that the base library has been installed, we can load the data present in any XML file using the **read_xml()** function, specifying the file name as an argument.

Check pandas version for the pd.read_xml() method:

With the Pandas version '1.2.4', **read_xml** does not work well, so you need to upgrade it to 1.3.0.

Update Pandas to the newest version, by using the following command:

pip install --upgrade pandas --user

pd.read_xml('file.xml') is available in version 1.3.0. and Higher.

Let's take, for example, an XML file like **library.xml**, whose textual content is the following:

```
<?xml version="1.0" encoding="UTF-8"?>
<library>
  <book category="crime">
    <title>Death on the Nile</title>
    <author>Agatha Christie</author>
    <year>1937</year>
    <country>United Kingdom</country>
  </book>
  <book category="crime">
    <title>The Hound of the Baskervilles</title>
    <author>Arthur Conan Doyle</author>
    <year>1902</year>
    <country>United Kingdom</country>
  </book>
  <book category="psychology">
    <title>Psychology and Alchemy</title>
    <author>Carl Gustav Jung</author>
    <year>1944</year>
    <country>Germany</country>
  </book>
  <book category="novel">
    <title>The Castel</title>
    <author>Franz Kafka</author>
    <year>1926</year>
    <country>Germany</country>
  </book>
</library>
```

Now we load the data present in this XML file using the function **read_xml()**, as shown as follows:

```
In [ ]: df = pd.read_xml('library.xml')
```

df

As a result, we will get the graphical representation of the DataFrame, as shown in *Figure 7.15*:

	category	title	author	year	country
0	crime	Death on the Nile	Agatha Christie	1937	United Kingdom
1	crime	The Hound of the Baskervilles	Arthur Conan Doyle	1902	United Kingdom
2	psichology	Psychology and Alchemy	Carl Gustav Jung	1944	Germany
3	novel	The Castel	Franz Kafka	1926	Germany

Figure 7.15: DataFrame obtained by reading the library.xml file

In the same way, it is possible to perform the opposite operation, that is, to save any DataFrame in XML format to a file. To do this, we will use the **to_xml()** method. As argument of the method, we will pass the name of the XML file that will be created in the workspace.

For example, we import data from the now familiar **books.csv** file to create a DataFrame. Then, we convert the values containing the dates to a specific type for the dates (we will see this in detail later in the chapter). And finally, we save it in the form of an XML file called **newbooks.xml**, as shown as follows:

```
In [ ]: df2 = pd.read_csv('books.csv')

        df2.PublicationDate = pd.to_datetime(df2.PublicationDate)

        df2.to_xml('newbooks.xml')
```

Also, in this case, when we check the workspace, we will find the new file created, named **newbooks.xml**. To see its contents, you can call the **read_xml()** function in the following way:

```
In [ ]: pd.read_xml('newbooks.xml')
```

As a result, we will obtain the DataFrame, as represented in *Figure 7.16*:

	index	ID	Title	Author	PublicationDate
0	0	001276A	The Rise of the Falcon	John Admiral	2018-04-25 00:00:00
1	1	023125B	Controlled mind	Robert Greens	2016-08-28 00:00:00
2	2	005556E	Only love remains	Greta Blooming	2015-02-17 00:00:00

Figure 7.16: DataFrame obtained by reading the newbooks.xml file

The XML files we have seen so far have one thing in common – they have an internal tabular structure that is perfectly suited to being imported into a DataFrame. But in reality, there is no standard XML structure and often the data inside could take more nested forms. In these cases, it is necessary to use the XSLT technology to transform these XML into a tabular structured format.

We modify the previous XML file by inserting a further nesting level by adding, for example, the plans of the library. But this time, we will use a variable containing the text of the modified XML file which we will call xml. This is an alternative way that saves us from reading XML files and working directly on the internal text in real time to carry out tests, as shown as follows:

```
In [ ]: xml = """"<?xml version="1.0" encoding="UTF-8"?>

<library>

  <floor val='1'>

    <book category="crime">

      <title>Death on the Nile</title>

      <author>Agatha Christie</author>

      <year>1937</year>

      <country>United Kingdom</country>

    </book>

    <book category="crime">

      <title>The Hound of the Baskervilles</title>

      <author>Arthur Conan Doyle</author>

      <year>1902</year>

      <country>United Kingdom</country>

    </book>

  </floor>

  <floor val='2'>

    <book category="psichology">

      <title>Psychology and Alchemy</title>
```

```
    <author>Carl Gustav Jung</author>

    <year>1944</year>

    <country>Germany</country>

  </book>

  <book category="novel">

    <title>The Castel</title>

    <author>Franz Kafka</author>

    <year>1926</year>

    <country>Germany</country>

  </book>

 </floor>

</library>

"""
```

In this case, we will always use the **read_xml()** function, but instead of the file, we will pass the variable containing the text in XML as an argument, as shown as follows:

In [ ]: pd.read_xml(xml)

If we run this command, we will get the following result, as shown in *Figure 7.17*:

	val	book
0	1	NaN
1	2	NaN

Figure 7.17: Something went wrong with reading the xml variable

As we can see in this case, the **read_xml()** method was unable to read the data of interest, as it is located in the deepest nesting levels. So, it is necessary to transform the data structure in XML into a tabular form that is well suited to our needs. As we said earlier, we can take advantage of the XSLT technology which, through a series of commands, is able to transform the structure of an XML file as we wish. XSLT is to be considered a real programming language.

So, to convert the XML text into a structure more suited to us, we will write the XSL code by saving it as text inside an **xsl** variable. The XSL code is also based on a series of tags which correspond to a series of commands that perform transformation operations, as shown as follows:

```
In [ ]: xsl = """<xsl:stylesheet version="1.0" xmlns:xsl="http://www.
w3.org/1999/XSL/Transform">
    <xsl:output method="xml" omit-xml-declaration="no" indent="yes"/>
    <xsl:strip-space elements="*"/>
    <xsl:template match="/library">
        <xsl:copy>
            <xsl:apply-templates select="floor"/>
        </xsl:copy>
    </xsl:template>
    <xsl:template match="floor">
        <xsl:apply-templates select="book"/>
    </xsl:template>
    <xsl:template match="book">
        <xsl:copy>
            <category><xsl:value-of select="@category"/></category>
            <title><xsl:value-of select="title"/></title>
            <author><xsl:value-of select="author"/></author>
            <year><xsl:value-of select="year"/></year>
            <country><xsl:value-of select="country"/></country>
        </xsl:copy>
    </xsl:template>
</xsl:stylesheet>
"""
```

At this point, the XSL text is passed to the optional stylesheet parameter of the **read_xml()** function which will deal with both the transformation of the incoming XML text and subsequently the conversion of the data inside, into a DataFrame, as shown as follows:

```
In [ ]: pd.read_xml(xml, stylesheet=xsl)
```

We will get a DataFrame as a result, as shown in *Figure 7.18*:

	category	title	author	year	country
0	crime	Death on the Nile	Agatha Christie	1937	United Kingdom
1	crime	The Hound of the Baskervilles	Arthur Conan Doyle	1902	United Kingdom
2	psichology	Psychology and Alchemy	Carl Gustav Jung	1944	Germany
3	novel	The Castel	Franz Kafka	1926	Germany

Figure 7.18: The DataFrame obtained from the xml variable after the XSLT conversion

As we can see, the result is now the same as that in the previous example.

Read and Write data in JSON

Another file format widely used for exchanging data, especially in the web world, is **JavaScript Object Notation (JSON)**. This format has proved so flexible that today, it is practically the most used format for exchanging data via HTTP between browsers and other applications.

In Pandas, to work with data in the JSON format, it is necessary to have the fsspec module installed. Also, for this package, it is critical to check if it has already been installed. Otherwise, use conda to install the package, as follows:

```
conda install fsspec
```

Or, more easily you can find and download it from Anaconda Navigator, as shown in *Figure 7.19*:

Figure 7.19: Installing the fsspec package from Anaconda Navigator

If you don't use Anaconda, you can still install the **fsspec** package via **pip**, as shown as follows:

```
pip install fsspec
```

Once the package is installed, we can start with the examples. Let's load the data from the **books.csv** file back into a DataFrame, as shown as follows:

```
In [ ]: df = pd.read_csv('books.csv')

        df
```

We will obtain the DataFrame as represented in *Figure 7.20*:

	ID	Title	Author	PublicationDate
0	001276A	The Rise of the Falcon	John Admiral	25-Apr-2018
1	023125B	Controlled mind	Robert Greens	28-Aug-2016
2	005556E	Only love remains	Greta Blooming	17-Feb-2015

Figure 7.20: DataFrame obtained by importing data from the books.csv file

Now that we have a DataFrame, we can save it in the JSON format by saving it directly to a **books.json** file, as shown as follows:

```
In [ ]: df.to_json('books.json')
```

If you check the workspace, you will find a new **books.json** file. If instead we are curious to see the data of our test DataFrame converted into the JSON format, we can use the standard out as done previously using **sys.stdout**, as shown as follows:

```
In [ ]:  import sys

         df.to_json(sys.stdout)
```

Out[ ]:

```
{"ID":{"0":"001276A","1":"023125B","2":"005556E"},"Title":{"0":"The Rise
of the Falcon","1":"Controlled mind","2":"Only love remains"}, "Author":
{"0":"John Admiral","1":"Robert Greens","2":"Greta Blooming"},"Publicati
onDate":{"0":"25-Apr-2018","1":"28-Aug-2016","2":"17-Feb-2015"}}
```

As we can see, the JSON structure is similar to a dict in Python, but with a nested key-value system.

Like all other file formats, reading JSON files to get a DataFrame as a result is also possible and is done with the **read_json()** function.

Let's convert the newly generated JSON file into a DataFrame, as shown as follows:

```
In [ ]: pd.read_json('books.json')
```

And as a result, we will get the DataFrame as represented in *Figure 7.21*:

	ID	Title	Author	PublicationDate
0	001276A	The Rise of the Falcon	John Admiral	25-Apr-2018
1	023125B	Controlled mind	Robert Greens	28-Aug-2016
2	005556E	Only love remains	Greta Blooming	17-Feb-2015

Figure 7.21: DataFrame obtained by importing data from the books.json file

Again, we have used JSON files with an internal tabular structure, but in reality, the data in JSON has a tree structure that only in a few cases is flattened to correspond to a tabular format. In reality, therefore, JSON data has a more complex structure with key-value pairs nested between them.

For example, we write a JSON structure with different nesting levels, such as the following, and assign it to the variable **jsondata**:

```
In [ ]: jsondata = {
"company": "BMW",
"site": "Munchen, Germany",
"production": "Motor Vehicles",
"products": [
{
"product": "Series 1",
"model": " 116d 5-Door Sport Pack"
},
{
"product": "Series 3",
"model": " 330E xDrive Sport Aut"
}
]
}
```

We can try to pass it as an argument to the **read_json** function to convert the data inside it into a DataFrame, as shown as follows:

```
In [ ]: pd.read_json(jsondata)
```

```
Out[ ]:
```

```
...
```

Invalid file path or buffer object type: <class 'dict'>

We get a message because the JSON format of the data is not convertible into a DataFrame as it is not in a tabular format, or it contains other features that do not conform to the standard JSON format (this is not the case). Fortunately, to overcome these problems, there is the **json_normalize()** function which allows you to convert any JSON format into a tabular one, which can be converted into a DataFrame. We then apply the **json_normalize()** function to the data in the JSON format contained in the **jsondata** variable, as shown as follows:

```
In [ ]: pd.json_normalize(jsondata)
```

This time, instead of an error message, we will get a DataFrame, as represented in *Figure 7.22*:

	company	site	production	products
0	BMW	Munchen, Germany	Motor Vehicles	[{'product': 'Series 1', 'model': ' 116d 5-Doo...

Figure 7.22: DataFrame resulting from the conversion of the json_normalize function

We have obtained a readable and convertible DataFrame, even if it does not yet have a tabular format. For best results, you can add the JSON file keys to specify how the JSON file should be tabulated. This way, we can make the JSON data passed as an argument perfectly tabular, as shown as follows:

```
In [ ]: pd.json_normalize(jsondata, "products",
["company","site","production"])
```

Finally, we will obtain a tabular DataFrame like the one represented in *Figure 7.23*:

	product	model	company	site	production
0	Series 1	116d 5-Door Sport Pack	BMW	Munchen, Germany	Motor Vehicles
1	Series 3	330E xDrive Sport Aut	BMW	Munchen, Germany	Motor Vehicles

Figure 7.23: DataFrame obtained from the jsondata variable

Write and read data in binary format

So far, we have seen many different file formats, but one thing united them all – their format is textual, regardless of the structure of the data stored inside. But with the

Pandas library, the possibilities for reading and writing files are not limited to this. In Python, as well as in Pandas, it is also possible to save data in binary format. One of the simplest techniques for doing this is to serialize data in binary format in a file using pickle serialization, a technique widely used in Python. Also, in this case, it is possible to write and read data in binary format through the following methods:

- **to_pickle()**
- **read_pickle()**

These follow a syntax very similar to that of the previous file formats.

We then load the data again from a sample CSV file, such as **books.csv** to get a test DataFrame, as shown as follows:

```
In [ ]: df = pd.read_csv('books.csv')

        df
```

We will obtain the following DataFrame as shown in *Figure 7.24*:

	ID	Title	Author	PublicationDate
0	001276A	The Rise of the Falcon	John Admiral	25-Apr-2018
1	023125B	Controlled mind	Robert Greens	28-Aug-2016
2	005556E	Only love remains	Greta Blooming	17-Feb-2015

Figure 7.24: DataFrame obtained from the books.csv file

This time, we will save the data of this test DataFrame in the binary format in a file with a generic extension (often .dat, but this is mandatory). We then use the **to_pickle()** method to generate a new binary file which we will call **newbooks.dat**, as shown as follows:

```
In [ ]: df.to_pickle('newbooks.dat')
```

Also, in this case, we will have the creation of a new file in our workspace. Now you can reload the data into it using the **read_pickle()** function:

```
In [ ]: pd.read_pickle('newbooks.dat')
```

As a result, we will obtain a DataFrame perfectly identical to the original one obtained from the test CSV file, as shown in *Figure 7.25*:

	ID	Title	Author	PublicationDate
0	001276A	The Rise of the Falcon	John Admiral	25-Apr-2018
1	023125B	Controlled mind	Robert Greens	28-Aug-2016
2	005556E	Only love remains	Greta Blooming	17-Feb-2015

Figure 7.25: DataFrame obtained from the newbooks.dat binary file

Final thoughts on saving data to file

In general, however, data storage is recommended to be carried out in one of the preceding text formats, mainly, because these formats are universal and used by many applications. So, storing files in the CSV, EXCEL, or JSON format is not just a way to save your results, but an efficient way to exchange data and information. In this way, it is possible to exchange data even with environments other than the Python-Pandas, thus, making data analysis universal.

Furthermore, the serialization of data in binary format is based on particular and pre-established algorithms that will only be used for a few years. When saving a data in binary format, the use of the data limited to certain environments and only for a few years must be considered, since it is difficult to guarantee that the data conversion format will remain unchanged over time, even for such widespread methods as Pickled serialization.

Interact with databases for data exchange

A completely different approach is to use databases as a data source. In business reality, data is almost always contained within databases that efficiently manage gigabytes of data. Databases are such a common technology nowadays that it is practically impossible not to deal with them when dealing with data analysis. It is, therefore, essential to know how to extract data from this kind of technology and then be able to convert them into a DataFrame.

The vast majority of current databases (MySQL, Oracle, PostgreSQL, SQLServer, and so on) are relational and use the SQL language for the extraction and manipulation of data in the form of tables. As an example, we will use the SQLite database, which is a simple and small solution that allows us to install and manage a database on our PC.

SQLite installation

The installation of the SQLite database is simple and fast. On the official website, you can download all the necessary files of the latest release (**https://www.sqlite. org/download.html**).

Look for the Precompiled Binaries version corresponding to your operating system and download it by clicking on the link. For example, on Windows, search for 'Precompiled Binaries for Windows' and download the following two compressed ZIP files:

- `sqlite-dll-win32-x86-xxxxxx.zip`

- `sqlite-tools-win32-x86-xxxxxx.zip`

Once downloaded, create an SQLite folder on C:\ and then extract the contents of the two ZIP files you just downloaded. At the end, you will find a series of files, as shown in *Figure 7.26*:

Figure 7.26: *SQLite files on Windows*

As for the other operating systems, the installation operations will be very similar. However, consult the official documentation for detailed installation instructions if you need them.

Open a command line session (for example, on Windows, press the **WIN** + **R** keys together and write **cmd**), and once opened, go to the C:\SQLite directory and type **sqlite3**. If the installation went correctly, you will connect to the database, as shown in *Figure 7.27*:

```
C:\SQLite>sqlite3
SQLite version 3.36.0 2021-06-18 18:36:39
Enter ".help" for usage hints.
Connected to a transient in-memory database.
Use ".open FILENAME" to reopen on a persistent database.
sqlite>
```

Figure 7.27: *Running SQLite via command line*

Now that you are connected to SQLite, you can run a series of commands. Enter `.help` to get a list of all available commands, as shown as follows:

```
sqlite> .help

.archive ...              Manage SQL archives

.auth ON|OFF              Show authorizer callbacks

.backup ?DB? FILE         Backup DB (default "main") to FILE

.bail on|off              Stop after hitting an error.  Default OFF

. . .
```

Creation of test data on SQLite

Now that we have SQLite on our computer, we can start entering the necessary data for our examples. Instead of using sqlite3 from the command line, to create a data table, you can use Python directly, thanks to the use of drivers that allow reading and writing of data directly from the Python shell. As for SQLite, the **sqlite3** driver exists in Python which is directly importable like any other library.

We then create a table directly on the database that will host the data, which we will exchange with Pandas for the generation of a DataFrame. Also, for the creation of tables in a relationship database like SQLite, we use SQL and then we directly write the rows necessary to define and create the **Fruits** table, as shown as follows:

```
In [ ]: import sqlite3

   query = """

     CREATE TABLE Fruits

     (fruit VARCHAR(20),

      weight REAL(20),

      amount INTEGER,

      price REAL,

      origin VARCHAR(20)

   );"""
```

At this point, we create a connection with the database inside SQLite, called **mydata**. Then, once the connection is established, we execute the query to create the table, and then we send the **commit()** function to make it effective, as shown as follows:

```
In [ ]: conn = sqlite3.connect('mydata.sqlite')
        conn.execute(query)
        conn.commit()
```

At this point, we have created an empty table. The next step will be to enter some data inside. This operation is also done with the SQL language that we will insert in the commands in Python to execute them, as shown as follows:

```
In [ ]: data = [('Apples',12.5,6,100.23,'Germany'),
            ('Cherries',4.5,3,200.50,'Turkey'),
            ('Ananas',19.4,4,300.85,'Madagascar'),
            ('Strawberries',7.8,12,250.33,'Italy'),
        ]


        stmt = "INSERT INTO Fruits VALUES (?,?,?,?,?)"
        conn.executemany(stmt, data)
        conn.commit()
```

Now that we have a table with data in the database, we can move on to the case of exporting these data through Pandas methods to convert them into a DataFrame and continue with our data analysis.

Again, we need the specific driver for each database model, which in our case is **sqlite3**. This, like most other SQL drivers, returns the data of a table in the form of a list of tuples, as shown as follows:

```
In [ ]: cursor = conn.execute('SELECT * FROM Fruits')
        rows = cursor.fetchall()
        rows
Out[ ]:
[('Apples', 12.5, 6, 100.23, 'Germany'),
 ('Cherries', 4.5, 3, 200.5, 'Turkey'),
 ('Ananas', 19.4, 4, 300.85, 'Madagascar'),
 ('Strawberries', 7.8, 12, 250.33, 'Italy')]
```

The data returned in the rows variable have the form of a list of tuples, and therefore, for the final conversion into a DataFrame, it must be appropriately manipulated within the constructor. As for the data, there is no problem, since a **DataFrame()**

constructor is able to optimally manage the lists of tuples and convert them into a DataFrame, but for the labels of the columns, it will be necessary to write an expression inline to pass them from the table to the DataFrame, as shown as follows:

```
In [ ]: pd.DataFrame(rows, columns=[x[0] for x in cursor.description])
```

We will then get a DataFrame like the one shown in *Figure 7.28*:

	fruit	weight	amount	price	origin
0	Apples	12.5	6	100.23	Germany
1	Cherries	4.5	3	200.50	Turkey
2	Ananas	19.4	4	300.85	Madagascar
3	Strawberries	7.8	12	250.33	Italy

Figure 7.28: DataFrame obtained from a table on SQLite database

Other data sources

In addition to files containing data in different formats and classic databases, there are many other types of data sources. Covering them all remains a task that is far beyond the scope of this book and would only lead to confusion due to an excess of information. It is natural that during the data analysis activity, when you work for certain companies, or in particular professional fields, you will be able to find highly specialized environments that make use of specific software and forms of data exchange. Also, in the professional sphere, in this rapidly developing environment, you may find yourself in front of *too new* or *too old* environments and strangely you will soon discover that the problems are the same. In 'too new' working environments, one will find innovative, highly efficient tools, but of which it will be difficult to find tools and documentation on the net and in the literature. Probably, the libraries in Python (and also in other languages) will not yet exist to work in these environments, or there will be prototype versions that are not as performing or still under development to guarantee full operability. The same goes for *too old* environments. Perhaps, in this case, it will be easier to find documentation about it, but in any case, there will be no tools, such as Python libraries, capable of interacting with these obsolete technologies.

In all these cases, the optimal solution remains to research as much as possible to find solutions in these specific areas, and sometimes it will be necessary to develop implementations in Python (or another programming language) to make up for where it is not possible to find something already ready. However, to acquire a good command of data exchange methods in the most common forms can still be a good backup to develop or understand new work environments in the field of data exchange.

Working with Time Data

One of the best reasons to use Pandas is its ability to recognize and manage time and date variables in the data values we work on. In the previous chapters, we saw some simple cases where the data was nothing more than string labels and numeric values. In reality, data can have many formats, and dates and times are almost omnipresent. In fact, in the collection of data, in their sampling, dates and times are introduced. It is this type of value that is indispensable for carrying out significant statistics and, therefore, in the analysis of the data, it is essential that the tools are able to recognize and use them.

The Pandas library manages this type of data based on the following two specific concepts:

- Date Times
- Time deltas

Date Times

Date Times are nothing more than the concept of date and time with which we generally indicate a certain instant. In the data on which we generally work, dates and times are reported as strings whose values have many different formats. Very often, depending on the country of origin, the order in which the years, months, and days of a date are reported (less often as regards the hours, minutes, and seconds) can vary greatly. Furthermore, these values can be expressed both numerically and literally, for example, the month of November can be specified as '11' or as 'Nov'. The year could have four digits, or for convenience, only report the last two, such as 2021 or 21. Additionally, these values are separated from each other by a widely varying separator character ('-', '/', or ':', and so on). It is, therefore, clear that it is difficult to have tools that are able to parse these values correctly.

Well, Pandas is a very powerful library in this area and it makes the work of data analysts a lot easier in recognizing and managing this data. Based on the already developed features of the datetime module of the standard library, Pandas has created a Timestamp class that efficiently implements this concept of Date Time.

Its constructor is, in fact, a powerful tool that accepts as a parameter a string of characters indicating the date and time, and is then able to convert it into a type of data created specifically in Pandas, **datetime64**. This value is actually the conversion of the date and time in string format to the corresponding number of nanoseconds. It can be understood how this value is extremely precise (given the very small-time unit chosen as a basis) and, therefore, it is also very suitable for scientific applications that require measurements in very short time spans.

Let's write a series of examples on recognizing and converting dates with the **Timestamp()** constructor, as follows:

```
In [ ]: pd.Timestamp('2021-11-30')
Out[ ]: Timestamp('2021-11-30 00:00:00')
```

```
In [ ]: pd.Timestamp('2021-Nov-30')
Out[ ]: Timestamp('2021-11-30 00:00:00')
```

```
In [ ]: pd.Timestamp('2021/11/30')
Out[ ]:Timestamp('2021-11-30 00:00:00')
```

It can deduced from the preceding examples that regardless of the format type, the **Timestamp()** constructor is able to recognize that it is the same date.

This constructor is also able to work on numeric formats and not only with strings. In this case, each argument will correspond in the order of years, months, days, hours, minutes, and seconds, as shown as follows:

```
In [ ]: pd.Timestamp(2021,11,30,0,0,0)
Out[ ]:Timestamp('2021-11-30 00:00:00')
```

In this case, it is also possible to avoid evaluating the time arguments that have zero as a value, as shown as follows:

```
In [ ]: pd.Timestamp(2021,11,30)
Out[ ]:Timestamp('2021-11-30 00:00:00')
```

So far, we have seen the constructor for generating these kinds of values. However, when importing data from external sources, we will need much more to convert the already defined data than to build it. In this case, the Pandas library provides us with the **to_datetime()** function which accepts, as an argument, a series of objects which will then be converted into DateTime values.

For example, we have a DataFrame like the following:

```
In [ ]: df = pd.DataFrame({'year': [2019, 2020, 2021],
                           'month': [10, 6, 4],
                           'day': [15, 10, 20]})

        print(df)
Out[ ]:
   year  month  day
0  2019     10   15
1  2020      6   10
2  2021      4   20
```

It can be converted to DateTime values using the **to_datetime()** function, as shown as follows:

```
In [ ]: ts = pd.to_datetime(df)

        print(ts)

        print(type(ts))
Out[ ]:
0    2019-10-15

1    2020-06-10

2    2021-04-20

dtype: datetime64[ns]


<class 'pandas.core.series.Series'>
```

As we can see, the function has converted a DataFrame into a Series of **datetime64** values.

Another possibility is, for example, that of converting strings that describe a date and a time but their format is too intelligible for the constructor. In fact, the **to_datetime()** function allows you to add as an optional parameter, the format in which you can specify the particular formatting that follows the string by means of indicators (called format codes, as for example, %S to indicate the seconds) and, thus, be able to parse. Also, by adding the optional errors parameter with the value 'raise', you will get an error message whenever the **to_datetime()** function fails to parse the string in a datetime64 value, as shown as follows:

```
In [ ]: t = pd.to_datetime('2021 USA 31--12', format='%Y USA %d--%m',
errors='raise')

        print(t)
```

```
Out[ ]: 2021-12-31 00:00:00
```

As we can see, thanks to the format codes, it is possible to make the **to_datetime** function recognize the single attributes of a date even in the case of strings that have particular formats with additional text characters. If we were to pass a series of strings, in which one of them does not match the format, the parsing will fail, and you will get an error message. To avoid this, you can specify 'ignore' in the optional **errors** parameter.

Table 7.1 shows some of the most common format codes, which can be useful in defining the format of a date and time:

Format Code	Description	Examples
%a	Weekday, abbreviated	Mon, Tues, …
%A	Weekday, full name	Monday, Tuesday
%w	Weekday, decimal	0=Sunday,1,2, …
%d	Day of month, zero-padded	01, 02, …, 30, 31
%b	Month, abbreviated	Jan, Feb, …
%B	Month, full name	January, February, …
%m	Month number, zero-padded	01, 02, …, 12
%y	Year, without century, zero-padded	01, 02, …, 99
%Y	Year, with century	1887, 1999, 2020, …
%H	Hour (24 hour), zero-padded	01, 02, …, 23, 24
%I	Hour (12 hour) zero-padded	01, …, 12
%p	AM or PM	AM, PM
%M	Minute, zero-padded	01, 02, …, 60
%S	Second, zero padded	01, 02, …, 60

Table 7.1: Most common format code

Let's see again an example of date conversions, using format codes. We specify the following Series in which we have a series of strings to convert to dates:

```
In [ ]: ts = pd.Series(['2019 USA 31--12','2020 ITA 20--11','2021 USA
10--10'])
        print(ts)
Out[ ]:
0    2019 USA 31--12
1    2020 ITA 20--11
2    2021 USA 10--10
dtype: object
```

Also, in this case, we use the **to_datetime()** function specifying a possible format that can interpret them all correctly (but in reality, this is not the case), as shown as follows:

```
In [ ]: t = pd.to_datetime(ts, format='%Y USA %d--%m', errors='ignore')
        print(t)
Out[ ]:
0    2019 USA 31--12
1    2020 ITA 20--11
2    2021 USA 10--10
dtype: object
```

After running these commands, we did not get any error message. In fact, we expected a conversion error since the second line of the Series contains a string that doesn't match the format entered in the **to_datetime()** function. Indeed, all the lines have kept the type of source data (object).

Another feature linked to the concept of date time is that this could be strictly linked to the geographical area of reference, that is specific to a TimeZone. That is, some values of type Timestamp also have a well-defined TimeZone inside them.

To add a reference TimeZone to the value of date time, add the optional parameter **tz** to the constructor specifying the TimeZone using the specific string.

Let's see some of the following as examples:

```
In [ ]: pd.Timestamp('2021-Nov-30 11:40', tz='UTC')
Out[ ]: Timestamp('2021-11-30 11:40:00+0000', tz='UTC')
```

```
In [ ]: pd.Timestamp('2021-Nov-30 11:40', tz='Europe/Stockholm')
```

```
Out[ ]: Timestamp('2021-11-30 11:40:00+0100', tz='Europe/Stockholm')
```

As we can see, the timezone has been added to the **TimeStamp** object, adding a time zone indicator at the end of the time. In the Europe/Stockholm timezone, we have **+0100,** which means one hour longer than UTC. The timezone can also be added later, after defining the variable. With the **tz_localize()** method, you can add the timezone specification passing the relative string as an argument, as shown as follows:

```
In [ ]: t = pd.Timestamp('2021-Nov-30 11:40PM')
        print(t)
        t = t.tz_localize(tz='America/Sao_Paulo')
        print(t)
```

```
Out[ ]:
```

```
2021-11-30 23:40:00
```

```
2021-11-30 23:40:00-03:00
```

Another interesting feature of timezones is that, given a precise DateTime, it is possible to calculate the corresponding time value in another timezone. We use the **tz_convert()** method with the TimeZone of interest to get the corresponding value, as shown as follows:

```
In [ ]: t2 = t.tz_convert('US/Eastern')
        print(t2)
```

```
Out[ ]: 2021-11-30 21:40:00-05:00
```

We have seen that by sending a variable of type DateTime to print, we obtain a string containing all the information such as date, time, and timezone. However, we often need to view and manage each of these individual items. All this is possible, thanks to the numerous attributes that the DateTime object has. With this, it will be possible to obtain only that partial information we need, such as, for example, the number of minutes, the year, or the hour, as shown as follows:

```
In [ ]: print(t.year)
        print(t.month)
        print(t.day)
        print(t.hour)
        print(t.minute)
        print(t.second)
```

```
    print(t.tz)
Out[ ]:
2021
11
30
23
40
0
America/Sao_Paulo
```

Seeing this system of attributes, one would be tempted to update one of them with another value. However, if you try to do this, you will get the following error message:

```
In [ ]: t.hour = 12
Out[ ]:
...
AttributeError: attribute 'hour' of 'datetime.datetime' objects is not writable
```

To modify or update a DateTime value, it will be necessary to use arithmetic methods that will involve another concept, Time Deltas.

Time Deltas

DateTimes are precise times to which a data can be assigned. Another concept of time on which Pandas is based are the Time Deltas, that are the measurements of time durations, that is, the time interval between two precise instants (DateTime). This concept is also fundamental to working with times and dates in a data analysis.

Pandas implements this concept through `Timedelta`, a class very similar to the one present in the datetime module of the standard library. This class also has its own constructor, and the definition of a time interval can be very simple and intuitive. For example, if we wanted to define the duration of a time equivalent to one day, it would be enough to write the following:

```
In [ ]: pd.Timedelta('1 Day')

Out[ ]: Timedelta('1 days 00:00:00')
```

In this case, if we wanted to update a Datetime value, for example, by increasing its value by an hour, it would be enough to create a **Timedelta** value equivalent to an hour and add it to the **Datetime** variable, thus, obtaining the updated value. It is, therefore, possible to perform arithmetic calculations with times using **Datetime** and **Timedelta** together, as shown as follows:

```
In [ ]: t = pd.Timestamp('2021-Nov-16 10:30AM')
        print(t)
        dt = pd.Timedelta('1 Hour')
        t = t + dt
        print(t)
Out[ ]:
2021-11-16 10:30:00
2021-11-16 11:30:00
```

```
The preceding lines can also be written more implicitly as follows:
In [ ]: t = pd.Timestamp('2021-Nov-16 10:30AM')
        t = t + pd.Timedelta('1 Hour')
        print(t)
Out[ ]:
2021-11-16 11:30:00
```

Another, more formal way of defining time intervals is to enter the relative amount and unit of time. For example, another way to define a day and time is to enter 1 as a numeric value, and use the optional unit parameter defining 'd' to define days as a unit of time, as shown as follows:

```
In [ ]: pd.Timedelta(1, unit="d")

Out[ ]:Timedelta('1 days 00:00:00')
```

Using smaller time units such as seconds, the manufacturer will convert them to the larger time units, thus, converting them to the corresponding values of days, hours, and minutes, as shown as follows:

```
In [ ]: pd.Timedelta(150045, unit="s")

Out[ ]: Timedelta('1 days 17:40:45')
```

There are also more complex ways to define time intervals, which are useful when you have multiple units together, such as days, minutes, and hours, as shown as follows:

```
In [ ]: pd.Timedelta('3D 5:34:23')
```

```
Out[ ]: Timedelta('3 days 05:34:23')
```

We have seen that **Timedelta** defines time intervals and are useful for performing arithmetic calculations on Timestamp objects. This concept is even more explicit when we consider the following example:

```
In [ ]: t1 = pd.Timestamp('2021-Jan-01 11:30AM')
        t2 = pd.Timestamp('2021-Mar-13 4:15PM')
        dt = t2 - t1
        print(dt)
        print(type(dt))
```

```
Out[ ]:
71 days 04:45:00


<class 'pandas._libs.tslibs.timedeltas.Timedelta'>
```

As we can see from the result, even by making the difference between two Timestamps, an object of type **Timedelta** is automatically generated as a result, without using the constructor.

There is also a data conversion function for Timedelta, called **to_timedelta()**. In this case, however, parsing is less flexible than **to_datetime**. In fact, there is no optional format parameter, and only the default formats that work with the constructor are recognized, as shown as follows:

```
In [ ]: ts = pd.Series(['00:22:33','00:13:12','00:24:14'])
        print(ts)
        dt = pd.to_timedelta(ts, errors='raise')
        print(dt)
```

```
Out[ ]:
0    00:22:33
1    00:13:12
```

```
2    00:24:14

dtype: object

0    0 days 00:22:33

1    0 days 00:13:12

2    0 days 00:24:14

dtype: timedelta64[ns]
```

Create arrays of time values

Now that we have seen what Timestamps and Timedelta are in Pandas, let's take a further step – seeing how it is possible to generate an array of this type of values in a simple and automatic way.

For this purpose, there is the **data_range()** function which allows us to create a predetermined number of values, starting from a given date (Timestamp), and then defining an appropriate time interval, generating a series of Datetime values all uniformly staggered.

For example, it is possible to generate an array of 10 consecutive days starting from a specific date (passed as the first argument) defining as optional parameters **freq = 'D',** to define the duration of 1 day from one value to another and, with periods, the number of values to generate. In this case, the number of consecutive days are 10, as shown as follows:

```
In [ ]: pd.date_range('2021/01/01', freq='D', periods=10)
Out[ ]:
DatetimeIndex(['2021-01-01', '2021-01-02', '2021-01-03', '2021-01-04',
               '2021-01-05', '2021-01-06', '2021-01-07', '2021-01-08',
               '2021-01-09', '2021-01-10'],
              dtype='datetime64[ns]', freq='D')
```

As we can see, the **data_range()** function creates a **DatetimeIndex** object containing 10 consecutive days starting from 1st January 2021.

Another possibility is to pass two different Timestamps, one starting and one ending, as arguments to the **data_range()** function. The default intervals are one day, as shown as follows:

```
In [ ]: pd.date_range("2021/01/01", "2021/01/10")
```

```
Out[ ]:
```

```
DatetimeIndex(['2021-01-01', '2021-01-02', '2021-01-03', '2021-01-04',

                '2021-01-05', '2021-01-06', '2021-01-07', '2021-01-08',

                '2021-01-09', '2021-01-10'],

             dtype='datetime64[ns]', freq='D')
```

If, on the other hand, we want a staggered time interval with different times, we must explicitly specify it with the **freq** parameter. Or we could decide to subdivide this interval by a certain number of parts; in this case, we will use the optional parameter, periods.

For example, we would like to create a Timestamp array with 5 minutes difference within the specified time limits, then we will specify **'5T'** to indicate 5 minutes to the optional **freq** parameter, as shown as follows:

```
In [ ]: pd.date_range("2021/01/01 8:00","2021/01/01 10:00", freq='5T')
```

```
Out[ ]:
```

```
DatetimeIndex(['2021-01-01 08:00:00', '2021-01-01 08:05:00',

                '2021-01-01 08:10:00', '2021-01-01 08:15:00',

                '2021-01-01 08:20:00', '2021-01-01 08:25:00',

                '2021-01-01 08:30:00', '2021-01-01 08:35:00',

                '2021-01-01 08:40:00', '2021-01-01 08:45:00',

                '2021-01-01 08:50:00', '2021-01-01 08:55:00',

                '2021-01-01 09:00:00', '2021-01-01 09:05:00',

                '2021-01-01 09:10:00', '2021-01-01 09:15:00',

                '2021-01-01 09:20:00', '2021-01-01 09:25:00',

                '2021-01-01 09:30:00', '2021-01-01 09:35:00',

                '2021-01-01 09:40:00', '2021-01-01 09:45:00',

                '2021-01-01 09:50:00', '2021-01-01 09:55:00',

                '2021-01-01 10:00:00'],

             dtype='datetime64[ns]', freq='5T')
```

Or we might want to divide this time interval into 10 equal parts, each delimited by a Timestamp. In this case, 10 is assigned to the optional parameter **periods**, as shown as follows:

```
In [ ]: pd.date_range("2021/01/01 8:00","2021/01/01 10:00", periods=10)
Out[ ]:
DatetimeIndex(['2021-01-01 08:00:00', '2021-01-01 08:13:20',
               '2021-01-01 08:26:40', '2021-01-01 08:40:00',
               '2021-01-01 08:53:20', '2021-01-01 09:06:40',
               '2021-01-01 09:20:00', '2021-01-01 09:33:20',
               '2021-01-01 09:46:40', '2021-01-01 10:00:00'],
              dtype='datetime64[ns]', freq=None)
```

In all these cases, we have seen the generation of an object of type **DatetimeIndex** containing a list of Datetime values. In many cases, this kind of object is useful for building Series or DataFrame. For example, it is quite common to use these values as Index, both in a Series and in a DataFrame, as shown as follows:

```
In [ ]: range = pd.date_range("2021/01/01 8:00","2021/01/01 10:00",
periods=10)
        tsi = pd.Series(np.random.randn(len(range)), index=range)
        print(tsi)
Out[ ]:
2021-01-01 08:00:00    1.479959
2021-01-01 08:13:20    0.408933
2021-01-01 08:26:40    0.106165
2021-01-01 08:40:00   -1.198836
2021-01-01 08:53:20    0.378987
2021-01-01 09:06:40    0.275445
2021-01-01 09:20:00   -1.735805
2021-01-01 09:33:20    0.076814
2021-01-01 09:46:40   -0.830684
2021-01-01 10:00:00    0.804353
dtype: float64
```

But they can also be used to populate their values automatically, as shown as follows:

```
In [ ]: ts = pd.Series(range)
        print(ts)
Out[ ]:
0    2021-01-01 08:00:00
1    2021-01-01 08:13:20
2    2021-01-01 08:26:40
3    2021-01-01 08:40:00
4    2021-01-01 08:53:20
5    2021-01-01 09:06:40
6    2021-01-01 09:20:00
7    2021-01-01 09:33:20
8    2021-01-01 09:46:40
9    2021-01-01 10:00:00
dtype: datetime64[ns]
```

In the first case, the use of index with datetime64 type values allows you to easily select rows relating to a particular time interval, as shown as follows:

```
In [ ]: tsi["2021/01/01 8:00":"2021/01/01 8:30"]
Out[ ]:
2021-01-01 08:00:00    1.479959
2021-01-01 08:13:20    0.408933
2021-01-01 08:26:40    0.106165
dtype: float64
```

Import Date Time values from file

So far, we have seen how Date Time data is generated out of thin air to fill Series or DataFrame. But most of the time, this kind of data will be imported from external data sources like files or database queries. In this chapter, we saw that there are many functions that allow us to convert this externally read data into DataFrame. We will, therefore, find in our newly generated DataFrame, one or more columns containing date or time values.

For example, we saw in a previous example, the case of a CSV file containing a column with strings that express dates, as shown as follows:

```
In [ ]: df = pd.read_csv('books.csv')
```

```
       print(df)
```

Out[ ]:

```
       ID              Title          Author  PublicationDate
0  001276A  The Rise of the Falcon    John Admiral      25-Apr-2018
1  023125B          Controlled mind   Robert Greens     28-Aug-2016
2  005556E        Only love remains   Greta Blooming    17-Feb-2015
```

As we can see, the **PublicationDate** column of the DataFrame contains dates. Actually, during the import, the **read_csv ()** method was not able to recognize these values by itself, and simply entered them with a generic object as the data type, as shown as follows:

In [ ]: **df.PublicationDate**

Out[ ]:

```
0     25-Apr-2018
1     28-Aug-2016
2     17-Feb-2015
```

Name: PublicationDate, dtype: object

To convert to **TimeStamp**, you can use the **to_datetime()** function that we saw earlier. We assign the result to the same column to overwrite it or to a new one, as shown as follows:

In [ ]: **df['PublicationDate'] = pd.to_datetime(df.PublicationDate)**

```
       print(df)
```

Out[ ]:

```
       ID              Title          Author  PublicationDate
0  001276A  The Rise of the Falcon    John Admiral      2018-04-25
1  023125B          Controlled mind   Robert Greens     2016-08-28
2  005556E        Only love remains   Greta Blooming    2015-02-17
```

In [ ]: **df.PublicationDate**

Out[ ]:

```
0     2018-04-25
```

```
1     2016-08-28

2     2015-02-17

Name: PublicationDate, dtype: datetime64[ns]
```

As you can see, the data type is now **datetime64**. In reality, **read_csv()** is a powerful function that has many optional parameters, including **parse_dates** which allows you to pass the column intended for a conversion parsing in datetime64. All this allows us to avoid carrying out this operation in two steps and, therefore, without the need to use the **to_datetime()** function. To the optional parameter **parse_dates**, you pass the list (even if it is a single element) of the index of the columns to be converted, as shown as follows:

```
In [ ]: df = pd.read_csv('books.csv', parse_dates = [3])

        print(df)

Out[ ]:

        ID                  Title        Author PublicationDate

0   001276A  The Rise of the Falcon     John Admiral      2018-04-25

1   023125B         Controlled mind    Robert Greens      2016-08-28

2   005556E        Only love remains   Greta Blooming      2015-02-17
```

As we can see, the dates were read as such during the import of the data in the CSV file, thus, obtaining in the DataFrame, already a column with **datetime64** type values.

Working with Text Data

Another type of data that we are dealing with is text data. This type of data is greatly underestimated, but it also requires an appropriate knowledge of various manipulation techniques and some basic knowledge to be able to better manage them within the Pandas library and in data analysis in general.

As with dates and times, when importing text data from an external file or database, it is generically classified as object data types, as shown as follows:

```
In [ ]: df = pd.read_csv('books.csv')

        print(df)

Out[ ]:

        ID                  Title        Author PublicationDate
```

```
0  001276A  The Rise of the Falcon    John Admiral    25-Apr-2018

1  023125B          Controlled mind   Robert Greens   28-Aug-2016

2  005556E        Only love remains   Greta Blooming  17-Feb-2015
```

Let's see in detail the values of the columns that contain textual data, as shown as follows:

```
In [ ]: print(df.ID)
Out[ ]:
0    001276A
1    023125B
2    005556E
Name: ID, dtype: object
```

```
In [ ]: print(df.Title)
Out[ ]:
0    The Rise of the Falcon
1            Controlled mind
2          Only love remains
Name: Title, dtype: object
```

```
In [ ]: print(df.Author)
Out[ ]:
0      John Admiral
1     Robert Greens
2    Greta Blooming
Name: Author, dtype: object
```

As we can see, all three columns containing the data of type text have been imported into the DataFrame as values of type object. You can always make sure that you can import them as strings by adding the optional **dtype** parameter inside the **read_csv()** function. We then set this parameter on the type of data string, as shown as follows:

```
In [ ]: df = pd.read_csv('books.csv', dtype='string')

        print(df)
```

```
Out[ ]:
        ID                 Title          Author  PublicationDate
0  001276A  The Rise of the Falcon   John Admiral      25-Apr-2018
1  023125B          Controlled mind  Robert Greens      28-Aug-2016
2  005556E       Only love remains  Greta Blooming     17-Feb-2015
```

In this case, however, all columns, including those of other types, will be considered to be of the string type, as shown as follows:

```
In [ ]: df.PublicationDate
Out[ ]:
0    25-Apr-2018
1    28-Aug-2016
2    17-Feb-2015
Name: PublicationDate, dtype: string
```

Then, at this point, the single column is converted with the correct type of data, as shown as follows:

```
In [ ]: df.PublicationDate = pd.to_datetime(df.PublicationDate)
        df.PublicationDate
Out[ ]:
0    2018-04-25
1    2016-08-28
2    2015-02-17
Name: PublicationDate, dtype: datetime64[ns]
```

Or, you can import everything as an object and then promptly convert each column with its data type. For example, to convert the values of a single column, you can use the **astype()** method, passing the single type of data as an argument, as shown as follows:

```
In [ ]: df.Title = df.Title.astype('string')
        df.Title
Out[ ]:
0    The Rise of the Falcon
1           Controlled mind
2         Only love remains
```

```
Name: Title, dtype: string
```

But why convert all text data to string type? Once you have converted a textual value into a data type string, you can take advantage of the many methods provided by Python for handling strings. This then provides us with a powerful tool for manipulating and managing textual data.

The methods of correcting the characters of the string

The simplest case is that of wanting to correct the formatting of a text, deciding, for example, to convert the characters from lowercase to uppercase or vice versa. There are a few methods that deal with this. For example, if we want to put all the letters in uppercase within a column, we use the **upper()** method, as shown as follows:

```
In [ ]: df.Title.str.upper()
Out[ ]:
0    THE RISE OF THE FALCON
1           CONTROLLED MIND
2          ONLY LOVE REMAINS
Name: Title, dtype: string
```

Whereas, if we want to use all lowercase characters, we will use the **lower()** method, as shown as follows:

```
In [ ]: df.Title.str.lower()
Out[ ]:
0    the rise of the falcon
1           controlled mind
2          only love remains
Name: Title, dtype: string
```

One of the most used methods in correcting imported text data is **strip()**. Often, when importing columns of text, you have problems with empty spaces. Some strings start with blanks, or at the end, have some blanks that increase their length unnecessarily. Well, these can be removed by some methods.

For example, let's add the following column to our DataFrame:

```
In [ ]: df['Comment'] = [' Too long for a child    ',
                  'Interesting      book  ',
```

                          '   Very Impressive']
          print(df)
Out[ ]:

          ID   Title   Author PublicationDate \
0   001276A   The Rise of the Falcon   John Admiral   2018-04-25
1   023125B   Controlled mind   Robert Greens   2016-08-28
2   005556E   Only love remains Greta Blooming   2015-02-17

                          Comment
0   Too long for a child
1   Interesting   book
2   Very Impressive

As we can see, the last column has comments that have some excess whitespace, both at the beginning and at the end of a text. There is, therefore, a need to correct these values. First, let's see the length of the various strings (including unnecessary spaces) using the **len()** method. These values will help us better check whether the spaces have been removed correctly or not, as shown as follows:

In [ ]: df.Comment.str.len()

Out[ ]:
0   24
1   22
2   18
Name: Comment, dtype: int64

We then apply the **strip()** method to remove unnecessary spaces both at the beginning and at the end of the string (remove leading and trailing whitespaces), as shown as follows:

In [ ]: df.Comment = df.Comment.str.strip()
          print(df.Comment)

Out[ ]:
0   Too long for a child
1   Interesting   book
2   Very Impressive
Name: Comment, dtype: object

```
In [ ]: print(df.Comment.str.len())
Out[ ]:
0    20
1    20
2    15
Name: Comment, dtype: int64
```

As we can see from the result, and by observing the reduced string lengths, after using the **strip()** method, all unnecessary spaces at the beginning and end of the strings have been removed. This is not true for useless spaces that divide words within a string. In fact, you see the string 'Interesting   book' which keeps three empty spaces between the two words. The **strip()** method does not affect the inside of a string in the slightest, but only controls the beginning and the end. If we have such needs, we can use the **replace()** method.

This method allows us to replace one or more characters with others. In this case, we can replace two consecutive spaces with no characters. It is as if we are telling Python to remove all cases where there are two consecutive spaces, as shown as follows:

```
In [ ]: df.Comment.str.replace('  ','')
Out[ ]:
0    Too long for a child
1       Interesting book
2        Very Impressive
Name: Comment, dtype: object
```

From the results obtained, we see that the spaces between the words have also been corrected.

The **replace()** method, in its more conventional use, therefore, serves to replace one or more characters with others. It can be used, for example, to remove or replace unwanted separator characters.

We call up the DataFrame we are working on, as follows:

```
In [ ]: df
```

We get the DataFrame, as shown in *Figure 7.29*:

	ID	Title	Author	PublicationDate	Comment
0	001276A	The Rise of the Falcon	John Admiral	2018-04-25	Too long for a child
1	023125B	Controlled mind	Robert Greens	2016-08-28	Interesting book
2	005556E	Only love remains	Greta Blooming	2015-02-17	Very Impressive

Figure 7.29: Example dataframe

For example, we may want to put commas to separate the name and surname of the authors of the books, as shown as follows:

```
In[ ]: df.Author = df.Author.str.replace(' ',',')
       print(df.Author)
```

```
Out[ ]:
0       John,Admiral
1       Robert,Greens
2       Greta,Blooming
Name: Author, dtype: string
```

Or, we can use it to replace one word with another, within a text, as shown as follows:

```
In [ ]: df.Comment.str.replace('book','novel')
```

```
Out[ ]:
0       Too long for a child
1       Interesting    novel
2               Very Impressive
Name: Comment, dtype: object
```

Methods for splitting strings

Another important string processing method, widely used in Pandas is `split()`. This method analyzes the words present in strings (by default, it includes many separator characters, such as spaces and commas), and separates them from each other obtaining a list of smaller strings, each corresponding to a single word, as shown as follows:

```
In [ ]: df.Title.str.split()
```

```
Out[ ]:
0       [The, Rise, of, the, Falcon]
1                   [Controlled, mind]
```

```
2           [Only, love, remains]
Name: Title, dtype: object
```

If, on the other hand, the words are separated by separator characters, such as a comma ',', it is possible to specify it as an argument of the method, as shown as follows:

```
In [ ]: df.Author.str.split(',')
Out[ ]:
0        [John, Admiral]
1      [Robert, Greens]
2     [Greta, Blooming]
Name: Author, dtype: object
```

As a result, the method returns the strings in the form of a list of words, enclosed in square brackets. A much more useful format for those who work with Pandas is to obtain a DataFrame formed by the words divided between them and placed in columns. To obtain this format, the optional expand parameter is added, making it equal to **True**, as shown as follows:

```
In [ ]: dfw = df.Author.str.split(',', expand=True)
        print(dfw)
Out[ ]:
         0          1
0    John    Admiral
1  Robert     Greens
2   Greta   Blooming


In [ ]: type(dfw)
Out[ ]:
pandas.core.frame.DataFrame
```

As we can see from the result, we got a DataFrame. But the most common operation practiced in the analysis of textual data is to obtain in our DataFrame, the addition of new columns with the values of the individual words. For example, we want to create two new columns in which we have the name and surname of the authors of the books separately, as shown as follows:

```
In [ ]: df[['Author_name','Author_surname']] = df.Author.str.split(',',
expand=True)

        del df['Author']

        df
```

We will get the DataFrame, as shown in *Figure 7.30*:

	ID	Title	PublicationDate	Comment	Author_name	Author_surname
0	001276A	The Rise of the Falcon	2018-04-25	Too long for a child	John	Admiral
1	023125B	Controlled mind	2016-08-28	Interesting book	Robert	Greens
2	005556E	Only love remains	2015-02-17	Very Impressive	Greta	Blooming

Figure 7.30: Example DataFrame

Another common operation with text data is the reverse to the one just performed. Instead of dividing the strings of one column into multiple columns, we want to do the opposite operation. We want to merge the strings of several columns into one. There is no need to use any string method to do this. It is sufficient to use the arithmetic operator sum to concatenate the string values of the individual columns together. You can also add character strings between the operators if you want to add separator characters. In our example, we want to introduce spaces and then we will add the string ' ', as shown as follows:

```
In [ ]: df['Author'] = df['Author_name'] + ' ' + df['Author_surname']

        df
```

You will get the DataFrame, as shown in *Figure 7.31*:

	ID	Title	PublicationDate	Comment	Author_name	Author_surname	Author
0	001276A	The Rise of the Falcon	2018-04-25	Too long for a child	John	Admiral	John Admiral
1	023125B	Controlled mind	2016-08-28	Interesting book	Robert	Greens	Robert Greens
2	005556E	Only love remains	2015-02-17	Very Impressive	Greta	Blooming	Greta Blooming

Figure 7.31: Example DataFrame

As you can see, we have restored the original situation, performing the reverse operation to the previous one.

Methods for concatenating columns of text

However, it is possible to do the same operation using a method for strings that allows their concatenation. So, with the `cat()` method, it is possible to merge the textual values of two columns of the DataFrame and possibly add a separator character with the optional **sep** parameter, as shown as follows:

```
In [ ]: df.Author_name.str.cat(df.Author_surname, sep=' ')
Out[ ]:
0       John Admiral
1       Robert Greens
2       Greta Blooming
Name: Author_name, dtype: string
```

```
Now, we can delete the source columns, as follows:
In [ ]: del df['Author_surname']
        del df['Author_name']
        df
```

We get the DataFrame, as shown in *Figure 7.32*:

	ID	Title	PublicationDate	Comment	Author
0	001276A	The Rise of the Falcon	2018-04-25	Too long for a child	John Admiral
1	023125B	Controlled mind	2016-08-28	Interesting book	Robert Greens
2	005556E	Only love remains	2015-02-17	Very Impressive	Greta Blooming

Figure 7.32: Example DataFrame

As we can see, the results are identical.

Separate alphanumeric from numeric characters in a column

A more complex example than the previous one is to separate alphanumeric from numeric characters in a column, which very often are joined together without any separator character.

In this case, the **replace()** method comes to our aid once again, which allows us to extract only the numeric characters from a column. This is because of a regex expression passed as an argument. If we want to eliminate all alphanumeric characters from our column, we can use the expression regex **([A-Z] +)**, as shown as follows:

```
In [ ]: df['ID1'] = df.ID.str.replace('([A-Z]+)', '', regex=True)
        print(df.ID1)
Out[ ]:
0    001276
1    023125
2    005556
Name: ID1, dtype: string
```

Whereas, if we want to extract only the alphanumeric part, we will use the same method, but this time, passing the expression regex **([0-9] +)**, as shown as follows:

```
In [ ]: df['ID2'] = df.ID.str.replace('([0-9]+)', '', regex=True)
        print(df.ID2)
Out[ ]:
0    A
1    B
2    E
Name: ID2, dtype: string
```

```
Now, let's delete the source column, as follows:
In [ ]: del df['ID']
        df
```

We will get the DataFrame, as shown in *Figure 7.33*:

	Title	PublicationDate	Comment	Author	ID1	ID2
0	The Rise of the Falcon	2018-04-25	Too long for a child	John Admiral	001276	A
1	Controlled mind	2016-08-28	Interesting book	Robert Greens	023125	B
2	Only love remains	2015-02-17	Very Impressive	Greta Blooming	005556	E

Figure 7.33: Example DataFrame

We have, thus, obtained two new columns in which we have separated the numeric characters from the alphanumeric ones.

An alternative method, but which gives similar results, is with the **extract()** method. This method also works through regex expressions and extracts from a column, the characters that correspond to the conditions imposed by the regex expression, as shown as follows:

```
In [ ]: df['ID'] = df.ID1.str.cat(df.ID2)

        df.ID.str.extract('([0-9]+)')
```

As a result, we get the Series as shown in *Figure 7.34*:

	0
0	001276
1	023125
2	005556

Figure 7.34: Column of numeric values extracted from df.ID

The same can be done to extract the alphanumeric part from the column. It is sufficient to change the regex expression to extract only the alphanumeric characters, as shown as follows:

```
In [ ]: df.ID.str.extract('([A-Z]+)')
```

The result is the Series represented in *Figure 7.35*:

	0
0	A
1	B
2	E

Figure 7.35: Column of alphanumeric values extracted from df.ID

Now that we have separated the alphanumeric from the numeric characters, we can delete the original column, as shown as follows:

```
In [ ]: del df['ID']
```

As we can see in *Figure 7.36*, the results of this operation are the same as the previous one:

	Title	PublicationDate	Comment	Author	ID1	ID2
0	The Rise of the Falcon	2018-04-25	Too long for a child	John Admiral	001276	A
1	Controlled mind	2016-08-28	Interesting book	Robert Greens	023125	B
2	Only love remains	2015-02-17	Very Impressive	Greta Blooming	005556	E

Figure 7.36: Example DataFrame

Adding characters to the rows of a column

In the previous examples, we saw how the **cat()** method allowed us to concatenate the strings of two columns together to form a new one. Another use of **cat()** is to add one or more characters to the end of each line in a column.

For example, let's add the acronyms of the nations to one of the columns we generated, as shown as follows:

```
In [ ]: df.ID2.str.cat(['USA','ITA','FRA'],sep='-')
Out[ ]:
0    A-USA
1    B-ITA
2    E-FRA
Name: ID2, dtype: string
```

This, however, supposes the insertion of a list or an external Series having the same number of rows as our DataFrame. If, on the other hand, we want to add the same sequence of characters for an entire column, we create a temporary column in the DataFrame, all with the same value, and then it is concatenated to the desired column, as shown as follows:

```
In [ ]: df['temp'] = 'USA'
        df.ID2 = df.ID2.str.cat(df['temp'],sep='-')
        del df['temp']
        print(df.ID2)
Out[ ]:
0    A-USA
1    B-USA
2    E-USA
Name: ID2, dtype: string
```

Let's see the result of these operations as follows:

```
In [ ]: df
```

As a result, we will obtain the DataFrame, as shown in *Figure 7.37*:

	Title	PublicationDate	Comment	Author	ID1	ID2
0	The Rise of the Falcon	2018-04-25	Too long for a child	John Admiral	001276	A-USA
1	Controlled mind	2016-08-28	Interesting book	Robert Greens	023125	B-USA
2	Only love remains	2015-02-17	Very Impressive	Greta Blooming	005556	E-USA

Figure 7.37: Example DataFrame

As you can see, these methods are malleable, and to carry out the same operation, you can find different possible solutions.

Recognition methods between alphanumeric and numeric characters

There are methods for strings that allow you to know if, within a string, we have only alphanumeric or numeric characters. For example, we previously separated the ID code column into two columns, one alphanumeric and one numeric. Often, DataFrames have many rows and it is not possible to ascertain whether the previous operation was successful on all rows. It could also be that one of the rows of the column contained an incorrect or non-uniform code and that, therefore, the regex expression was not sufficient to completely separate the alphanumeric characters from the numeric ones. To make sure of this, you can use the `isdigit()` method which parses each row of a column, making sure it contains only numeric characters, as shown as follows:

```
In [ ]: df.ID1.str.isdigit()
Out[ ]:
0    True
1    True
2    True
Name: ID1, dtype: boolean
```

The same goes for the opposite, that is, if you want to make sure that each row of a column contains only alphanumeric characters, you can use the `isalnum()` method, as shown as follows:

```
In [ ]: df.ID2.str.isalnum()
Out[ ]:
0    False
1    False
```

```
2    False
Name: ID2, dtype: boolean
```

Searching methods in strings

There are also many other methods for strings that are capable of performing recursive searches within textual data. For example, you could check for the presence of a word within each line, with the **find()** method, as shown as follows:

We verify the presence of the word **'love'** within the titles of the books in our DataFrame as follows:

```
In [ ]: df.Title.str.find('love')
Out[ ]:
0    -1
1    -1
2    5
Name: Title, dtype: Int64
```

As can be seen from the result, a series of numbers is obtained, whose values correspond to the position of the word **'love'** within each row of the column. If it is present, then a positive integer is obtained, and if it is not present, the value -1 is obtained.

If, on the other hand, our search is essentially focused on knowing whether the word is present or not within a column, it can be written as follows:

```
In [ ]: df.Title.str.find('love') > -1
Out[ ]:
0    False
1    False
2    True
Name: Title, dtype: boolean
```

As you can see from the preceding example, the **find()** method returns a positive value if it has found the searched word, and the number will correspond to the position of the word within the line of text. To obtain a Boolean Series instead, it is sufficient to check if the returned values are greater than 0.

Conclusion

In this chapter, you received all the information you need to get data from the outside world. Text files, data in JSON or XML format, and even tables in databases, are excellent data sources from which to draw the data we need. This is thanks to the many specific methods and functions that you saw in the chapter and which, at the same time, allow you to import and convert data in DataFrame in one step. Furthermore, now with the second part of this chapter, you have become aware that data is not limited to simple numerical values, but also textual, some of which can be considered strings, and other types of data that are more complex such as dates and times. Thanks to a series of examples, you have an overview of how to manipulate these types of objects to fit and clean them for the purposes of your analysis.

In the next chapter, we will see some exceptions and special cases that you can run into when dealing with real data obtained from external data sources.

Questions

1. What are the differences between the concepts of Date Time and Delta Time?

2. What are the utilities of converting textual data of type object into strings?

Multiple choice questions

1. Which of these assertions is false for df.to_csv(sys.stdout, index=False, header=True)?

   A. The values in the CSV file are separated by the character ','.

   B. The first values for each row on the CSV file correspond to the row indices of the DataFrame.

   C. The first row on the CSV file corresponds to the column labels of the DataFrame.

2. Using the sqlite3 driver to query SQLite, what kind of return value do you get from conn.execute('SELECT * FROM MyTable')?

   A. a DataFrame

   B. a dict

   C. a list of tuples

3. Which of the following formats is suitable for converting the string '12-Apr @21:14' to DateTime?

   A. format='%d-%m @%H:%M'

    B.   format='%d-%m @%I:%M'

    C.   format='%d-%b @%H:%M'

4. Which of the following options is unable to extract a sequence of numeric characters from a column with ID label?

    A.   df.ID.str.replace('([0-9]+)', '', regex=True)

    B.   df.ID.str.extract('([0-9]+)')

    C.   df.ID.str.replace('([A-Z]+)', '', regex=True)

Solution

1: B; 2: A; 3: C; 4: C

Key Terms

Importing files, XML, JSON, Excel Spreadsheet, Date Time, Time delta, Strings.

References/Further Readings

- *Python Data Analytics With Pandas, NumPy, and Matplotlib, Fabio Nelli, Apress*

- *https://pandas.pydata.org/pandas-docs/stable/user_guide/io.html*

## CHAPTER 8

Day 6 - Troubleshooting Challenges with Real Datasets

In the previous chapters, we learned how to obtain missing values during our operations. In the world of real data, you will rarely get datasets where there is no missing value. It is, therefore, very important to understand how to manage these values, given that if not properly treated, this type of value can lead to calculation and analysis problems, preventing us from carrying out our work. In this chapter, we will address the issue of missing values in detail, deepening our knowledge on this kind of data and on how to manage it.

But that's not all, there are other problems that can be encountered during the creation and analysis of the DataFrame. In the second part of this chapter, we will see some special cases, such as Sparse DataFrame, the replacement or elimination of redundant data, and in particular, we will discover the concept of **Tidy data**.

Structure

In this chapter, we will cover the following topics:

- Handling missing data
- Data Replacing
- Data Duplicated
- Renaming Axis Labels

- Sparse DataFrames
- TIDY data

Objective

After studying this chapter, you will master some basic concepts for preparing and cleaning real-world datasets after importing them. A correct arrangement of the values within the columns is essential if you want to perform the data analysis in the most correct way. So, having deepened the techniques of missing values, you can remove, or at least manage, this type of value. In addition, you will learn some fundamental techniques and concepts to correctly set up a DataFrame, cleaning up both redundant values, grouping, or separating values in columns. Furthermore, thanks to the Tidy data concept, you will understand if the structure of a newly imported DataFrame responds correctly to particular requirements, and thanks to appropriate techniques, you will be able to order its internal structure and the values connected to it.

Handling Missing Data

Let's start this chapter with Missing Data. This concept is not strictly related to the Panda library, but exists in many contexts. In databases, these are indicated with the value NULL. Some programming languages use NA, or empty strings ' '. While in Python, different ways are used to represent missing values – NaN, NAN, or nan, (which all stand for 'Not a Number'), but they are all equivalent to each other. Furthermore, other built-in values, such as None, can also be considered as a missing value.

Missing values in Python are mainly defined and managed by the NumPy library. All three of the previously described shapes can be imported individually from the library, as shown as follows:

```
In [ ]: from numpy import NaN, NAN, nan
```

While for these three values, there are no particular differences; other types of data considered or used as such, in reality, are not the only one. In fact, values such as 0 or ' ' (empty space) are not missing values at all, since they are still equal values and within the data sets, the latter could be confused or generate errors during the calculation or analysis of some data. For example, 0 is a number, and not a 'Not a Number', and therefore, can be included in the calculation of averages, for example, without generating an error, but strongly interfering with the result. The same thing with ' ', which being a string could interfere with some interpretations of the data.

How NaNs are formed

Missing values, or NaNs, are more common than one might think and are generated in our DataFrame on several occasions. One of these is during data import.

When importing data from an external source to generate a DataFrame, for example, using the **read_csv()** function – this is when it finds cells with missing values and automatically assigns their NaN value.

To do this, let's create a CSV file with a text editor and save it as **countries.csv**. We write the following data inside:

```
Country,Population,Capital,Area

USA,329.5,Washington,3796

Russia,144.1,Moscow,

Sweden,,Stockholm,450

UK,67.22,Not Known,242

Japan,125.8,Tokyo,

Egypt,102.3,Not Known,1010
```

As you can see, we have not specifically inserted some values within the columns. We import the data of this file into a DataFrame through the **read_csv()** method, as shown as follows:

```
In [ ]: df = pd.read_csv('countries.csv')
        df
```

We will then get a DataFrame, like the one shown in *Figure 8.1*:

	Country	Population	Capital	Area
0	USA	329.50	Washington	3796.0
1	Russia	144.10	Moscow	NaN
2	Sweden	NaN	Stockholm	450.0
3	UK	67.22	Not Known	242.0
4	Japan	125.80	Tokyo	NaN
5	Egypt	102.30	Not Known	1010.0

Figure 8.1: DataFrame obtained from countries.csv

As we can see, in the CSV file, where no values were specified, the NaN values have been inserted.

In **read_csv()**, as in all other external file reading functions, there are the following three optional parameters that manage the reading of the missing values:

- na_values
- na_filter
- keep_default_na

The **na_values** parameter allows you to specify the additional missing values (NaN, NA, and nan are the default ones). In fact, it could happen that within the imported dataset, there are fields with particular values that explicitly indicate a missing value. In these cases, it would be appropriate to add these values within this parameter, helping the **read_csv()** function to recognize these kinds of values as missing values.

In the countries.csv sample file, not all country capitals have been indicated. Where they were not present, **'Not Known'** was specified as the value. So, instead of leaving this value inside our DataFrame, we convert it to NaN during the import phase, as shown as follows:

```
In [ ]: df = pd.read_csv('countries.csv', na_values=['Not Known'])
        df
```

This time, we will get a DataFrame, as shown in *Figure 8.2*:

	Country	Population	Capital	Area
0	USA	329.50	Washington	3796.0
1	Russia	144.10	Moscow	NaN
2	Sweden	NaN	Stockholm	450.0
3	UK	67.22	NaN	242.0
4	Japan	125.80	Tokyo	NaN
5	Egypt	102.30	NaN	1010.0

Figure 8.2: DataFrame obtained from countries.csv with the na_values parameter

As we can see, where the string **'Not Known'** used to be, now there is NaN.

The **na_filter** parameter is of the Boolean type and, by default, is set to **True**. This parameter is useful for deactivating the missing value recognition mode, and therefore, if set to **False**, the NaN insertion system is deactivated, and the data is imported and they are in the source file.

For example, let's set the following up when importing data from our **countries. csv** example file:

```
In [ ]: df = pd.read_csv('countries.csv', na_filter=False)

        df
```

We will get a DataFrame like the one shown in *Figure 8.3*:

	Country	Population	Capital	Area
0	USA	329.5	Washington	3796
1	Russia	144.1	Moscow	
2	Sweden		Stockholm	450
3	UK	67.22	Not Known	242
4	Japan	125.8	Tokyo	
5	Egypt	102.3	Not Known	1010

Figure 8.3: DataFrame obtained from countries.csv with na_filter disabled

As we can see from the result, the NaN values are no longer present in the DataFrame, but the empty spaces in the CSV file remain so even within the DataFrame.

The **keep_default_na** parameter is also of the Boolean type and is set by default to **True**. In this case, setting it to **False** does not disable the missing values filter, but only those defined in **na_values**.

Let's try this setting by importing our countries.csv file, as shown as follows:

```
In [ ]: df = pd.read_csv('countries.csv', na_values=['Not Known'], keep_
default_na=False)

        df
```

We will get the DataFrame, as shown in *Figure 8.4*:

	Country	Population	Capital	Area
0	USA	329.5	Washington	3796
1	Russia	144.1	Moscow	
2	Sweden		Stockholm	450
3	UK	67.22	NaN	242
4	Japan	125.8	Tokyo	
5	Egypt	102.3	NaN	1010

Figure 8.4: DataFrame obtained from countries.csv with keep_default_na on False

As we can see, we have obtained an intermediate situation with respect to the two previous cases. The empty spaces within the CSV file are kept as such, whereas, with regards to the 'Not Known' values, they are recognized as missing values.

Other operations that generate NaN

In addition to the recognition of particular values within the datasets imported into a DataFrame, the NaN values can be subsequently generated automatically during data processing. In fact, in the previous chapters, we saw that some operations carried out on the DataFrame generate NaNs within the results, as follows:

- Reindexing (Chapter 4)
- Shifting (Chapter 5)
- Merging (Chapter 6)

One of the most common examples is when Reindexing a DataFrame (see *Chapter 4 - (Day 2) Working within a DataFrame, Basic Funcionalities*). In this kind of operation, when you reorganize the indexes within a DataFrame, if you insert a new index (both row and column), you will have, as a result, a new DataFrame in which there are entire rows or columns of missing values, precisely in correspondence with these indices.

For example, let's import the contents of the **books.csv** file, as shown as follows:

```
In [ ]: df = pd.read_csv('books.csv')
        df
```

You get a DataFrame like the one shown in *Figure 8.5*:

	ID	Title	Author	PublicationDate
0	001276A	The Rise of the Falcon	John Admiral	25-Apr-2018
1	023125B	Controlled mind	Robert Greens	28-Aug-2016
2	005556E	Only love remains	Greta Blooming	17-Feb-2015

Figure 8.5: DataFrame obtained from books.csv

We subject the newly imported DataFrame to reindexing, setting a new order of the column indexes, and inserting a new **Price** label, as shown as follows:

```
In [ ]: df2 = df.reindex(['ID','Author','Title','Price'],axis=1)
        df2
```

You will get the DataFrame like the one represented in *Figure 8.6*:

	ID	Author	Title	Price
0	001276A	John Admiral	The Rise of the Falcon	NaN
1	023125B	Robert Greens	Controlled mind	NaN
2	005556E	Greta Blooming	Only love remains	NaN

Figure 8.6: Result of the reindexing of the DataFrame

As we can see, a new Price column filled with NaN values was automatically generated. In this case, the management is really simple; if we insert a new label in the Reindexing, it is because we want to add a new column.

Thus, the values are enhanced with a Series that is already set, or new ones are defined, as shown as follows:

```
In [ ]: df2['Price'] = [10.00, 20.00, 15.00]
        df2
```

You get the DataFrame like the one in *Figure 8.7*:

	ID	Title	Author	PublicationDate	Price
0	001276A	The Rise of the Falcon	John Admiral	25-Apr-2018	10.0
1	023125B	Controlled mind	Robert Greens	28-Aug-2016	20.0
2	005556E	Only love remains	Greta Blooming	17-Feb-2015	15.0

Figure 8.7: Corrected DataFrame after Reindexing

Another operation very similar to the previous one is Shifting, in which NaN values are generated when moving rows or columns (see *Chapter 5 - (Day 3) Working within a DataFrame, Advanced Funcionalities*).

In fact, you can make a shift on the test DataFrame, as shown as follows:

```
In [ ]: df.shift(1)
```

We will obtain the shift of all rows downwards, with the loss of the last row, and the generation of a new row at the beginning fully valued with NaN values, as shown in *Figure 8.8*:

	ID	Title	Author	PublicationDate
0	NaN	NaN	NaN	NaN
1	001276A	The Rise of the Falcon	John Admiral	25-Apr-2018
2	023125B	Controlled mind	Robert Greens	28-Aug-2016

Figure 8.8: Result of the shifting of the test DataFrame

Also, in this case, it is possible to remedy either by eliminating the row or by enhancing it with appropriate values.

In both the previous cases, it is already possible to value the missing values with an appropriate value, without the need to value them later (if this is what is desired). This can be done with the optional **fill_value** parameter, as shown as follows:

```
In [ ]: df.reindex(['ID','Author','Title','Price'],
                    axis=1, fill_value= 0.00)
```

The result obtained is shown in *Figure 8.9*:

	ID	Author	Title	Price
0	001276A	John Admiral	The Rise of the Falcon	0.0
1	023125B	Robert Greens	Controlled mind	0.0
2	005556E	Greta Blooming	Only love remains	0.0

Figure 8.9: The DataFrame no longer has NaN values

The same thing is achieved by inserting **fill_value** in the shifting, as shown as follows:

```
In [ ]: df.shift(1, fill_value='Empty')
```

In fact, the DataFrame in *Figure 8.10* is obtained in which the NaN values have been replaced by an indicative value **Empty**:

	ID	Title	Author	PublicationDate
0	Empty	Empty	Empty	Empty
1	001276A	The Rise of the Falcon	John Admiral	25-Apr-2018
2	023125B	Controlled mind	Robert Greens	28-Aug-2016

Figure 8.10: The DataFrame no longer has NaN values

Other operations that add NaN values into the resulting DataFrame are operations that involve two DataFrames (see *Chapter 6 - (Day 4) Working with two or more DataFrames*).

For example, by merging between two DataFrames, there will be some NaNs where there is no correspondence between the two objects.

To work with merging, we import the data for a second DataFrame from the **books_store.csv** file, as shown as follows:

```
In [ ]: df1 = pd.read_csv('books_store.csv')

        df1
```

The internal values of those are represented in *Figure 8.11*:

	ID	Title	Price	Amount
0	001276A	The Rise of the Falcon	25.0	23
1	023125B	Controlled mind	15.0	33
2	035721C	Walking on Mars	27.0	54
3	005556E	Only love remains	33.0	43

Figure 8.11: The DataFrame imported from the books_store.csv file

As you can see, a dataset of values suitably correlated to the test DataFrame was chosen as the second DataFrame. They are, in fact, the same books but containing different information.

At this point, we perform the merging between the two DataFrames, as shown as follows:

```
In [ ]: pd.merge(df,df1, on = ['ID','Title'], how='right')
```

The result is the DataFrame as shown in *Figure 8.12*:

	ID	Title	Author	PublicationDate	Price	Amount
0	001276A	The Rise of the Falcon	John Admiral	25-Apr-2018	25.0	23
1	023125B	Controlled mind	Robert Greens	28-Aug-2016	15.0	33
2	035721C	Walking on Mars	NaN	NaN	27.0	54
3	005556E	Only love remains	Greta Blooming	17-Feb-2015	33.0	43

Figure 8.12: The DataFrame imported from the books_store.csv file

As you can see, with regards to the book, where there is no correspondence (we do not know the author and the date of publication), the NaNs are entered where the data is missing. In this case, either you look for this information punctually and replace the NaNs with the correct values, or you will have to ignore all those lines (books) that have these values.

Working with Missing values

In the previous sections, we saw how the missing NaN values are generated within the DataFrame. Once their presence has been ascertained, there are several solutions on how to manage them. Broadly speaking, they can be grouped into two different approaches, as follows:

- Remove them
- Fill them with other values

In this regard, the Pandas library provides a whole series of methods and functions that allow us to perform operations on NaN values, as follows:

- `isnull()`
- `notnull()`
- `dropna()`
- `fillna()`

Find and count the missing values

First, it will be necessary to check the presence of the missing values and their position in the DataFrame structure. In the real world, DataFrames reach enormous sizes with thousands of rows and columns, making it impossible to search visually. In this regard, there are a number of functions that come to our aid. If you want to count the total number of missing values within a DataFrame or limitedly a specific column, you can use the **count_nonzero()** function of Numpy in conjunction with the `isnull()` method.

Let's reload the data from the countries.csv file for our examples, as shown as follows:

```
In [ ]: df = pd.read_csv('countries.csv')
        df
```

The test DataFrame is like the one shown in *Figure 8.13*:

	Country	Population	Capital	Area
0	USA	329.50	Washington	3796.0
1	Russia	144.10	Moscow	NaN
2	Sweden	NaN	Stockholm	450.0
3	UK	67.22	Not Known	242.0
4	Japan	125.80	Tokyo	NaN
5	Egypt	102.30	Not Known	1010.0

Figure 8.13: *The DataFrame imported from countries.csv*

To check how many NaN values are present in the DataFrame, we therefore, use the combination of **count_nonzero()** and **isnull()**, as shown as follows:

```
In [ ]: np.count_nonzero(df.isnull())
```

```
Out[ ]: 3
```

If instead we want to know the number of NaN values limited to a column, we will use the following code:

```
In [ ]: np.count_nonzero(df['Area'].isnull())
```

```
Out[ ]: 2
```

Another way is to use the **value_counts()** method on a Series, as shown as follows:

```
In [ ]: df['Area'].value_counts(dropna=False)
Out[ ]:
NaN        2
3796.0     1
450.0      1
242.0      1
1010.0     1
Name: Area, dtype: int64
```

You get a frequency table of the values within the DataFrame, including NaN.

Drop missing values

One of the two possible approaches when dealing with the presence of NaN values within our DataFrame is to remove them. In fact, we often do not know or want to manage this missing information and, therefore, it is better to delete it. In this regard, the **dropna()** method can be used to eliminate the missing values, as shown as follows:

In [ ]: df.dropna()

In *Figure 8.14*, we can see the test DataFrame where all the rows, with even a single NaN value, have been removed:

	Country	Population	Capital	Area
0	USA	329.50	Washington	3796.0
3	UK	67.22	Not Known	242.0
5	Egypt	102.30	Not Known	1010.0

Figure 8.14: The DataFrame in which the NaNs were removed

The **dropna()** method can also work more loosely, telling it to only drop lines where all values are NaN. This is possible by passing the optional parameter **how = 'all'**.

Filling in of Missing Values

The other approach is instead to enhance the NaN values with other appropriate values. In this case, you can use the **fillna()** method to replace the NaN values with another value, passing it as an argument.

For example, if we want to replace all the NaNs in the DataFrame with the **Empty** value, we can write the following code:

In [ ]: df.fillna('Empty')

We will get a DataFrame in which all NaN values have been replaced with the string **Empty**, as shown in *Figure 8.15*:

	Country	Population	Capital	Area
0	USA	329.5	Washington	3796.0
1	Russia	144.1	Moscow	Empty
2	Sweden	Empty	Stockholm	450.0
3	UK	67.22	Not Known	242.0
4	Japan	125.8	Tokyo	Empty
5	Egypt	102.3	Not Known	1010.0

Figure 8.15: The DataFrame in which the NaNs were replaced with Empty

It is also possible to specify a different value to be used in place of NaN, specifically for each column. In this case, a **dict** is passed as an argument.

In our case, we will insert in the **dict**, as key, the name of the columns containing the NaN values, and as value, the values to be used in their place, as shown as follows:

```
In [ ]: df.fillna({'Population':0.0, 'Area': 10.0})
```

You will get a DataFrame in which, in each column, the NaN values have been valued in a different way, as shown in *Figure 8.16*:

	Country	Population	Capital	Area
0	USA	329.50	Washington	3796.0
1	Russia	144.10	Moscow	10.0
2	Sweden	0.00	Stockholm	450.0
3	UK	67.22	Not Known	242.0
4	Japan	125.80	Tokyo	10.0
5	Egypt	102.30	Not Known	1010.0

Figure 8.16: *The DataFrame in which the NaNs were replaced with column-specific values*

These methods return a copy of the referenced object. But they can be applied directly to the calling DataFrame if we specify the optional **inplace** parameter set to **True**.

If you modify the previous method with the following command, the operation of replacing the NaN values will be irreversible:

```
In [ ]: #df.fillna('Empty', inplace=True)
```

We put the comment symbol, because for the continuation of the examples, we need to work again with the test DataFrame containing the NaN values.

Fill Forward or Backward

Remaining in the approach of replacing NaN values, there is also the possibility of inserting values that try to follow the trend of the other elements of the column. There are two possible ways that allow this possibility – fill forward and fill backward. In fill forward, the last known value is used to fill in the missing value.

In this case, we still use the **fillna()** method, but we specify the optional **method** parameter to indicate the specific method, which in this case, is **ffill** (Fill Forward), as shown as follows:

```
In [ ]: df.fillna(method='ffill')
```

As a result, we will have the DataFrame as shown in *Figure 8.17*:

	Country	Population	Capital	Area
0	USA	329.50	Washington	3796.0
1	Russia	144.10	Moscow	3796.0
2	Sweden	144.10	Stockholm	450.0
3	UK	67.22	Not Known	242.0
4	Japan	125.80	Tokyo	242.0
5	Egypt	102.30	Not Known	1010.0

Figure 8.17: The DataFrame in which the NaNs were replaced with values from the previous row

As we can see, each NaN value has been replaced by the previous row value in the same column.

As for the Fill Backward, the behavior is the opposite. It will be the value of the next row to replace the NaN values. To set this, you specify **bfill** in the optional **method** parameter, as shown as follows:

```
In [ ]: df.fillna(method='bfill')
```

As a result, we will have the DataFrame as shown in *Figure 8.18*:

	Country	Population	Capital	Area
0	USA	329.50	Washington	3796.0
1	Russia	144.10	Moscow	450.0
2	Sweden	67.22	Stockholm	450.0
3	UK	67.22	Not Known	242.0
4	Japan	125.80	Tokyo	1010.0
5	Egypt	102.30	Not Known	1010.0

Figure 8.18: The DataFrame in which the NaNs were replaced with values from the next row

As we can see from the result, in this case, the NaN values will be replaced with the values of the next row in the same column.

The two approaches just seen are some of the possibilities that can be applied with the Pandas library. For example, you can replace NaN values with the results of column value statistics, calculated directly by passing **fillna()**, with methods such as **mean()** or **median()** as the argument of the method, as shown as follows:

```
In [ ]: df.fillna(df.mean())
```

The result is the DataFrame as shown in *Figure 8.19*:

	Country	Population	Capital	Area
0	USA	329.500	Washington	3796.0
1	Russia	144.100	Moscow	1374.5
2	Sweden	153.784	Stockholm	450.0
3	UK	67.220	Not Known	242.0
4	Japan	125.800	Tokyo	1374.5
5	Egypt	102.300	Not Known	1010.0

Figure 8.19: The DataFrame in which the NaNs were replaced with the averages of the column values

As we can see from the result, the NaN values have been replaced with the averages of the values present in the corresponding columns.

Interpolate

Still continuing with the different possibilities of managing the approach to replacing NaN values, interpolation must also be considered. This technique uses the values in the column to fill in the missing values with calculated values to interpolate the trend of the values in the column. To do this, we use the **interpolate()** method, as shown as follows:

```
In [ ]: df.interpolate()
```

The result is the DataFrame as shown in *Figure 8.20*:

	Country	Population	Capital	Area
0	USA	329.50	Washington	3796.0
1	Russia	144.10	Moscow	2123.0
2	Sweden	105.66	Stockholm	450.0
3	UK	67.22	Not Known	242.0
4	Japan	125.80	Tokyo	626.0
5	Egypt	102.30	Not Known	1010.0

Figure 8.20: The DataFrame in which the NaNs were replaced with interpolated values

By default, the interpolation in Pandas fills the values linearly, but here too, you can change this behavior by adding the optional **method** parameter and specifying the interpolation method.

Conversion of data types in the presence of NaN

Finding ourselves working with NaN values, it can often happen that we are faced with unexpected behaviors.

First, we saw that there can be several ways to express missing values, as follows:

- None (from Python)
- np.nan (from NumPy)
- pd.NA (from Pandas)

But if we pass it inside some lists of values, for example integers, we will find some surprises, as shown as follows:

```
In [ ]: pd.Series([1, 4, None, 5, 12])
Out[ ]: 0    1.0
1    4.0
2    NaN
dtype: float64
```

```
In [ ]: pd.Series([1, 4, np.nan, 5, 12])
Out[ ]: 0    1.0
1    4.0
2    NaN
3    5.0
4    12.0
dtype: float64
```

As we can see from the results regarding **None** and **np.nan**, there was an implicit casting which caused our integers to be converted to floating numbers. Whereas, for **pd.NA**, we have a different behavior. That is, if we pass a list of integers to the Series constructor, we have, as a result, the recognition of those values as integers (**dtype64**). But if there is a **pd.NA** within that list, then all the values will be converted to the generic data type object, as shown as follows:

```
In [ ]: pd.Series([1, 4, 5, 12])
```

```
Out[ ]: 0     1
1     4
2     5
3     12
dtype: int64


In [ ]: pd.Series([1, 4, pd.NA, 5, 12])
Out[ ]: 0       1
1       4
2     <NA>
3       5
4      12
dtype: object
```

To overcome this problem, we define the type of data we want in the optional **dtype** parameter of the **Series()** constructor, as shown as follows:

```
In [ ]: pd.Series([1, 4, pd.NA, 5, None, np.nan], dtype='Int64')
Out[ ]: 0       1
1       4
2     <NA>
3       5
4     <NA>
5     <NA>
dtype: Int64
```

Another method is to convert the list into a Python **IntegerArray** object. To do this, use the **array()** function, passing it the list as an argument, as shown as follows:

```
In [ ]: pd.array([1, 4, pd.NA, 5, None, np.nan])
Out[ ]: <IntegerArray>
[1, 4, <NA>, 5, <NA>, <NA>]
Length: 6, dtype: Int64


In [ ]: pd.array([1.0, 4.0, pd.NA, 5.0, None, np.nan])
Out[ ]: <FloatingArray>
```

```
[1.0, 4.0, <NA>, 5.0, <NA>, <NA>]
Length: 6, dtype: Float64
```

As we can see from the results, the system is perfectly capable of recognizingthe different types of missing values, and adapt them from time to time..

The same goes for a list of Boolean values in which missing values are present. We can study the conversion of data during the transition from List to Series, as shown as follows:

```
In [ ]: pd.Series([True, False, None, True, False])
Out[ ]:

0    True
1    False
2    None
3    True
4    False
dtype: object


In [ ]: pd.Series([True, False, np.nan, True, False])
Out[ ]:
0    True
1    False
2    NaN
3    True
4    False
dtype: object


In [ ]: pd.Series([True, False, pd.NA, True, False])
Out[ ]:

0    True
1    False
2    <NA>
```

```
3      True
4      False
dtype: object
```

As we can see, in all cases, there is no recognition of Boolean data types and there is a conversion of the values passed as generic data of type object. Also in this case, the type of data can be defined in the constructor, as shown as follows:

```
In [ ]: pd.Series([True, False, pd.NA, True, None, np.nan, False],
dtype='boolean')
Out[ ]: 0      True
1      False
2      <NA>
3      True
4      <NA>
5      <NA>
6      False
dtype: boolean
```

Or, you can use the **array()** function, as shown as follows:

```
In [ ]: pd.array([True, False, pd.NA, True, None, np.nan, False])
<BooleanArray>
[True, False, <NA>, True, <NA>, <NA>, False]
Length: 7, dtype: boolean
```

As you can see, in both cases, there is a correct data conversion.

Other common operations for correcting newly imported DataFrame

In the previous sections of this chapter, we saw that one of the main problems when importing data sets from external sources is to find some missing values valued as NaN. We saw how to overcome this type of problem, but this is only one of the operations to be performed when importing new data. In this section, we will see some common operations that do not involve NaN values, but that obviate other undesired values present in the DataFrame (incorrect, unwanted, or duplicated values).

Data Replacing

One of these operations to be carried out on a DataFrame just generated from imported data is **Data Replacing**. In addition to the NaNs within the DataFrame, there may be values that for our analysis could be uncomfortable. So, in these cases, it will be necessary to replace them with other values more suited to us. The Pandas library provides us with the **replace()** method that allows us to replace values with others more in keeping with our analysis standards.

For example, let's load a dataset containing a series of garments with the description of the size and color, as shown as follows:

```
In [ ]: df = pd.read_csv('clothing.csv')
        df
```

You will get the DataFrame as shown in *Figure 8.21*:

	Type	Color	Size
0	Tshirt	Black	M
1	Socks	Red	L
2	Sweater	Blue	S
3	Sweater	Bluex	M
4	Tshirt	White	M
5	Sweater	Carmine	XL
6	Socks	Red	L
7	Tshirt	Black	M
8	Socks	Brown	S

Figure 8.21: *The DataFrame obtained from the clothing.csv file*

As we can see, the DataFrame presents a series of garments with the color and size. Looking at the colors carefully, we will find the Carmine color and the Bluex color. In the first case, for example, we would like to simplify such a specific color into a more general one such as **Red**. In the second case, however, it is certainly a data entry error and, therefore, must be corrected with **Blue**.

So, to make these corrections, we use the **replace()** method, as shown as follows:

```
In [ ]: df.replace('Carmine', 'Red',inplace=True)
        df.replace('Bluex','Blue',inplace=True)
        df
```

We will obtain the DataFrame with the correct values as shown in *Figure 8.22*:

	Type	Color	Size
0	Tshirt	Black	M
1	Socks	Red	L
2	Sweater	Blue	S
3	Sweater	Blue	M
4	Tshirt	White	M
5	Sweater	Red	XL
6	Socks	Red	L
7	Tshirt	Black	M
8	Socks	Brown	S

Figure 8.22: *The DataFrame obtained from the clothing.csv file with the correct values*

In these kind of operations, unless you are performing some tests, it is always better to use the optional **inplace** parameter set to **True**, to make the changes permanent.

Data Duplicated

Another common case present in newly imported datasets is that of presenting rows with duplicate data. Again, you will need to make corrections, removing all duplicate data. However, given the size of the datasets and consequently of the DataFrame generated, being able to understand whether or not duplicate data exist within them can be problematic if it is not done with the correct tools. In this regard, in the Pandas library, the **duplicated()** method exists, which helps us in the search for duplicate rows (or duplicate values limited to a column).

We apply this method to our test DataFrame, as shown as follows:

```
In [ ]: df.duplicated()
Out[ ]:

0    False
1    False
2    False
3    False
```

```
4    False

5    False

6     True

7     True

8    False
```

dtype: bool

This method returns a Boolean Series with True values indicating that there are duplicate rows. As you can see from the result, there are two duplicate lines, in positions 6 and 7. The next step will, therefore, be their removal. Also, in this case, there is a special method that does the **drop_duplicates()**, as shown as follows:

In [ ]: df.drop_duplicates()

The result shown in *Figure 8.23* is obtained:

	Type	Color	Size
0	Tshirt	Black	M
1	Socks	Red	L
2	Sweater	Blue	S
3	Sweater	Blue	M
4	Tshirt	White	M
5	Sweater	Red	XL
8	Socks	Brown	S

Figure 8.23: *The DataFrame no longer has duplicate rows*

This method keeps the first observed value by default. You can vary this behavior by adding the optional **keep = 'last'** parameter, leaving the last replicated instead and deleting the previous ones, as shown as follows:

In [ ]: df.drop_duplicates(keep='last', inplace=True)

   Df

We will obtain the DataFrame as shown in *Figure 8.24*:

	Type	Color	Size
2	Sweater	Blue	S
3	Sweater	Blue	M
4	Tshirt	White	M
5	Sweater	Red	XL
6	Socks	Red	L
7	Tshirt	Black	M
8	Socks	Brown	S

Figure 8.24: The DataFrame no longer has duplicate rows

Also, in this case, it is advisable to add the optional parameter **inplace** to **True** to make the corrections permanent.

Renaming Axis Indexes

Another operation often necessary when importing a new dataset in the form of a DataFrame is to change the labels of the columns and rows. Like the values within the DataFrame, the labels present in the indexes may also be invalid or irrelevant.

Let's take the previously used **books.csv** file and import it with the **read_csv()** method, as shown as follows:

```
In [ ]: df = pd.read_csv('books.csv')

        df
```

We will get a DataFrame like the one shown in *Figure 8.25*:

	ID	Title	Author	PublicationDate
0	001276A	The Rise of the Falcon	John Admiral	25-Apr-2018
1	023125B	Controlled mind	Robert Greens	28-Aug-2016
2	005556E	Only love remains	Greta Blooming	17-Feb-2015

Figure 8.25: The DataFrame imported from the books.csv file

As we can see, the **read_csv()** method has added a progressive sequence of integers as labels, but in reality, the imported dataset already has identifying values inside it for each row – the ID column. So, a more correct way to import these values is by adding the optional **index_col** parameter specifying the number of the column that will be used as index labels, as shown as follows:

```
In [ ]: df = pd.read_csv('books.csv', index_col=0)

        df
```

This time, we will get a DataFrame with the index labels enhanced with data from the dataset, as shown in *Figure 8.26*:

ID	Title	Author	PublicationDate
001276A	The Rise of the Falcon	John Admiral	25-Apr-2018
023125B	Controlled mind	Robert Greens	28-Aug-2016
005556E	Only love remains	Greta Blooming	17-Feb-2015

Figure 8.26: The DataFrame imported from the books.csv file with index valued

By checking the various labels (both of index and columns) present in the newly imported DataFrame, corrections or changes could be made according to our analysis needs.

In this regard, there is the **rename()** method which allows us to modify the names of the labels in a flexible way.

For example, a single column label can be punctually corrected. Let's correct **PublicationDate** by creating a space between the two words. You can, therefore, act at the column level by adding the optional columns parameter and specifying a **dict** which indicates the label to be replaced as key and the new value as value, as shown as follows:

```
In   [   ]:   df.rename(columns   =   {'PublicationDate':'Publication'},
inplace=True)

        df
```

We will obtain the DataFrame as shown in *Figure 8.27*:

ID	Title	Author	Publication
001276A	The Rise of the Falcon	John Admiral	25-Apr-2018
023125B	Controlled mind	Robert Greens	28-Aug-2016
005556E	Only love remains	Greta Blooming	17-Feb-2015

Figure 8.27: DataFrame where one of the column labels has been renamed

As you can see, the fix worked perfectly. We added the optional **inplace** parameter set to True, to make the change permanent.

But the **rename()** method can also be used recursively. By inserting some string functions, it is possible to modify all the labels at the same time (both of index and columns). You use the optional parameters index and columns and specify the string function to change the corresponding label, by inserting the following code:

```
In [ ]: df.rename(index=str.lower, columns=str.upper, inplace=True)

        df
```

You will get the DataFrame with all the labels changed for both index and columns, as shown in *Figure 8.28*:

ID	TITLE	AUTHOR	PUBLICATION
001276a	The Rise of the Falcon	John Admiral	25-Apr-2018
023125b	Controlled mind	Robert Greens	28-Aug-2016
005556e	Only love remains	Greta Blooming	17-Feb-2015

Figure 8.28: DataFrame with modified labels

In addition to the **rename()** method, other methods can be used, such as **map()** which allows us to apply a function defined by us to all labels.

For example, we could extract the first five characters from the index labels excluding all the others, as shown as follows:

```
In [ ]: limiter = lambda x: x[:5]

        df.index = df.index.map(limiter)

        df
```

We will obtain the DataFrame as shown in *Figure 8.29*:

ID	TITLE	AUTHOR	PUBLICATION
00127	The Rise of the Falcon	John Admiral	25-Apr-2018
02312	Controlled mind	Robert Greens	28-Aug-2016
00555	Only love remains	Greta Blooming	17-Feb-2015

Figure 8.29: DataFrame with modified labels

Sparse DataFrames

It is not uncommon, especially in the scientific field, that many imported datasets converted into DataFrame prove to be almost totally empty. That is, most of the values present within the DataFrame do not have values and are enhanced with missing values. In this case, they are called Sparse DataFrames. These types of datasets are much more common than one might imagine, and generally have very large dimensions. The factor to be considered immediately is that given their size, the Sparse DataFrame occupy large amounts of memory, and that they do so unnecessarily, since for the most part, they are empty. Also, in these cases, Pandas comes to our aid with some useful tools.

As an example, let's create a Sparse DataFrame. First, we define an array filled with random values. And then we empty it by filling it for the most part with missing values. For example, we can replace all values less than 1 with missing values, as shown as follows:

```
In [ ]: arr = np.random.randn(10000)
        arr[arr < 1] = np.nan
        df = pd.DataFrame(arr.reshape(100,100))
        df
```

You will get a Sparse DataFrame as shown in *Figure 8.30*:

	0	1	2	3	4	5	6	7	8	9	...	90	91	92	93	94	95
0	NaN	NaN	NaN	NaN	1.559401	NaN	1.468812	NaN	NaN	NaN	...	1.353886	1.470546	NaN	2.027072	NaN	1.908858
1	NaN	1.276342	NaN	NaN	NaN	NaN	NaN	NaN	NaN	NaN	...	NaN	2.371007	NaN	NaN	1.125632	NaN
2	NaN	NaN	1.619231	NaN	2.106197	2.010218	NaN	NaN	1.591981	NaN	...	NaN	NaN	NaN	NaN	NaN	NaN
3	NaN	NaN	NaN	NaN	NaN	NaN	NaN	NaN	NaN	NaN	...	NaN	2.182267	NaN	NaN	1.485204	NaN
4	NaN	NaN	NaN	NaN	NaN	NaN	NaN	NaN	1.107637	NaN	...	NaN	NaN	NaN	NaN	NaN	NaN
...																	
95	NaN	NaN	1.253838	NaN	NaN	NaN	NaN	NaN	NaN	NaN	...	NaN	NaN	NaN	NaN	NaN	2.215013
96	NaN	NaN	NaN	NaN	NaN	NaN	NaN	2.753961	NaN	NaN	...	NaN	NaN	1.488350	1.182738	NaN	NaN
97	NaN	NaN	1.354572	NaN	NaN	NaN	1.431137	1.436382	NaN	NaN	...	NaN	NaN	NaN	NaN	NaN	NaN
98	NaN	NaN	NaN	NaN	NaN	NaN	NaN	NaN	NaN	NaN	...	NaN	1.624369	NaN	NaN	NaN	NaN
99	NaN	NaN	NaN	NaN	NaN	NaN	NaN	1.538846	NaN	2.329964	...	NaN	NaN	2.296871	1.798333	NaN	NaN

100 rows × 100 columns

Figure 8.30: Sparse DataFrame

We got a DataFrame in which most of the values are missing. To find out how much memory this DataFrame occupies, you can use the following code:

```
In [ ]: '{:0.2f} bytes'.format(df.memory_usage().sum() / 1e3)
Out[ ]: '80.13 bytes'
```

We therefore, have 80.13 bytes occupied in memory. As for the Pandas library, there is a more efficient way to manage this kind of DataFrame, and in this regard, there is a type of data, **SparseDtype**, created specifically to manage Sparse DataFrames. We then convert our DataFrame into a Sparse, as shown as follows:

```
In [ ]: sdf = df.astype(pd.SparseDtype("float", np.nan))
```

Once the conversion is done, we can get an idea of how much this DataFrame is "Sparse". To do this, we can use the **sparse.density** attribute which gives us a percentage value of the data density within the DataFrame, as shown as follows:

```
In [ ]: sdf.sparse.density
```

```
Out[ ]: 0.1549
```

There is, therefore, about 15% of data valued within the DataFrame. However, this remains a high value; there can be much emptier Sparse DataFrame. If you take a look at the newly generated **sdf** DataFrame, apparently you don't notice any differences from the original **df**. We see the differences in the amount of memory that **sdf** DataFrame occupies, as shown as follows:

```
In [ ]: '{:0.2f} bytes'.format(sdf.memory_usage().sum() / 1e3)
```

```
Out[ ]: '18.72 bytes'
```

As we can see from the obtained value, the occupied memory space is considerably less. There is, therefore, a much more efficient management of the memory with regards to the Sparse DataFrame. This is a very important factor when dealing with DataFrame with tens of thousands of rows and columns.

Tidy Data

The DataFrame taken as an example in the previous chapters were already simple and tidy and did not require a whole series of preliminary operations before starting work on them. Real world datasets, that is, those that are obtained from acquisitions on external data sources, are often not so *tidy* and much less ordered. This means spending a significant amount of time on a whole series of operations that allow us to prepare our data for analysis.

TIDY DATA is a concept coined by Hadley Wickham in her paper in the Journal of Statistical Software. In this work, he defines a set of rules that describe how the data in a table should be to make analyzing the data easier.

In particular, he introduced the following three basic principles:

- Each row is an observation
- Each column is a variable
- Each type of observation unit is a table.

Any table that does not meet these three principles can be considered *messy*.

To understand intuitively what a variable really is, you will first have to understand the difference between a variable name and the value of a variable. The names of the variables will be the labels of the columns, while the values will be those measures or characteristics detected for each observation (row of the table), which will populate the values of a column.

Let's define the following DataFrame:

```
In [ ]: df = pd.DataFrame( [[34,22,14],
                            [22,43,22],
                            [14,32,15],
                            [15,22,15]],
               columns=['Pens','Notebooks','USBSticks'],
               index=['Sales','HelpDesk',
                    'HumanResource','Store'])
       df
```

We will obtain, as a result, the DataFrame as shown in *Figure 8.31*:

	Pens	Notebooks	USBSticks
Sales	34	22	14
HelpDesk	22	43	22
HumanResource	14	32	15
Store	15	22	15

Figure 8.31: Will this DataFrame be messy or tidy?

This DataFrame appears simple and intuitive, but in the definition *messy-tidy*, it is not so, because both the labels of the columns and of the rows are values of variables and not names of variables. In fact, we have **Departments** and **Gadgets**.

Therefore, some operations on our DataFrame will be necessary to make sure that the column names will be transposed to become the values of a single column, and the same thing for the row indexes.

Methods for inversion of Stacked Data

There are a number of functions widely used to perform this kind of transformation in order to obtain a TIDY table at the end, which are as follows:

- stack()

- `melt()`

They are useful for converting column names (horizontally) to values of a vertical column. That is, they convert variables into values.

There are also complementary methods that perform the reverse operation, i.e., convert the values of a column into a series of columns, which are as follows:

- `unstack()`
- `pivot()`

That is, they convert values into variables.

Example with the stack() method

Back to our example DataFrame, we can then apply the **stack()** method, as shown as follows:

```
In [ ]: df.stack()
Out[ ]:
Sales           Pens        34
                Notebooks   22
                USBSticks   14
HelpDesk        Pens        22
                Notebooks   43
                USBSticks   22
HumanResource   Pens        14
                Notebooks   32
                USBSticks   15
Store           Pens        15
                Notebooks   22
                USBSticks   15
dtype: int64
```

As we can see, we got a MultiIndex Series. We therefore, have the values of the variables all vertically distributed – only they are still indices. We must, therefore, convert them to values of a column, and to do this, we can use the **reset_index()** method, as shown as follows:

```
In [ ]: df2 = df.stack().reset_index()
        df2
```

And you get the stacked DataFrame as shown in *Figure 8.32*:

	level_0	level_1	0
0	Sales	Pens	34
1	Sales	Notebooks	22
2	Sales	USBSticks	14
3	HelpDesk	Pens	22
4	HelpDesk	Notebooks	43
5	HelpDesk	USBSticks	22
6	HumanResource	Pens	14
7	HumanResource	Notebooks	32
8	HumanResource	USBSticks	15
9	Store	Pens	15
10	Store	Notebooks	22
11	Store	USBSticks	15

Figure 8.32: The stacked DataFrame

Now, we just have to give the right labels to the columns that are nothing more than the names of the variables, as shown as follows:

```
In [ ]: df2.columns = ['Department','Gadgets','Amount']
        df2
```

We modify the DataFrame as shown in *Figure 8.33*:

	Department	Gadgets	Amount
0	Sales	Pens	34
1	Sales	Notebooks	22
2	Sales	USBSticks	14
3	HelpDesk	Pens	22
4	HelpDesk	Notebooks	43
5	HelpDesk	USBSticks	22
6	HumanResource	Pens	14
7	HumanResource	Notebooks	32
8	HumanResource	USBSticks	15
9	Store	Pens	15
10	Store	Notebooks	22
11	Store	USBSticks	15

Figure 8.33: Il DataFrame è diventato TIDY

As we can see, with a few operations, we have obtained a TIDY DataFrame.

Example with the melt() method

We can also obtain the same result with the `melt()` method, as shown as follows:

```
In [ ]: df2 = df.reset_index()

        df2 = df2.rename(columns={'index': 'Department'})

        df2.melt(id_vars=['Department'],

              value_vars=['Pens','Notebooks','USBSticks'],

              var_name='Gadgets',

              value_name='Amount')
```

As a result, we will get the DataFrame as shown in *Figure 8.34*:

	Department	Gadgets	Amount
0	Sales	Pens	34
1	HelpDesk	Pens	22
2	HumanResource	Pens	14
3	Store	Pens	15
4	Sales	Notebooks	22
5	HelpDesk	Notebooks	43
6	HumanResource	Notebooks	32
7	Store	Notebooks	22
8	Sales	USBSticks	14
9	HelpDesk	USBSticks	22
10	HumanResource	USBSticks	15
11	Store	USBSticks	15

Figure 8.34: The melted DataFrame

We obtained the same result as in the previous example, also in this case, obtaining a TIDY DataFrame.

Columns that contain values, not variables

Often it happens to find tables in which the column labels have ranges of possible values of a given variable.. This way of distributing data is known as **wide** data.

For this example, we will import a dataset contained in the **CountrySalaries.csv** file, as shown as follows:

```
In [ ]: df = pd.read_csv('CountrySalaries.csv')

        df
```

The values of the dataset will, thus, be converted into a DataFrame, as shown in *Figure 8.35*:

	Country	<$10K	$10-30K	$30-50K	$50-70K	>70K
0	France	3456	4768	9897	8756	512
1	UK	2865	5694	8754	9342	345
2	Italy	3560	5670	7990	7831	452
3	Spain	3421	4670	6832	8882	346

Figure 8.35: The DataFrame obtained from CountrySalaries.csv

To convert it into "long" and "tidy" data format, we will have to do a series of operations (unpivot, melt, gather), Pandas has a **melt()** function that allows reshaping a DataFrame in a tidy format. It accepts the following parameters:

- **id_vars** is a container (**list, tuple, ndarray**) in which the variables that remain such are inserted.

- **value_vars** identifies the columns you want to unpivot. By default, they are those not considered in in **id_vars**.

- **var_name** is a string for the new column where **value_vars** are *melted down*. By default, it is called **variable**.

- **value_name** is a string for the name of the new column representing the **varname** values. By default, it is **value**.

We perform the melting of the DataFrame with the **melt()** method, as shown as follows:

```
In [ ]: df.melt(id_vars=['Country'],

              var_name='SalaryRange',
```

```
value_name='Employees' )
```

The DataFrame is obtained as shown in *Figure 8.36*:

	Country	SalaryRange	Employees
0	France	<$10K	3456
1	UK	<$10K	2865
2	Italy	<$10K	3560
3	Spain	<$10K	3421
4	France	$10-30K	4768
5	UK	$10-30K	5694
6	Italy	$10-30K	5670
7	Spain	$10-30K	4670
8	France	$30-50K	9897
9	UK	$30-50K	8754
10	Italy	$30-50K	7990
11	Spain	$30-50K	6832
12	France	$50-70K	8756
13	UK	$50-70K	9342
14	Italy	$50-70K	7831
15	Spain	$50-70K	8882
16	France	>70K	512
17	UK	>70K	345
18	Italy	>70K	452
19	Spain	>70K	346

Figure 8.36: *The melted DataFrame*

Also, in this case, we have obtained a Tidy DataFrame by applying a simple operation.

Several variables in the same column

Tidy DataFrame should have a single column for each single variable as the rules specify. In this case, we can load as an example, the data contained in the **Measures. csv** file, as shown as follows:

```
In [ ]: df = pd.read_csv('Measures.csv')

        df
```

You will get the DataFrame as shown in *Figure 8.37*:

	Sensor	Measure	Value
0	234	Temp	25°C
1	234	X	34.56
2	234	Y	12.47
3	321	Temp	27°C
4	321	X	52.11
5	321	Y	38.16
6	456	Temp	12°C
7	456	X	24.16
8	456	Y	28.12

Figure 8.37: The melted DataFrame

Also in this case, we have some characteristics that deviate this DataFrame from the concept of Tidy. First, it would be better if the DataFrame was ordered differently. For example, we have multiple values of different nature specified under the same sensor number. Furthermore, the Measure column clearly contains variables since it recursively repeats the same values specifying the same three types of measure. So, in reality, the first thing to do is to sort out the values based on the true indices, and then perform some value-to-index conversions. This can be done with the **set_index()** method.

We convert the values of the Sensor and Measure columns into indices, as shown as follows:

```
In [ ]: df1 = df.set_index(['Sensor','Measure'])

        df1
```

The DataFrame will be transformed in its structure, as shown in *Figure 8.38*:

		Value
Sensor	Measure	
234	Temp	25°C
	X	34.56
	Y	12.47
321	Temp	27°C
	X	52.11
	Y	38.16
456	Temp	12°C
	X	24.16
	Y	28.12

Figure 8.38: First transformation of the DataFrame

Now, let's carry out the unstacking operation, creating a row for each type of sensor, and new columns for each type of measurement. To do this, use the **unstack()** method and apply it to the **Measure** column, as shown as follows:

```
In [ ]: df2 = df1.unstack('Measure')
        df2
```

We will get the DataFrame, as shown in *Figure 8.39*, as a result:

	Value		
Measure	Temp	X	Y
Sensor			
234	25°C	34.56	12.47
321	27°C	52.11	38.16
456	12°C	24.16	28.12

Figure 8.39: Second transformation of the DataFrame

Now, we need to apply a further transformation to our DataFrame. We could consider the labels of the Sensor index to be variable values. We can then convert the labels back to column values through the **reset_index()** method, as shown as follows:

```
In [ ]: df2.reset_index(col_level = -1)
```

The result is the DataFrame as shown in *Figure 8.40*:

Measure	Sensor	Value Temp	X	Y
0	234	25°C	34.56	12.47
1	321	27°C	52.11	38.16
2	456	12°C	24.16	28.12

Figure 8.40: The Tidy DataFrame

As we can see, we have finally transformed the initial DataFrame from Messy.

Columns that contain multiple variables

Sometimes a column in a dataset can contain the values of multiple variables. This feature also moves our DataFrame away from the Tidy concept. In this case, you need to perform a value separation operation using string methods such as **split()**.

For this example, we will import the data from the **PokerHands.csv** file, as shown as follows:

```
In [ ]: df = pd.read_csv('PokerHands.csv')

        Df
```

In this file, there are some cards present in the different poker hands. There are five columns each corresponding to a card. As values, we have the value of the card (K stands for King, Q for Queen, J for Jack, A for Ace) and then a single character indicating the sign H stands for Hearts, D for Diamonds, S for Spare, and C stands for Clubs. The data is represented in the imported DataFrame as shown in *Figure 8.41*:

	Hand	1st	2nd	3rd	4th	5th
0	1	4 C	10 H	Q H	K S	7 S
1	2	7 C	A H	Q H	K S	7 S
2	3	J D	Q D	A D	6 S	9 H
3	4	J D	Q D	A D	10 D	K D
4	5	5 H	8 D	10 C	J C	K H

Figure 8.41: The DataFrame obtained from the PokerHands.csv file

So in this case too, we find ourselves in a Messy DataFrame to be processed to make it Tidy. In this case, it will only be necessary to separate the card values from the signs. These are simply string manipulations that we discussed extensively in the previous chapter (see *Chapter 7 - Day 5 - Working with data sources and real-word datasets*).

We separate the sign from the value from the Column corresponding to the first card, as shown as follows:

```
In [ ]: df[['1st_V','1st_S']] = df['1st'].str.split(' ', expand=True)

        df
```

And we will get the changes as shown in *Figure 8.42*:

	Hand	1st	2nd	3rd	4th	5th	1st_V	1st_S
0	1	4 C	10 H	Q H	K S	7 S	4	C
1	2	7 C	A H	Q H	K S	7 S	7	C
2	3	J D	Q D	A D	6 S	9 H	J	D
3	4	J D	Q D	A D	10 D	K D	J	D
4	5	5 H	8 D	10 C	J C	K H	5	H

Figure 8.42: First changes applied to the DataFrame obtained from the PokerHands.csv file

We make the same changes for all the other columns (the other four cards), as shown as follows:

```
In [ ]: df[['2nd_V','2nd_S']] = df['2nd'].str.split(' ', expand=True)

        df[['3rd_V','3rd_S']] = df['3rd'].str.split(' ', expand=True)

        df[['4th_V','4th_S']] = df['4th'].str.split(' ', expand=True)

        df[['5th_V','5th_S']] = df['5th'].str.split(' ', expand=True)

        del df['1st']

        del df['2nd']

        del df['3rd']

        del df['4th']

        del df['5th']
```

```
df.index = df['Hand']

del df['Hand']

df
```

And we will get a Tidy DataFrame, as shown in *Figure 8.43*:

Hand	1st_V	1st_S	2nd_V	2nd_S	3rd_V	3rd_S	4th_V	4th_S	5th_V	5th_S
1	4	C	10	H	Q	H	K	S	7	S
2	7	C	A	H	Q	H	K	S	7	S
3	J	D	Q	D	A	D	6	S	9	H
4	J	D	Q	D	A	D	10	D	K	D
5	5	H	8	D	10	C	J	C	K	H

Figure 8.43: The Tidy DataFrame starting from the PokerHands.csv file

Variables in both rows and columns

Another case that you can run into when importing external data is a particular way in which data is reported on external data sources. The data is collected in ranges of values divided into columns.

To better understand this mode, let's load, for example, the data contained in the **CountrySalaries2.csv** file, as shown as follows:

```
In [ ]: df = pd.read_csv('CountrySalaries2.csv')

        df
```

The values of this will be imported into the DataFrame, as shown in *Figure 8.44*:

	Country	Sex	<$10K	$10-30K	$30-50K	$50-70K	>70K
0	France	F	3456	4768	9897	8756	512
1	France	M	2416	4528	9965	6556	124
2	UK	F	2865	5694	8754	9342	345
3	UK	M	3465	5494	7865	7842	545
4	Italy	F	3560	5670	7990	7831	452
5	Italy	M	1460	3470	4590	2331	245
6	Spain	F	3421	4670	6832	8882	346
7	Spain	M	6521	3370	5515	3466	351

Figure 8.44: The DataFrame obtained from the CountrySalaries2.csv file

Also, in this case, we find ourselves with a *messy* DataFrame. To overcome this problem, you can begin to change the structure of the DataFrame by applying a melting with the `melt()` method, as shown as follows:

```
In [ ]: df.melt( id_vars=['Country','Sex'],

            var_name='SalaryRange',

            value_name='Employees' )
```

With this operation, we will transform the DataFrame structure, as shown in *Figure 8.45*:

	Country	Sex	SalaryRange	Employees
0	France	F	<$10K	3456
1	France	M	<$10K	2416
2	UK	F	<$10K	2865
3	UK	M	<$10K	3465
4	Italy	F	<$10K	3560
5	Italy	M	<$10K	1460
6	Spain	F	<$10K	3421
7	Spain	M	<$10K	6521
8	France	F	$10-30K	4768
9	France	M	$10-30K	4528
10	UK	F	$10-30K	5694
11	UK	M	$10-30K	5494
12	Italy	F	$10-30K	5670
13	Italy	M	$10-30K	3470
14	Spain	F	$10-30K	4670
15	Spain	M	$10-30K	3370

Figure 8.45: First transformation of the DataFrame obtained from the CountrySalaries2.csv file

As we can see from the result, the ranges of values that were previously column labels have been transformed into values and inserted all within the same **SalaryRange** column. The other related values are sorted accordingly. Now a further operation is carried out which will modify the structure bringing it back from 'long' to 'wide'. To do this, use the **pivot_table()** function by grouping all the values by **Country** and dividing the values again on different columns, as shown as follows:

```
In [ ]: df2 = df.pivot_table(index=['Country'],columns='Sex')

        df2
```

With this operation, the DataFrame is transformed into the structure, as shown in *Figure 8.46*:

	$10-30K		$30-50K		$50-70K		<$10K		>70K	
Sex	F	M	F	M	F	M	F	M	F	M
Country										
France	4768	4528	9897	9965	8756	6556	3456	2416	512	124
Italy	5670	3470	7990	4590	7831	2331	3560	1460	452	245
Spain	4670	3370	6832	5515	8882	3466	3421	6521	346	351
UK	5694	5494	8754	7865	9342	7842	2865	3465	345	545

Figure 8.46: Second transformation of the DataFrame obtained from the CountrySalaries2.csv file

After this transformation, we returned with a structure similar to the one we started with, but in reality, we now have a Tidy DataFrame. In fact, now there is a row for each country and the DataFrame contains only numerical values, all comparable to each other. While the subdivisions of sex within each range have been converted into the second level index on the columns.

Groups of Variables in the columns

Another common case in newly imported datasets is that they can have groups of variables in their column names. Again, let's take the data contained in the `Aftershaves.csv` file as an example, as shown as follows:

```
In [ ]: df = pd.read_csv('Aftershaves.csv')
        df
```

These values are imported into the DataFrame, as shown in *Figure 8.47*:

	Product	Component_1	Component_2	Component_3	Vol_1	Vol_2	Vol_3
0	BlackSpirit	Menthol	Essence3	Essence4	250	135	25
1	MountainBreath	Pinene	Limonene	Essence3	240	255	15
2	LoveFlame	Geraniol	Eugenol	Essence4	145	275	50

Figure 8.47: The DataFrame obtained from the Aftershaves.csv file

For this example, the `wide_to_long()` function may be useful to stack the table, as shown as follows:

```
In [ ]: df2 = pd.wide_to_long(df, stubnames=['Component','Vol'],
```

```
            i=['Product'],

            j='Component_num',

            sep = '_' )

    df2
```

This will obtain the DataFrame as shown in *Figure 8.48*:

		Component	Vol
Product	**Component_num**		
BlackSpirit	1	Menthol	250
MountainBreath	1	Pinene	240
LoveFlame	1	Geraniol	145
BlackSpirit	2	Essence3	135
MountainBreath	2	Limonene	255
LoveFlame	2	Eugenol	275
BlackSpirit	3	Essence4	25
MountainBreath	3	Essence3	15
LoveFlame	3	Essence4	50

Figure 8.48: *The DataFrame transformed from wide to long*

The **wide_to_long()** function works quite specifically. Its main parameter is **stubnames**, which is a list of strings. Each string represents a single grouping column.

Names of columns with multiple variables

A "messy" feature of DataFrames is when column names contain several variables. Again, we can import the data into the **Incomes.csv** file, as shown as follows:

```
In [ ]: df = pd.read_csv('Incomes.csv')

        df
```

The values of these will be collected in a DataFrame like the one shown in *Figure 8.49*:

	City	2020_ZONE1	2020_ZONE2	2020_ZONE3	2021_ZONE1	2021_ZONE2	2021_ZONE3
0	Milan	34000	15000	25000	17000	23000	8000
1	Paris	18000	21000	24000	19000	31000	11000
2	London	21000	22000	17000	23000	25000	13000
3	Tokyo	25000	18000	21000	20000	18000	15000

Figure 8.49: The DataFrame transformed from wide to long

As we can see, the names of the columns contain various information, such as the year and the area. This situation can be improved by carrying out a series of operations. First, we can do a melting, as shown as follows:

```
In [ ]: df2 = df.melt(id_vars=['City'],

                var_name='time_area',

                value_name='Income')

        df2
```

We will obtain a 'long' DataFrame like the one shown in *Figure 8.50*:

	City	time_area	Income
0	Milan	2020_ZONE1	34000
1	Paris	2020_ZONE1	18000
2	London	2020_ZONE1	21000
3	Tokyo	2020_ZONE1	25000
4	Milan	2020_ZONE2	15000
5	Paris	2020_ZONE2	21000
6	London	2020_ZONE2	22000
7	Tokyo	2020_ZONE2	18000
8	Milan	2020_ZONE3	25000
9	Paris	2020_ZONE3	24000
10	London	2020_ZONE3	17000
11	Tokyo	2020_ZONE3	21000
12	Milan	2021_ZONE1	17000
13	Paris	2021_ZONE1	19000
14	London	2021_ZONE1	23000
15	Tokyo	2021_ZONE1	20000

Figure 8.50: First transformation of the test DataFrame

As we can see from the result, we have converted the column labels to `time_area` column values. So, now we can make some changes to these values by dealing with the classic string manipulation operations, as shown as follows:

```
In [ ]: df2['year']= df2['time_area'].str[0:4]

        df2['zone']=df2['time_area'].str[-1]

        df2
```

We will obtain as a result the DataFrame as shown in *Figure 8.51*:

	City	time_area	Income	year	zone
0	Milan	2020_ZONE1	34000	2020	1
1	Paris	2020_ZONE1	18000	2020	1
2	London	2020_ZONE1	21000	2020	1
3	Tokyo	2020_ZONE1	25000	2020	1
4	Milan	2020_ZONE2	15000	2020	2
5	Paris	2020_ZONE2	21000	2020	2
6	London	2020_ZONE2	22000	2020	2
7	Tokyo	2020_ZONE2	18000	2020	2
8	Milan	2020_ZONE3	25000	2020	3
9	Paris	2020_ZONE3	24000	2020	3
10	London	2020_ZONE3	17000	2020	3
11	Tokyo	2020_ZONE3	21000	2020	3
12	Milan	2021_ZONE1	17000	2021	1
13	Paris	2021_ZONE1	19000	2021	1
14	London	2021_ZONE1	23000	2021	1
15	Tokyo	2021_ZONE1	20000	2021	1
16	Milan	2021_ZONE2	23000	2021	2
17	Paris	2021_ZONE2	31000	2021	2
18	London	2021_ZONE2	25000	2021	2

Figure 8.51: Second transformation of the test DataFrame

As we can see from the result, we have extracted the values of interest (year and zone) from the names of the initial column labels and collected them in two separate columns (year and zone). At this point, we can delete the **time_area** column which is now useless, as shown as follows:

```
In [ ]: df2.drop(['time_area'], axis = 1)
```

The result is the DataFrame shown in *Figure 8.52*:

	City	Income	year	zone
0	Milan	34000	2020	1
1	Paris	18000	2020	1
2	London	21000	2020	1
3	Tokyo	25000	2020	1
4	Milan	15000	2020	2
5	Paris	21000	2020	2
6	London	22000	2020	2
7	Tokyo	18000	2020	2
8	Milan	25000	2020	3
9	Paris	24000	2020	3
10	London	17000	2020	3
11	Tokyo	21000	2020	3
12	Milan	17000	2021	1
13	Paris	19000	2021	1
14	London	23000	2021	1
15	Tokyo	20000	2021	1
16	Milan	23000	2021	2
17	Paris	31000	2021	2

Figure 8.52: Third transformation of the test DataFrame

Conclusion

In this chapter, we became aware of the various problems encountered when dealing with newly imported datasets from external sources. We know how to recognize missing values, their role, and are familiar with the various approaches with which to manage this kind of values – a choice that will depend on the purpose of our analysis. Moreover, thanks to the examples carried out, we have seen the most common operations on a newly imported DataFrame in order to make it as clean and understandable as possible, following the concepts of Tidy or Messy DataFrame. Now, the data processing part is finished, and the whole overview of Pandas methods and functions is at our disposal.

In the next chapter, we will deal with the data visualization part, creating graphs and histograms to be included in reports, thanks to the use of additional graphic libraries such as matplotlib.

Questions

1. What are the utilities in defining a missing value within a dataset and why do you prefer to identify it with a single NaN value?

2. Can information be obtained from the NaNs contained within a DataFrame?

3. What can be the causes of the presence of datasets with the most disparate structures and why instead there is not a well-defined standard for all the datasets?

4. What are the utilities in converting DataFrame into Tidy form?

Multiple choice questions

1. Which of these values cannot be considered, by default, a missing value on Pandas?

   A. np.nan

   B. NULL

   C. NaN

2. Which function is useful for managing the dtype when importing a list of values in which there are missing values inside?

   A. convert()

   B. astype()

   C. pd.array()

3. Which of the following statements is true for the drop_duplicates() method?

   A. By default, it removes all rows that have the same values

   B. By default, it removes all duplicate rows leaving the last occurrence

   C. By default, it removes all duplicate lines following the first occurrence

4. In the tidying of a DataFrame, which method can be useful to convert the column names into values of a column?

    A. unstack()

    B. melt()

    C. pivot()

5. In the tidying of a DataFrame, which method can be useful to convert the values of a column into a series of columns?

    A. unstack()

    B. stack()

    C. melt()

Solution

1: B; 2: C; 3: C; 4: B; 5: A

Key Terms

Sparse data, Missing values, Tidy data, Duplicated Data.

References/Further Readings

- *https://pandas.pydata.org/pandas-docs/stable/user_guide/*
- *Tidy Data, Journal of Statistical Software Vol.59 (2014), Hadley Wickham*

## CHAPTER 9

Day 7 – Data Visualization and Reporting

Here we are, finally on the last day of our week of complete immersion in the world of the Pandas bookshop. In the previous chapters, we gradually covered all the topics relevant to Pandas data structures and the many possible operations that can be performed on them, furthering our data analysis purposes. In this chapter, we will see the final part of the topic, that is, how to view our results in graphic format in order to be able to quickly summarize the information contained within the data. In this regard, there are graphic libraries in Python that greatly facilitate this task. Indeed, they are so integrated with the Pandas library that they perform many operations automatically, thus, becoming excellent tools for our work. We will then conclude the chapter with some examples of reporting, in which we will be able to publish our works in a summarized way and deliver them to third parties.

Structure

In this chapter, we will cover the following topics:

- Matplotlib
- Seaborn
- Pandas Profiling
- HTML and PDF reporting

Objective

After studying this chapter, we will complete all the skills necessary to perform data analysis with the Pandas library and the various technologies related to it. We will be introduced to the Matplotlib and Seaborn graphic libraries in order to create typical data analysis graphs (liner plots, scatters, histograms, bar diagrams, and pie diagrams). Finally, with some examples, we will become familiar with the reporting of the results of the data analysis through the three basic operations – summarize, view, and publish.

Matplotlib

The graphics library most used today with Python and Pandas in general is Matplotlib. In particular, this library was designed for visualizing data using graphs. Python is, in fact, a library that has gained a lot of ground in the scientific communities, and therefore, certainly could not lack a valid tool for the creation of the most commonly used charts such as linear plots, scatter plots, bar diagrams, pie diagrams, and box plots, as shown in *Figure 9.1*:

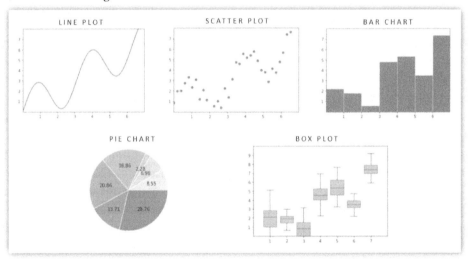

Figure 9.1: *Some examples of the most common plots and charts used in data analysis*

The matplotlib library has also become one of Pandas' basic libraries, and as we will see later, it is so integrated into it that it will be possible to use it by calling the display functions directly from a DataFrame. Also, with regard to Jupyter Notebook, the same is true. The display of the graphs is perfectly integrated into the cell structure of the Notebook, allowing the execution of the code inside a cell In []: and the direct representation of the graph obtained as a result in Out []:, all interactively.

The success and choice of matplotlib as Pandas' basic library is its peculiarity – you can view the data within a DataFrame in a few lines of code. You import the library, choose the type of chart to use, and pass the data as an argument. And that's it – our graph is represented. Let's see these simple steps together, to realize how easy it is to work this way.

During this section of the chapter, we will start from simple data in the form of lists generated with NumPy to display them with the different types of most common charts. When we become familiar with the matplotlib library, we will see how to use a DataFrame and its data inside to create the various charts.

Making a Line Plot with Matplotlib

The type of graph that we most commonly have in mind is that of a line plot, in which the data is displayed on Cartesian coordinates in the form of a line. Often when using this type of chart, you are dealing with data describing a function, as shown as follows:

```
y = function(x)
```

In this, the data described with coordinates **(x, y)** follow a specific relationship in the graph.

First, if we want to work with charts, we need to import the library, as shown as follows:

```
In [ ]: import matplotlib.pyplot as plt
```

We therefore, define two lists of **x** and **y** values that follow a certain linear trend, as shown as follows:

```
In [ ]: x = np.linspace(0, 10, 50)

        y = 2 * np.sin(2 * x) + x
```

We have defined 50 points **(x, y),** which will define a certain linear trend along the Cartesian coordinates. Now, all you have to do is represent them graphically with matplotlib. The thing is simple, as it only takes three lines of code, as shown as follows:

```
In [ ]: fig, ax = plt.subplots()

        ax.plot(x, y)

        plt.show()
```

As a result, we will the line plot as represented in *Figure 9.2*:

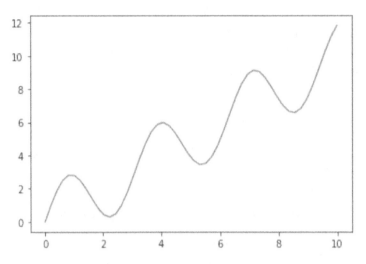

Figure 9.2: *Line Plot of a data series (x, y)*

As we can see, we have a graph with Cartesian coordinates, in which a blue line is represented that follows the trend of a sinusoidal function whose values increase linearly. The first line is the declaration of the **subplots()** function which generates the layout where the graph will be drawn and eventually define the subdivision of the layout into different panels to represent multiple charts at the same time (subplots). This function returns two objects **Figure** and **Axes**, which are respectively the layout and the array of subplots on which to draw the graphic elements (in our case, a single plot). The second line is the call to the plot() function in which the lists of the x and y coordinates of the data to be represented are passed, in order to draw a line that connects these points. These will be represented on the calling plot (**ax** is single in this case). And finally, we have the last line, which contains the **show()** function which displays the graph on the screen on **Out []** if we are working on Jupyter Notebook.

But what about everything else? In this code, we have not defined the color and thickness of the line anywhere, nor have we written how to represent the numbers and the cleats along the two Cartesian axes, and more. Good. This is the beauty and comfort of matplotlib; it allows us to have a graph with only three lines of code. All other information follows default values that nothing prevents us from modifying by adding additional code. In this way, we will have more and more control of the chart represented, gradually adding lines of code in which we will define how to represent the various graphic elements.

For example, in our case, we could add two new arguments to the **plot ()** function, such as the color of the line and its thickness. This can be done by defining values (other than the default ones) of the optional color and linewidth parameters.

Furthermore, by adding the **set()** function, we can define the Cartesian axes of the plot, modifying the range of **x** and **y** to be represented (parameters **xlim** and **ylim**) and the number of cleats to be affixed (parameters **xticks** and **yticks**). We modify the code as follows:

```
In [ ]: fig, ax = plt.subplots()
        ax.plot(x, y, color='red', linewidth=2.0)
        ax.set(xlim=(0, 7), xticks=np.arange(1, 7),
             ylim=(0, 8), yticks=np.arange(1, 8))
        plt.show()
```

By running this code, we will see some changes made to the chart obtained previously, as shown in *Figure 9.3*:

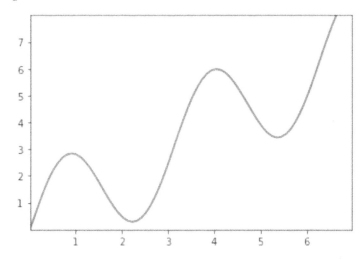

Figure 9.3: *Line Plot of a data series (x, y) with some modifications*

As we can see, the line is now represented in red, and the graph is represented in a smaller area than the previous one (some points remain outside the range and are not represented).

With the same logic, we can continue to modify and enrich our chart. For example, we can add a legend and another line that indicates the linear increase of the sinusoidal function. Thus, we modify the previous code by adding new elements, as shown as follows:

```
In [ ]: fig, ax = plt.subplots()
        y2 = x
        ax.plot(x, y, color='red', linewidth=2.0)
        ax.plot(x, y2, '--', color='blue', linewidth=2.0 )
```

```
ax.set(xlim=(0, 7), xticks=np.arange(1, 7),
        ylim=(0, 8), yticks=np.arange(1, 8))
ax.legend(['y=f(x)','y=x'])
plt.show()
```

We have added a new list **y2** which represents the linear increase of the sinusoidal function. To display it in the chart, we will use another **plot()** function in which we will specify a different color and the sequence of characters '-' which specify how the line should be dashed. We also add a legend with the **legend()** function, passing as an argument, a list containing the labels relating to each function (they follow the order in which the **plot()** functions are called).

By executing the code, we will obtain further modifications to our line plot as shown in *Figure 9.4*:

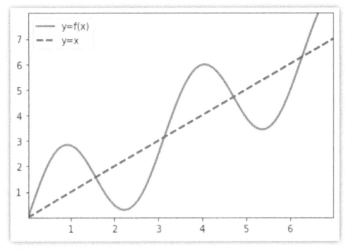

Figure 9.4: *Line Plot of a data series (x, y) with other modifications and legend*

As we can guess, the changes go on for a long time. It is sufficient to know all the ways of representing the individual elements and how they are expressed in the code through the matplotlib functions. A coverage of all possible functions and the optional parameters related to them is a huge task that cannot be covered in a single chapter. For further information on this, I highly recommend going to the official website of the library (**https://matplotlib.org/**) full of examples and detailed explanations on each function and parameter.

Making a Scatter Plot

Another very common type of chart is the Scatter Plot. In this type of graph, we still have a Cartesian axis system, but the data are represented as single points. Scatter plots are useful when you have a lot of points and you do not know whether there is a possible relationship between them. We therefore, prefer to leave them as single points and only consider later whether or not a relationship exists.

We add an error on the y axis to the previous data, in order to simulate the collection of real data by pretending not to know any relationship. We will do this by modifying the values of y with the np.random.normal() function. This function adds a random error to the y-list data that follows a normal distribution around the real value with standard deviation equal to **0.5**, as shown as follows:

```
In [ ]: x = np.linspace(0, 10, 50)
        y = 2 * np.sin(2 * x) + x
        ye = np.random.normal(y,0.5)
```

Again, the implementation is very simple and consists of only three lines of code, as shown as follows:

```
In [ ]: fig, ax = plt.subplots()
        ax.scatter(x, ye)
        plt.show()
```

The only difference with the previous code is that, this time, the **scatter()** function is called instead of **plot()**. This function, in fact, tells matplotlib to represent the points as a scatter plot. For the rest, everything is identical. By executing the code, we will obtain a scatter plot like the one in *Figure 9.5*:

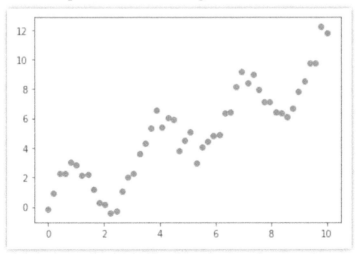

Figure 9.5: Scatter plot

Here too, there are many default values; in fact, the blue color and the representation system of the Cartesian axes have remained identical to the previous one. Also, in this case, it is possible to modify and enrich the graphic elements that make up the chart. For example, let's modify the previous code as follows:

```
In [ ]: fig, ax = plt.subplots()
        sizes = np.random.uniform(15, 500, len(x))
        colors = np.random.uniform(0, 30, len(x))
        ax.scatter(x, ye, s=sizes, c=colors)
        ax.plot(x, y, ':', color='red', linewidth=2.0)
        ax.set(xlim=(2, 8), xticks=np.arange(2, 8),
               ylim=(2, 8), yticks=np.arange(2, 8))
        plt.show()
```

In the default scatter plot, all points have the same color and size. In this case, we modify that rule by varying these characteristics randomly using the **Numpy** `np.random.uniform()` function. However, these characteristics are often used to represent further variables of the points represented. Even if we have represented our data in the form of a scatter plot with the **scatter()** function, it is also possible to superimpose a line plot in the same graph. For example, we might want to draw the base function line used to generate the points. We will then use the **plot()** function passing in the original values of y. Furthermore, as in the previous case, we modify the intervals of the Cartesian axes to represent, focusing only on a restricted part.

If we execute the modified code, we will obtain a scatter plot like the one represented in *Figure 9.6*:

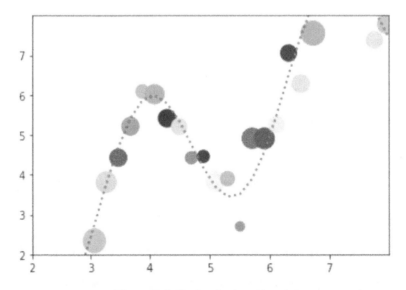

Figure 9.6: *Customized scatter plot*

As we can see, the possibilities are many. The ability to be able to modify the graphs by displaying the best information we are looking for is a skill that can only be gained with experience and a lot of exercise (intuition aside).

Making a Bar Chart

Another widely used type of chart is the Bar Chart. This type of graph is widely used in economics and marketing and is very useful for comparing values between categories of data, or even for following the trend of a discrete variable over time intervals such as months or years.

For this type of example, let's slightly modify the data to display the following:

```
In [ ]: x = 1 + np.arange(7)
        y = 2 * np.sin(2 * x) + x
```

In this case, we have reduced the dimensions of x to 7 elements (from 1 to 7), in order to display 7 bars in the chart, each with their respective value given by the function used in the previous examples.

To represent a bar chart of the newly created data, we will use the bar() function, specific for this type of chart, as shown as follows:

```
In [ ]: fig, ax = plt.subplots()
        ax.bar(x, y)
        plt.show()
```

Also, in this case, the code uses the default values and remains condensed into three simple lines. By executing, it we will obtain the bar chart as shown in *Figure 9.7*:

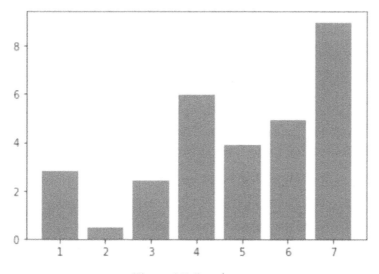

Figure 9.7: Bar chart

Also, in this case, it is possible to make changes and enrichments to the elements that make up the graph. I leave the task to the reader.

Making a Pie Chart

Another widely used chart in economics and marketing is the Pie Chart. This type of chart generally uses the same data as bar charts, but with respect to them, it is useful to understand how much the different categories of data cover the percentage of a whole, which is the sum of their values.

Then, using the same previous data, we can create a pie chart by replacing the **bar** () function with t0he **pie** () function, which, in the default mode, requires only the value of the various categories, represented by the elements of **y**, as shown as follows:

```
In [ ]: fig, ax = plt.subplots()
        ax.pie(y)
        plt.show()
```

By executing the code, the pie chart is obtained, as shown in *Figure 9.8*:

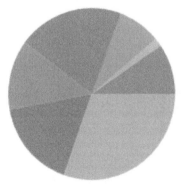

Figure 9.8: *Default Pie chart*

As we can see, the default graphic representation is very simple, perhaps too essential to be able to derive information from it. Changes to the default model are, therefore, necessary to add essential information to understand the nature of the data.

Let's modify the following code by adding many elements:

```
In [ ]: fig, ax = plt.subplots()
        colors = plt.get_cmap('Oranges')(np.linspace(0.2,
                                          0.7, len(x)))
        ax.pie(y,
```

```
        radius=1,
        colors=colors,
        wedgeprops={"linewidth": 1,
                    "edgecolor": "white"},
        autopct="%.2f")
ax.legend(x, bbox_to_anchor=(0, 1),
        loc='best', ncol=1)
plt.show()
```

First of all, the colors used in the default pie chart are very different from each other, and do not favor legibility. They can be replaced with a shade of a specific color, for example, orange (but you can use all colors as a base). To do this, we use the **get_cmap()** function specifying the base color as an argument. With **np.linspace()**, we can create as many shades of a color as there are elements (slices of cake) to represent.

Furthermore, to increase the readability of the various slices of the cake, a white space can be inserted between them. This can be done by adding the optional **wedgeprops** parameter, which in turn, has further configurable parameters such as **linewidth** and **edgecolor** which are the width and color of the dividing line between the slices.

A further enrichment of the pie chart would be to associate the numerical value to each corresponding slice. This can be done by adding the optional **autopct** parameter to the **pie()** function and then specifying the format to display. Finally, you can add a legend to display the seven categories and their corresponding colors with the **legend()** function that we have already seen earlier.

By executing the code, the pie chart is obtained as shown in *Figure 9.9*:

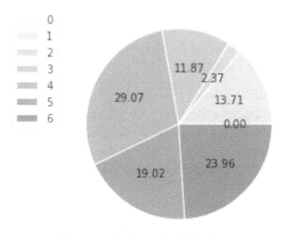

Figure 9.9: Customized Pie chart

As you can see, the results have improved significantly.

Making a Box Plot

Finally, we close our examples of chart types with a Box Plot. This type of chart is very similar to a bar chart but has the ability to further represent the distribution of values for each category. In fact, for each category (or element on the x-axis), not a single x value is represented, but an entire distribution of a population of data. Each category is represented in the graph by a box with a line (median or 50% of the values), and the two quartiles Q1 and Q3 (respectively 25% and 75% of the population) as bottom and top sides. There are also two *whiskers* which represent the range covered by the population values that fall within the *fences*. The upper fence is the highest threshold value which corresponds to Q3 + 1.5 (Q3 - Q1), beyond which, the population values are not considered valid (**outliers**). While the lower fence, which corresponds to the value Q1-1.5 (Q3-Q1), is the lowest threshold value beyond which the values are considered anomalous. *Figure 9.10* can help us better understand this representation:

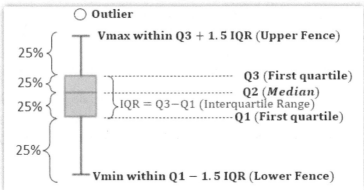

Figure 9.10: Graphical representation of a statistical distribution (box and whiskers)

The calculations of the distribution, the median values, and the two quartiles are performed automatically; the same thing for the whiskers and the outliers. So, there is no need to perform any calculations.

To be able to go on with this example, we will only need to specify the statistical populations that we will derive directly from the values previously used to generate the bar chart. To help us with this, we will use random generators like **np.random.uniform()** and **np.random.normal()** from the Numpy library. Eventually, we will get a D-list with 7 different populations of 100 values, each with its own different distribution, as shown as follows:

```
In [ ]: x = 1 + np.arange(7)

        y = tuple(2 * np.sin(2 * x) + x)
```

```
s = tuple(np.random.uniform(0.5,1.5,7))
D = np.random.normal(y,s,(100, 7))
```

Once the populations have been defined, we finally pass to the generation of the corresponding Box plot, this time using the **boxplot()** function, as shown as follows:

```
In [ ]: fig, ax = plt.subplots()

        ax.boxplot(D)

        plt.show()
```

By executing these three lines of code, we will obtain the box plot, as represented in *Figure 9.11*:

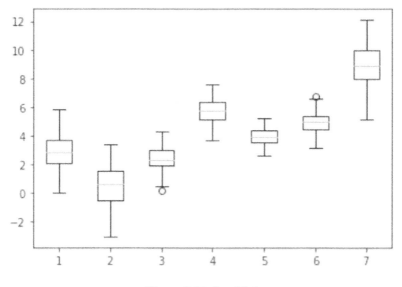

Figure 9.11: *Box Plot*

As we can see, the default representation of the Box Plot is excellent and gives us all the information we need without adding further details.

Using the data in a DataFrame with Matplotlib

Now that we have seen how to obtain the most common charts using the matplotlib library, we can move on to the next step, that is, to use the data within a DataFrame. Let's see how to integrate the results obtained with Pandas along with the graphics library.

In *Chapter 7, (Day 5) - Working with Data Source and Real Datasets*, we saw many examples of DataFrame generated by external sources. Let's take one of these to work with matplotlib. For example, let's take the data from a Wikipedia page, obtaining the meteorological data from an HTML table within the page.

Let's write the following code:

```
In [ ]: url = 'https://en.wikipedia.org/wiki/Rome'
        dfs = pd.read_html(url, match='Climate data')
        temperatures = dfs[0]
        temperatures
```

We obtain a DataFrame in which the results of the meteorological data of the city of Rome, collected between 1971 and 2000, will be reported, as partially shown in *Figure 9.12:*

	Month	Jan	Feb	Mar	Apr	May	Jun	Jul
0	Record high °C (°F)	20.2(68.4)	23.6(74.5)	27.0(80.6)	28.3(82.9)	33.1(91.6)	36.8(98.2)	40.0(104.0)
1	Average high °C (°F)	12.6(54.7)	14.0(57.2)	16.5(61.7)	18.9(66.0)	23.9(75.0)	28.1(82.6)	31.5(88.7)
2	Daily mean °C (°F)	7.4(45.3)	8.4(47.1)	10.4(50.7)	12.9(55.2)	17.3(63.1)	21.2(70.2)	24.2(75.6)
3	Average low °C (°F)	2.1(35.8)	2.7(36.9)	4.3(39.7)	6.8(44.2)	10.8(51.4)	14.3(57.7)	16.9(62.4)
4	Record low °C (°F)	−9.8(14.4)	−6.0(21.2)	−9.0(15.8)	−2.5(27.5)	3.7(38.7)	8.2(43.2)	9.8(49.6)
5	Average precipitation mm (inches)	69.5(2.74)	75.8(2.98)	59.0(2.32)	76.2(3.00)	49.1(1.93)	40.7(1.60)	21.0(0.83)

Figure 9.12: DataFrame from Wikipedia Web Page

Like all datasets imported from external sources, this DataFrame, before being used, will need some cleaning operations, and some modifications to prepare the data within it for analysis. Taking a quick look at the content of the DataFrame, we have the average values of temperatures together with other meteorological values such as annual precipitation and daily sunshine hours, all relating to each month of the year. The last row instead contains the same value for all columns – a string that describes the source of the data and the range of years in which the data was collected. Since these values are repetitive and are not of our interest, they must be removed by deleting the entire row from the DataFrame.

Continuing to take a look inside the DataFrame, we see that all the columns are similar, except for the first **Month** column. Instead, this presents some explanatory strings of the type of value present on the line. From the previous chapters, it will be clear to us that this kind of value should not occupy a column, but rather be used as labels in the row index. One of the operations to do will, therefore, be to modify the DataFrame by converting the **Month** column into index.

The other columns are labeled with the different months of the year. But if we move to the end, we will find a **Year** column. This column is also of no interest to us, and we will, therefore, have to remove it.

We then write the code to perform the aforementioned operations, as shown as follows:

```
In [ ]: temperatures = temperatures.droplevel(0, axis=1)

        temperatures = temperatures.drop([8])

        temperatures = temperatures.set_index('Month')

        del temperatures['Year']

        temperatures
```

We make the necessary changes, and we will obtain the DataFrame, as shown in *Figure 9.13*:

Month	Jan	Feb	Mar	Apr	May	Jun	Jul	Aug	Sep	Oct	Nov	Dec
Record high °C (°F)	20.2(68.4)	23.6(74.5)	27.0(80.6)	28.3(82.9)	33.1(91.6)	36.8(98.2)	40.0(104.0)	39.6(103.3)	37.6(99.7)	31.4(88.5)	26.0(78.8)	22.8(73.0)
Average high °C (°F)	12.6(54.7)	14.0(57.2)	16.5(61.7)	18.9(66.0)	23.9(75.0)	28.1(82.6)	31.5(88.7)	31.7(89.1)	27.5(81.5)	22.4(72.3)	16.5(61.7)	13.2(55.8)
Daily mean °C (°F)	7.4(45.3)	8.4(47.1)	10.4(50.7)	12.9(55.2)	17.3(63.1)	21.2(70.2)	24.2(75.6)	24.5(76.1)	20.9(69.6)	16.4(61.5)	11.2(52.2)	8.2(46.8)
Average low °C (°F)	2.1(35.8)	2.7(36.9)	4.3(39.7)	6.8(44.2)	10.9(51.4)	14.3(57.7)	16.9(62.4)	17.3(63.1)	14.3(57.7)	10.5(50.9)	5.9(42.4)	3.1(37.6)
Record low °C (°F)	−9.8(14.4)	−6.0(21.2)	−9.0(15.8)	−2.5(27.5)	3.7(38.7)	6.2(43.2)	9.8(49.6)	8.6(47.5)	5.4(41.7)	0.0(32.0)	−7.2(19.0)	−5.4(22.3)
Average precipitation mm (inches)	69.5(2.74)	75.8(2.98)	59.0(2.32)	76.2(3.00)	49.1(1.93)	40.7(1.60)	21.0(0.83)	34.1(1.34)	71.8(2.83)	107.0(4.21)	109.9(4.33)	84.4(3.32)
Average precipitation days (≥ 1 mm)	7.6	7.4	7.8	8.8	5.6	4.1	2.3	3.2	5.6	7.7	9.1	8.5
Mean monthly sunshine hours	120.9	132.8	167.4	201.0	263.5	285.0	331.7	297.6	237.0	195.3	129.0	111.6

Figure 9.13: *The DataFrame after the first changes*

Now, the DataFrame is much cleaner and tidier. But it still has some unwanted features. The temperatures inside the various columns have two scales, one in degrees Celsius and one in degrees Fahrenheit in brackets. We must, therefore, eliminate the values in Fahrenheit. The values inside the DataFrame, even if they seem numeric, are still strings. So, we can use the string manipulation operations we saw in the previous chapters.

We write the following code to remove the round brackets and the value contained in them from the DataFrame:

```
In [ ]: temperatures = temperatures.apply(lambda x: x.str.split('(').str.
get(0))

        temperatures
```

We will get the DataFrame as shown in *Figure 9.14*:

	Jan	Feb	Mar	Apr	May	Jun	Jul	Aug	Sep	Oct	Nov	Dec
Month												
Record high °C (°F)	20.2	23.6	27.0	28.3	33.1	36.8	40.0	39.6	37.6	31.4	26.0	22.8
Average high °C (°F)	12.6	14.0	16.5	18.9	23.9	28.1	31.5	31.7	27.5	22.4	16.5	13.2
Daily mean °C (°F)	7.4	8.4	10.4	12.9	17.3	21.2	24.2	24.5	20.9	16.4	11.2	8.2
Average low °C (°F)	2.1	2.7	4.3	6.8	10.8	14.3	16.9	17.3	14.3	10.5	5.8	3.1
Record low °C (°F)	-9.8	-6.0	-9.0	-2.5	3.7	6.2	9.8	8.6	5.4	0.0	-7.2	-5.4
Average precipitation mm (inches)	69.5	75.8	59.0	76.2	49.1	40.7	21.0	34.1	71.8	107.0	109.9	84.4
Average precipitation days (≥ 1 mm)	7.6	7.4	7.8	8.8	5.6	4.1	2.3	3.2	5.6	7.7	9.1	8.5
Mean monthly sunshine hours	120.9	132.8	167.4	201.0	263.5	285.0	331.7	297.6	237.0	195.3	129.0	111.6

Figure 9.14: The DataFrame after the first changes

Now that we have all the numbers within the different columns, we can think of converting these values to floats. But first, let's see what happens when we run the following code:

```
In [ ]: temperatures.astype(float)
```

We will get the following error code:

```
Out[ ]: ...
```

```
#ValueError: could not convert string to float: '-9.8'
```

```
#Your string contains a unicode en-dash, not an ASCII hyphen.
```

From the error message, we understand that instead of the negative sign, an incorrect character (dash) was used. We must, therefore, first replace this character with the correct one and then carry out the conversion. To do this, we can use regex expressions with the **replace()** function as we saw in the previous chapters, and then run the **astype()** function for data type conversion, as shown as follows:

```
In [ ]: temperatures = temperatures.apply(lambda x: x.str.replace(r'[^\
x00-\x7F]+','-', regex=True))
        temperatures = temperatures.astype(float)
        temperatures
```

This time, the code is executed correctly, obtaining the DataFrame as represented in *Figure 9.15:*

Month	Jan	Feb	Mar	Apr	May	Jun	Jul	Aug	Sep	Oct	Nov	Dec
Record high °C (°F)	20.2	23.6	27.0	28.3	33.1	36.8	40.0	39.6	37.6	31.4	26.0	22.8
Average high °C (°F)	12.6	14.0	16.5	18.9	23.9	28.1	31.5	31.7	27.5	22.4	16.5	13.2
Daily mean °C (°F)	7.4	8.4	10.4	12.9	17.3	21.2	24.2	24.5	20.9	16.4	11.2	8.2
Average low °C (°F)	2.1	2.7	4.3	6.8	10.8	14.3	16.9	17.3	14.3	10.5	5.8	3.1
Record low °C (°F)	-9.8	-6.0	-9.0	-2.5	3.7	6.2	9.8	8.6	5.4	0.0	-7.2	-5.4
Average precipitation mm (inches)	69.5	75.8	59.0	76.2	49.1	40.7	21.0	34.1	71.8	107.0	109.9	84.4
Average precipitation days (≥ 1 mm)	7.6	7.4	7.8	8.8	5.6	4.1	2.3	3.2	5.6	7.7	9.1	8.5
Mean monthly sunshine hours	120.9	132.8	167.4	201.0	263.5	285.0	331.7	297.6	237.0	195.3	129.0	111.6

Figure 9.15: The DataFrame further modified

At this point, we can clean up the index labels, restricting everything to the essential words only. We will write the following code that removes degrees Celsius and the words enclosed in parentheses from the strings:

```
In [ ]: temperatures.index = temperatures.index.str.split('(').str.
get(0).str.replace('°C','').str.strip()

        temperatures
```

We get the DataFrame as represented in *Figure 9.16*:

Month	Jan	Feb	Mar	Apr	May	Jun	Jul	Aug	Sep	Oct	Nov	Dec
Record high	20.2	23.6	27.0	28.3	33.1	36.8	40.0	39.6	37.6	31.4	26.0	22.8
Average high	12.6	14.0	16.5	18.9	23.9	28.1	31.5	31.7	27.5	22.4	16.5	13.2
Daily mean	7.4	8.4	10.4	12.9	17.3	21.2	24.2	24.5	20.9	16.4	11.2	8.2
Average low	2.1	2.7	4.3	6.8	10.8	14.3	16.9	17.3	14.3	10.5	5.8	3.1
Record low	-9.8	-6.0	-9.0	-2.5	3.7	6.2	9.8	8.6	5.4	0.0	-7.2	-5.4
Average precipitation mm	69.5	75.8	59.0	76.2	49.1	40.7	21.0	34.1	71.8	107.0	109.9	84.4
Average precipitation days	7.6	7.4	7.8	8.8	5.6	4.1	2.3	3.2	5.6	7.7	9.1	8.5
Mean monthly sunshine hours	120.9	132.8	167.4	201.0	263.5	285.0	331.7	297.6	237.0	195.3	129.0	111.6

Figure 9.16: A clean DataFrame

The last modification to do is to transpose the DataFrame. We know as a rule that variables must be divided by column, and here they are found by row. Whereas, the occurrences, which can be considered as the months of the year, are found by column. We then make the transposition of the DataFrame by writing the following code:

```
In [ ]: dft = temperatures.transpose()

        dft
```

We get the definitive DataFrame, as shown in *Figure 9.17*:

Month	Record high	Average high	Daily mean	Average low	Record low	Average precipitation mm	Average precipitation days	Mean monthly sunshine hours
Jan	20.2	12.6	7.4	2.1	-9.8	69.5	7.6	120.9
Feb	23.6	14.0	8.4	2.7	-6.0	75.8	7.4	132.8
Mar	27.0	16.5	10.4	4.3	-9.0	59.0	7.8	167.4
Apr	28.3	18.9	12.9	6.8	-2.5	76.2	8.8	201.0
May	33.1	23.9	17.3	10.8	3.7	49.1	5.6	263.5
Jun	36.8	28.1	21.2	14.3	6.2	40.7	4.1	285.0
Jul	40.0	31.5	24.2	16.9	9.8	21.0	2.3	331.7
Aug	39.6	31.7	24.5	17.3	8.6	34.1	3.2	297.6
Sep	37.6	27.5	20.9	14.3	5.4	71.8	5.6	237.0
Oct	31.4	22.4	16.4	10.5	0.0	107.0	7.7	195.3
Nov	26.0	16.5	11.2	5.8	-7.2	109.9	9.1	129.0
Dec	22.8	13.2	8.2	3.1	-5.4	84.4	8.5	111.6

Figure 9.17: A clean and tidy DataFrame

Now that we have a DataFrame ready to be used, we can decide to represent its data with matplotlib. We have previously seen how to use matplotlib to represent values contained within lists. With Pandas, things are slightly different. There is no need to convert the values of rows and columns into lists. Since matplotlib is strongly integrated with Panda, structured data such as Series and DataFrame have functions themselves that allow you to directly call the matplotlib functions.

For example, to represent the trend of the record temperatures in the different months of the year (the first line of the DataFrame), you can directly launch the following code:

```
In [ ]: dft['Record high'].plot()
```

Here, we called the **plot()** function directly from the selection of the first column of the DataFrame (which is a Series) to represent its values in a Line Plot, like the one shown in *Figure 9.18*:

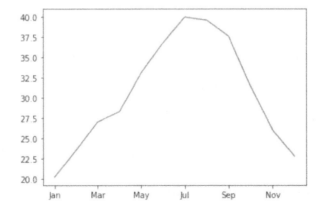

Figure 9.18: Record temperatures during the various months of the year

We got a default Line Plot. The column values are passed as Series directly without converting them into a list, and also the column labels are read as ticks and represented along the *x*-axis – all automatically.

The same thing is to be done if we want to represent more columns in the same chart. It is sufficient to extend the selection to the columns to be represented. In this case, it is a DataFrame that calls the **plot()** function. But Matplotlib is able to recognize the different columns and distribute each one on a different line, as shown as follows:

```
In [ ]: dft.iloc[:, 0:5].plot()
```

By executing, we will obtain the Line Plot like the one represented in *Figure 9.19*:

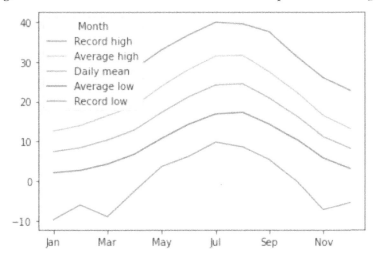

Figure 9.19: *All temperatures during the various months of the year*

We, therefore, have the months on the x-axis and the different meteorological measures divided by column. Furthermore, you can see that a legend is displayed automatically, where each column is shown with its label and the corresponding color.

But what if we wanted to modify the default charts, modifying and adding parameters as we did in the previous examples? Well, this operation is also very simple. We enclose the call to the plot() function between the **plt.figure()** and **plt.show()** functions and insert the other functions and parameters as previously done.

We then move the legend to the top, above the chart, and divide the internal items into three lines by modifying the **legend()** function, through the parameters **loc, ncol** and **bbox_to_anchor**. We then add a black dotted line at the zero value, with the addition of the **axhline()** function, as shown as follows:

In [ ]: plt.figure()

```
dft.iloc[:, 0:5].plot() # Graphic a DataFrame
plt.axhline(0, color="k", linestyle = ':');
plt.legend(loc='upper center',
        bbox_to_anchor=(0.5, 1.20),
        ncol=3, fancybox=True, shadow=True)
plt.show()
```

We will get an updated Line Plot like the one shown in *Figure 9.20*:

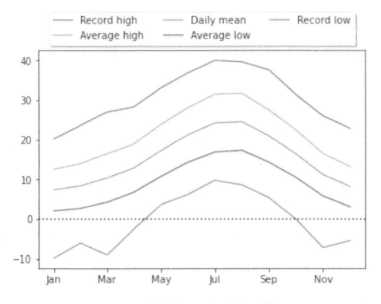

Figure 9.20: Customized Line Plot

Let's now consider the other types of charts that we saw at the beginning of the chapter. For example, to obtain a bar plot, the plot function can be used again, specifying the type of chart using the optional kind parameter, as in the following code:

In [ ]: dft['Daily mean'].plot(kind='bar')

Or, we can use the **plot** attribute instead and then call the **bar()** function, as shown as follows:

In [ ]: dft['Daily mean'].plot.bar()

In both cases, we will get the default Bar chart as shown in *Figure 9.21*:

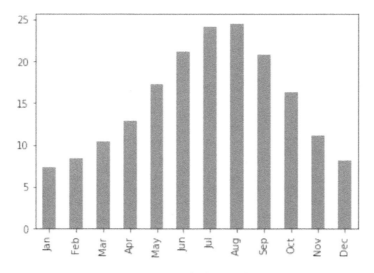

Figure 9.21: Default Bar chart

In this case, we passed a Series to the Bar Chart display. But you can pass a DataFrame, such as selecting the first columns, for example, as shown as follows:

```
In [ ]: dft.iloc[:, 0:4].plot.bar()
```

In this case, you will get a **MultiBar Chart**, where, for each category, there are several bars, as shown in *Figure 9.22*:

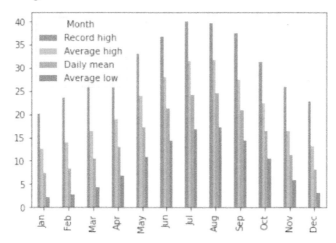

Figure 9.22: Default MultiBar chart

In these cases, the graph may become difficult to read due to the bars being too small and close together. To enlarge the layout of the graph to be displayed, the dimensions can be specified using the optional **figsize** parameter. We then enlarge the layout horizontally using the following code:

```
In [ ]: dft.iloc[:, 0:4].plot.bar(figsize=(10,4))
```

We will get a MultiBar chart with the most spaced bars along the horizontal axis, as shown in *Figure 9.23*:

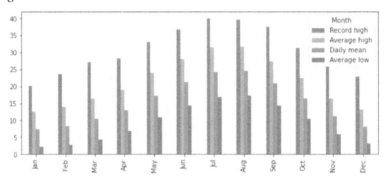

Figure 9.23: MultiBar chart enlarged horizontally

If instead we wanted to represent a horizontal bar chart, just replace the function **bar()** with **barh()**, specific for this type of chart, as shown as follows:

```
In [ ]: dft.iloc[:, 0:4].plot.barh(figsize=(4,10))
```

And we will get the same bar chart, but this time, the bars are oriented horizontally, and the months are on the vertical axis, as shown in *Figure 9.24*:

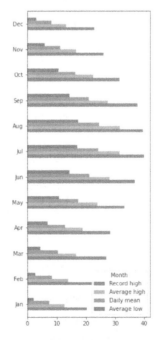

Figure 9.24: Horizontal MultiBar chart

Also, with regard to the Pie Charts, the discourse is almost similar. In this case, the **pie()** function on the plot attribute is used. Let's enlarge the pie dimensions compared to the default ones and add a **cmap** to create a gradation of shades on a blue base. Also, we want to see the corresponding values of each slice of the pie. To do this, we insert the following code:

```
In [ ]: plt.figure()
        colors = plt.get_cmap('Blues')(np.linspace(0.2,
                    0.7, len(dft['Daily mean'])))
        dft['Daily mean'].plot.pie(
            figsize=(5,5),
            autopct="%.2f",
            colors= colors
        );
        plt.show()
```

By executing the code, we will obtain a Pie Chart like the one represented in *Figure 9.25*:

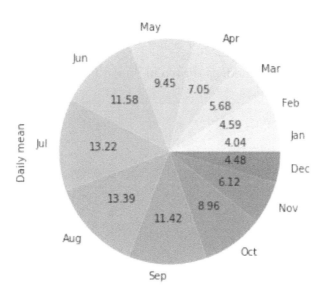

Figure 9.25: *Customized Pie Chart*

If we launch the **pie()** function, instead of on a Series, or on a DataFrame (or a selection of multiple columns), we will be able to obtain an interesting behavior by adding the optional subplots parameter, as shown in the following code:

```
In [ ]: dft.iloc[:, 5:7].plot.pie(subplots=True, figsize=(8, 4),
legend=None)
```

This will allow you to view multiple Pie Charts simultaneously on different subplots, each relating to a column of the DataFrame, as shown in *Figure 9.26*:

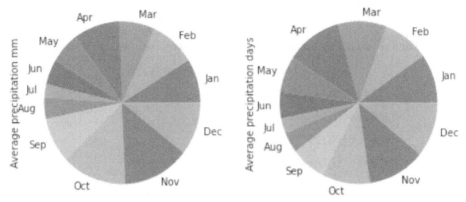

Figure 9.26: More Pie Charts on subplots

Finally, we conclude the series of examples with a scatter plot, which is obtained with the **scatter()** function, in which two columns of the DataFrame must be specified as parameters **x** and **y**, as shown as follows:

```
In [ ]: dft.plot.scatter(x='Daily mean', y='Average low')
```

The scatter plot will be obtained, as shown in *Figure 9.27*:

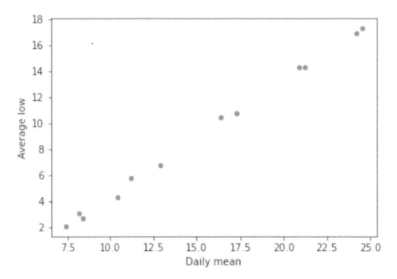

Figure 9.27: Scatter plot

Introduction to Seaborn

In the previous section, we saw the Matplotlib library that allows Python to display the data contained in lists and how this integrates perfectly with Pandas. Now, we will see a library created specifically to work with Pandas – the **Seaborn** library.

This library was developed using matplotlib as a basis, and therefore, inherits the default display behaviors, automatic and with the presence of internal calculations that help statistical processing. Seaborn, however, does this in a much more complex way, being able to process very complex operations, such as cluster analysis and statistical aggregation automatically, by passing only a DataFrame as argument. It is clear that this data-oriented ability also leads to a complexity in use. In fact, it will be necessary to fully understand the various modes of representation of the Seaborn library that go far beyond the simple graphical representations of bar diagrams and pie charts as seen with Matplotlib.

In this section, we will talk about an introduction to Seaborn, since a discussion of it would require a separate book, such is the complexity of its use. But given that it is an important tool for the data analyst and for Pandas, it is therefore, essential to know this library and understand what its potential may be. So, at the end of this chapter, for those who want to learn more about its use, it is recommended to consult the official website (**https://seaborn.pydata.org/**).

For the creation of graphics with the seaborn library, there is no need to explicitly import matplotlib, since it does so implicitly. The library is then imported directly, as shown as follows:

In [ ]: import seaborn as sns

For this library, we will use a DataFrame obtained by importing the data present from a CSV file, **MoneySpent.csv**. Given the large number of lines, we will only display the first five with the **head()** function, as shown as follows:

In [ ]: df = pd.read_csv('MoneySpent.csv')

df.head()

The first five lines of the DataFrame will be represented, as shown in *Figure 9.28*:

	Amount	Age	Sex
0	160	25	M
1	170	34	F
2	200	36	M
3	60	67	M
4	130	56	F

Figure 9.28: First five lines of the DataFrame

From what you can see, the DataFrame shows the sum of thick money from different subjects identified by age and gender.

To display a graph with Seaborn, use the **relplot()** function. As you can see, the function is called directly from the library, and therefore, to pass the DataFrame to it, we will have to use the optional data parameter. Then, with regards to the Cartesian coordinates of the values to be displayed, two columns of the DataFrame will be chosen with the optional parameters **x** and **y**. In our example, we will put the age values on the *x*-axis and the money spent on the *y*-axis. In the DataFrame, there is also the **Sex** column which divides the subjects into two categories (**M** for male and **F** for female). We will be able to use these values to display the two categories in a different way. We therefore, use the hue parameter to give two different colors to the points corresponding to the two sexes, as shown as follows:

So, let's write the following code:

```
In [ ]: sns.relplot(data=df,x='Age',y='Amount',hue='Sex')
```

We will get a scatter plot, as shown in *Figure 9.29*:

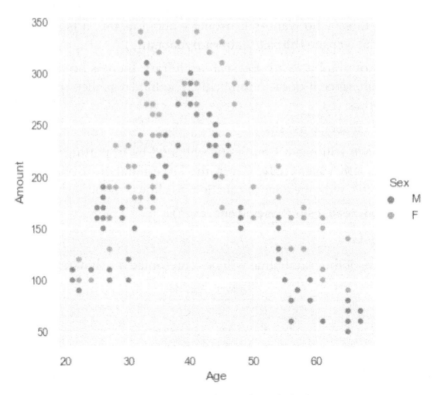

Figure 9.29: *Scatter plot made with Seaborn*

As we can see, even with the Seaborn library, we have the construction of a chart in which many graphics are created by default. We have a legend, the Cartesian axes with the cleats automatically optimized according to the entered values (intervals of 10 from 20 to 80 for the *x*-axis and intervals of 50 for the *y*-axis), a white grid on a gray background, and the writing of labels which show the names of the columns involved – all built automatically.

If, on the other hand, we want to view the data in the form of a Line Plot (the Scatter Plot is the default mode), we add the optional kind parameter in which we specify the `line` type. For the rest, we leave everything as the same, as shown in the following code:

```
In [ ]: sns.relplot(data=df, kind='line',

               x='Age',y='Amount', style='Sex',

               hue='Sex')
```

We then get a Line Plot like the one shown in *Figure 9.30*:

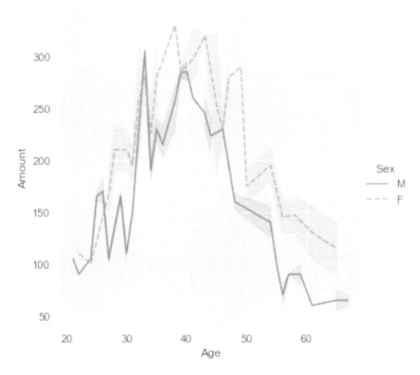

Figure 9.30: *Line plot made with Seaborn*

As we can see, there are two lines, one for each sex. Along the stroke of the lines, we sometimes have areas covered by the same color. These indicate an uncertainty interval in that stretch, given by the presence of several values along that stretch. This calculation is done automatically and is implicitly represented in the graph.

This potential for automatic calculation of areas of uncertainty can be exploited in a more accentuated way by using another graphical representation mode, which in Seaborn, can be called with the `lmplot()` function. With `lmplot()`, you get a scatter plot, in which the interpolation line of the data and the area of uncertainty are automatically calculated, i.e., it performs the regression, as shown as follows:

```
In [ ]: sns.lmplot( data=df[df['Age']> 46],

            x='Age', y='Amount', hue='Sex')
```

Knowing the trend of the values of our DataFrame from the previous charts, we limit the representation of data only to individuals over the age of 46, as they have a general tendency to increase. In fact, by executing the previous line of code, we get a graph, as shown in *Figure 9.31*:

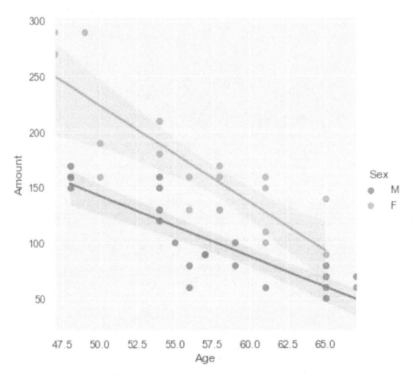

Figure 9.31: Lmplot made with Seaborn

As we can see, two straight lines have been calculated from the basic scatter plot that interpolate the linear trend of expenses due to the two different sexes.

A similar reasoning can be made for the data taken from subjects under the age of 46. In this case, we will have an ascending trend of the points of the scatter plot, as shown as follows:

```
In [ ]: sns.lmplot(data=df[df['Age']< 46],

              x='Age', y='Amount', hue='Sex')
```

In fact, you will get a graph like the one shown in *Figure 9.32*, in which the trend of the two lines is increasing:

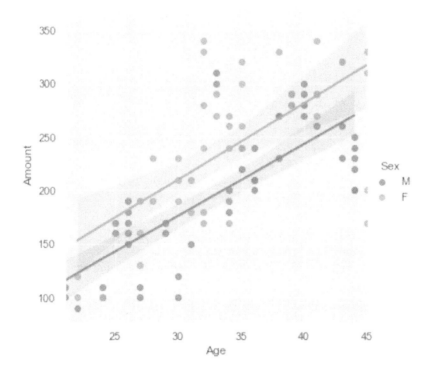

Figure 9.32: *Lmplot made with Seaborn*

Another basic graphical representation mode offered by Seaborn is that for the analysis of data distributions, carried out by the **displot()** function. For example, by passing our DataFrame to this function, we can study the age distribution of the subjects within it. By inserting **kde** as an optional parameter, you will also get the result of the calculation of the kernel destiny estimate, which will be added graphically to the chart, as shown as follows:

```
In [ ]: sns.displot(data=df, x='Age', kde=True)
```

In fact, by executing the row, a Bar Plot will be obtained with the distribution of subjects based on age groups and a Line Plot will also be superimposed on the trend of the population distribution by means of the **kde** calculation. You can see the result in *Figure 9.33*:

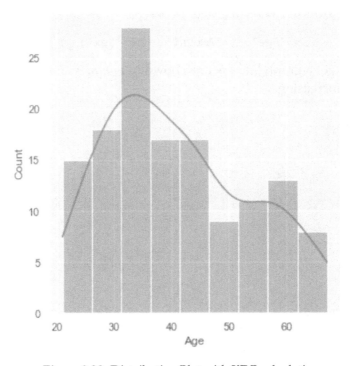

Figure 9.33: *Distribution Plot with KDE calculation*

The same example can be made more complex by dividing the population into two different groups based on their sex. This can be easily done by defining the optional **hue** parameter and assigning it the **Sex** column of the DataFrame, as shown as follows:

```
In [ ]: sns.displot(data=df, x='Age', hue='Sex', kde=True)
```

By executing the previous command, you will get a Bar plot in which the bars of the counts will be superimposed, thus, showing the excess of one of the sexes over the other, and two lines describing the population distribution of the two sexes. See the result in *Figure 9.34*:

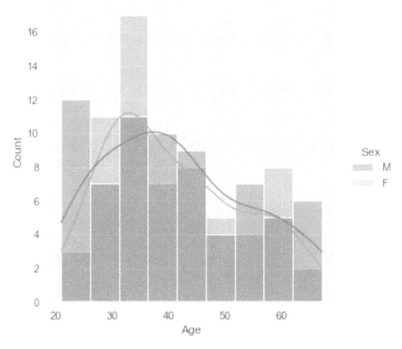

Figure 9.34: *Distribution Plot on two populations*

Another alternative way of creating graphs for distributions is that of a step diagram, with a stepped line that marks the cumulative sum of the subjects as they age. In this type of representation, it can be seen how much each age group contributes to the total of subjects. To obtain this type of graph, we still use **displot()** as a function, even if we specify the type **ecdf** in the parameter kind, as shown as follows:

```
In [ ]: sns.displot(data=df, kind='ecdf',
                x='Age', hue='Sex', rug=True)
```

By running the code, we will get a graph, as shown in *Figure 9.35*:

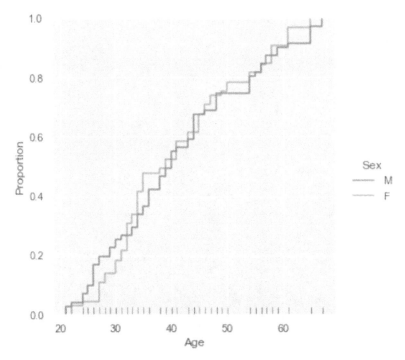

Figure 9.35: *Distribution Plot with steps on two populations*

As for the types of graphical representations and data charts we focus here, we covered the simplest cases to introduce the reader to the use of the library. But the library has much more complex graphic types. From the examples carried out, it is easy to understand how there are types of graphical representation of data that implicitly include the calculation of increasingly complex statistics, with the creation of very captivating and very useful charts from an analytical point of view. At the same time, the use of these representations requires an in-depth preliminary study of their characteristics. We need to consider their implicit calculations and take into account the data structure that the DataFrame must have to meet these requirements.

The Seaborn library provides the data analyst with powerful graphical tools. The purpose of this section was to introduce the reader to the potential of this library. For a complete use of these potentialities, the reader is asked to deepen his studies on the pages of the official website and on the numerous examples reported therein.

Reporting

In this second part of the chapter, we will introduce some examples of the Reporting phase, which corresponds to the final part of the data analysis. In fact, after having taken the data from external sources, we converted them into DataFrame and then the various manipulations and cleaning of the values within them were carried out. Then, we moved on to the graphical display of the results to obtain a visual representation of the information contained in them. Finally, after all the work is performed, it will be necessary to make a report of our work, in which the results of our analysis will be documented.

Reports will generally be published and available in various formats. For example, it will be possible to keep the Notebooks with our codes and our data, interspersed with comments and descriptive textual parts, but also HTML pages that will be published on web servers, for Intranet or Internet use. And finally, our reports will be printed in the form of PDF documents, a very popular format, even for those who are not precisely a data analyst.

Data Profiling and Reporting

There are many topics and applications regarding Reporting, but one of them is Summarizing or Data Profiling, that is, being able to describe a summary of the data obtained as a result (generally a DataFrame) complete with all the descriptive statistics and many other related information.

The most trivial example of all is the one we saw in previous chapters using the describe() function. We continue to work with the DataFrame obtained in the previous section, importing the data from the CSV file MoneySpent.csv, as shown as follows:

```
In [ ]: df = pd.read_csv('MoneySpent.csv')

        df.describe()
```

We obtain a summary representation of the statistics that distinguish the DataFrame, as shown in *Figure 9.36*:

	Amount	Age
count	136.000000	136.000000
mean	193.750000	41.080882
std	75.913572	12.333667
min	50.000000	21.000000
25%	130.000000	32.000000
50%	190.000000	39.000000
75%	260.000000	49.250000
max	340.000000	67.000000

Figure 9.36: Dataframe statistics obtained from describe()

But this result is too simple and trivial to be included in a report. To obtain more complete results, there is a Python module that extends the functionality of Pandas and allows the generation of statistics and other descriptive characteristics of a DataFrame in a professional and graphically acceptable way. This module is called **Pandas Profiling**. This module also integrates perfectly with Jupyter Notebook and allows the generation of reports directly on it in an interactive way.

This module is available in the Anaconda distribution, and then to install it, you can go to Anaconda Navigator, select the environment you are working on (in my case, **mypandas**) and search for the **pandas-profiling** module among the not installed packages, as shown in *Figure 9.37*:

Figure 9.37: *Installation of the pandas-profiling module*

Press the **Apply** button and start installing the package together with the dependencies. Once installed, we will be able to include the module in our code on Jupyter Notebook, as shown as follows:

```
In [ ]: import pandas_profiling as pdp
```

Unfortunately, in some cases (like mine), depending on the versions of the various packages, you get the following error message:

```
[Pandas-profiling] ImportError: cannot import name 'ABCIndexClass' from
'pandas.core.dtypes.generic'
```

This error is due to a conflict between the various versions of Pandas and the module. In Pandas version 1.3, the **ABCIndexClass** class was renamed as **ABCIndex**. To work around this problem, you can make a small change in the code of one of the packages. In the file, it will be the following:

"~/[your_conda_env_path]/lib/site-packages/visions/dtypes/boolean.py"

In my case, it is equivalent to the following:

"C:\Users\MyUser\anaconda3\Lib\site-packages\visions\dtypes\boolean.py"

The line is searched as follows:

```
from pandas.core.dtypes.generic import ABCIndexClass, ABCSeries
```

Then we replace **ABCIndexClass** with **ABCIndex**. You save the file, and everything is fine. Importing the module no longer generates error messages.

We write the following code to generate the profiling report of our DataFrame:

```
In [ ]: profile = pdp.ProfileReport(df,
                       title='Money spent by day',
                       explorative = True)
        profile
```

By running the previous code, we will see a series of processes started, represented by green bars that indicate the progress of the various processes, such as summarizing the DataFrame, generating the report, and finally printing the results on the HTML file, as shown in *Figure 9.38*:

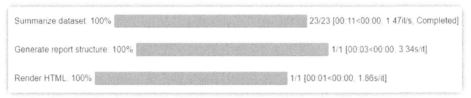

Figure 9.38: Data Profiling output during HTML report generation

After some time, you will get an HTML report that can be consulted directly from the Notebook, and which will include a series of panels containing various information on our DataFrame. Some of these panels can be seen in the following figures, such as the general overview of the DataFrame, as shown in *Figure 9.39*:

Overview

Overview   Warnings ❶   Reproduction

Dataset statistics		Variable types	
Number of variables	3	NUM	2
Number of observations	136	CAT	1
Missing cells	0		
Missing cells (%)	0.0%		
Duplicate rows	9		
Duplicate rows (%)	6.6%		
Total size in memory	10.0 KiB		
Average record size in memory	74.9 B		

Figure 9.39: Overview of the Dataframe values

Or, a **Variables** panel that describes the general statistics of the various columns, as shown in *Figure 9.40*:

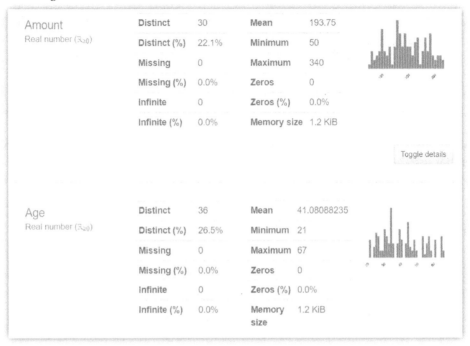

Figure 9.40: *Statistics of some columns of the DataFrame*

Reporting in HTML and PDF

Another way of reporting our results is to generate HTML or PDF files to be published outside our work environment. HTML formats will be useful for publications on Web Server, while PDF documents will be available on any platform.

There are many ways to do this kind of work online. In the case presented here, we will use the **jinja2** library to generate HTML files with our results published there. In this case, we will start with an HTML template on which the library will insert the values of our DataFrame.

We will then edit an HTML template from a text editor which will be saved as **myTemplate.html**, as shown as follows:

```
<!DOCTYPE html>
<html>
<head lang="en">
    <meta charset="UTF-8">
```

```
    <title>{{ title }}</title>
<style>
table, th, td {
  border: 1px solid white;
  border-collapse: collapse;
}
tr {
      border: 3px solid white;
      border-right: 2px solid white
}
tr:nth-child(1) {
    background: #faab09 !important;
    color: white;
}
tr:nth-child(even) {
  background: #f3e495;
}
tr:nth-child(odd) {
  background: #ffdc6a;
}
</style>
</head>
<body>
    <h2>Money spent by day</h2>
    <img src="{{ matplot }}">
    {{ dataframe }}
    </body>
</html>
```

As we can see from the template, inside the HTML tags, there are some variables enclosed in pairs of curly brackets. These will be replaced by **jinja2** with the values generated in real time, such as the page title, the values of our DataFrame, and a Scatter plot generated with the Matplotlib library.

We will create the template and import the classes from the library that we will need to generate the HTML file (there is no need to install **jinja2**). Then, we will create an environment on which we will load the template with the Environment constructor and its **get_template()** function, as shown as follows:

```
In [ ]: from jinja2 import Environment, FileSystemLoader
        env = Environment(loader=FileSystemLoader('.'))
        template = env.get_template('myReport.html')
```

Let's now create a PNG image of the Scatter Plot of our DataFrame generated with matplotlib. This image will then be loaded into the HTML page, as shown as follows:

```
In [ ]: plot = df.plot.scatter(x='Age', y='Amount')
        fig = plot.get_figure()
        filename = 'file:///C:/Users/nelli/Documents/myPandas/graph.png'
        fig.savefig('graph.png')
```

I have defined the path corresponding to my Jupyter Notebook workspace in the filename variable. Replace it with the path of your workspace. The generated image will be saved as a **graph.png** file.

At this point, we generate the final HTML file, replacing the title with the string **'Spent by Day'**, the **matplot** variable with the path of the PNG image file and the **dataframe** variable with our DataFrame converted into HTML, thanks to the **to_html()** function provided by Pandas, as shown as follows:

```
In [ ]: template_vars = {'title' : 'Spent by Day',
                    'dataframe': df.to_html(),
                    'matplot' : filename
                }
        html_out = template.render(template_vars)
        html_file = open('myReport.html','w')
        html_file.write(html_out)
        html_file.close()
```

If we go to see the directory of our workspace, we will find a new file **myReport. html**. If we open it from the browser, we will see an HTML page containing the data of our DataFrame, as shown in *Figure 9.41*:

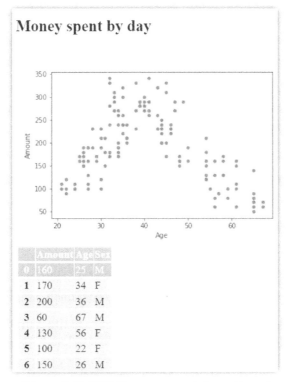

Figure 9.41: HTML page generated as a Report

Now, the final step will be to print the HTML page as a PDF file directly on our workspace. There are several libraries that perform this type of operation (not very convenient though). I chose **pdfkit**, a module based on the **wkhtmltopdf** application. The module is not available in the Anaconda distribution and, therefore, you will need to install it via the console with the **pip** command.

Open an Anaconda console and activate the work environment (in my case, it is **mypandas**). Then install the **pdfkit** module, as shown as follows:

```
(base) C:\Users\nelli>conda activate mypandas
```

```
(mypandas) C:\Users\nelli>
```

```
(mypandas) C:\Users\nelli>pip install pdfkit
```

But it's not done yet. In order to work with this module, it is necessary to install the **wkhtmltopdf** application on our computer. To install it on Windows, go to the official download release page (**https://wkhtmltopdf.org/downloads.html**). Download the executable package and install.

On Debian/Ubuntu systems, to install the application, enter from the command-line, the following:

```
sudo apt-get install wkhtmltopdf
```

Once the application is installed, you can continue by entering the code needed to convert the HTML page into a PDF document, as shown as follows:

```
In [ ]: path_wkthmltopdf =
            'C:\Programmi\wkhtmltopdf\\bin\wkhtmltopdf.exe'
        config = pdf.configuration(wkhtmltopdf=path_wkthmltopdf)
        options = {
            "enable-local-file-access": None
        }
        pdf.from_file('myReport.html', 'myReport.pdf',
            configuration=config, options = options)
```

By running the code, you will get a new **MyReport.pdf** file with the same contents of the source HTML file.

Conclusion

With this chapter, we concluded all the topics on the Pandas library and on the data analysis related to it. In this chapter, we saw that there are graphic libraries, such as matplotlib, which allow us to create charts in which to view our data. We saw how this library is able to integrate optimally with Pandas working directly on structured data such as Series and DataFrame. Then, we saw a quick introduction to another graphics library, Seaborn, created specifically to work with Pandas, very powerful but more complex than matplotlib. Finally, we saw how to create reports with some examples, such as summarizing a DataFrame or publishing our results in HTML and PDF.

In the next chapter, we will see what is beyond all this and what the next steps may be after completing the reading and study of this book.

Questions

1. Is Matplotlib a graphics library that only makes charts, or can it also be used for something else?

2. Are there rules that allow us to identify which type of chart is the most suitable for representing our data?

3. What can be the usefulness of specialized graphics libraries such as Seaborn, compared to Matplotlib? Mention the advantages and disadvantages.

4. For those who work professionally and have to deliver results, what could be the best methods to transfer the information processed by our analysis?

Multiple Choice Questions

1. Which of these charts is best suited to represent a population of data samples?

   A. Line Plot

   B. Bar Chart

   C. Box Plot

2. Which of these functions on Matplotlib does not allow us to graph our data as a Bar Chart?

   A. plot(kind='bar')

   B. barplot()

   C. bar()

3. With which optional parameter is it possible to change the size of a chart?

   A. figsize

   B. ax.size

   C. fig.size

4. What is the use of profiling with a DataFrame?

   A. In the automatic generation of charts

   B. In summarizing the statistics obtained from a DataFrame in the form of HTML pages

   C. In the production of HTML pages containing our results.

5. Which of these libraries is not used for HTML reporting?

   A. pdfkit

   B. jinja2

   C. matplotlib

Answers

1: C; 2: B; 3: A; 4: B; 5: A

Key Terms

Matplotlib, Line Plot, Scatter Plot, Bar chart, Pie Chart, Box Plot, Seaborn, Pandas Profiling, Reporting, PDFkit.

References/Further Readings

- https://pandas-profiling.github.io/pandas-profiling/docs/master/rtd/
- https://seaborn.pydata.org/examples/index.html
- https://matplotlib.org/stable/tutorials/index
- https://jinja.palletsprojects.com/en/3.0.x/
- https://pdfkit.org/

CHAPTER 10
Beyond Pandas

Having concluded the study path of the Pandas library in 7 days, I wanted to add another chapter that would introduce the reader to what can be *Beyond Pandas*. There are many choices to take on the study path, and I wanted to present you with some alternatives to help you better understand your next steps in the growth of skills in data analysis. Furthermore, I wanted to specify, in detail, the professional figure of the Data Scientist and the skills that he should master.

Structure

In this chapter, we will cover the following topics:

- Pandas Insights
- Data Scientist
- Statistical analysis
- Machine Learning
- Deep Learning
- Big Data
- Data Engineer

Objective

After studying this chapter, you will have a more complete picture of the possible choices of study and in-depth analysis that can be undertaken after the conclusion of the book. You will have the knowledge of the reference Python libraries for each topic, to be able to start studying and practicing them. In addition, you will have a better understanding of the professional figures related to data analysis such as the Data Scientist and the Data Engineer.

Where to learn more about Pandas?

The first thing to do after learning everything in the book will be to deepen the subject, look in more detail at the information that has remained unclear, clarify doubts, and possibly go and look for more complex topics not yet covered.

There are many books on the subject that more or less cover the same topics covered in this book, so to go beyond the concepts acquired, I suggest you take other paths.

The official Pandas documentation

The first thing to do is to consult the official Pandas documentation (**https://pandas.pydata.org/docs/**). Once the web page is open, you will find all the possible documentation divided into 4 parts, as shown in *Figure 10.1*:

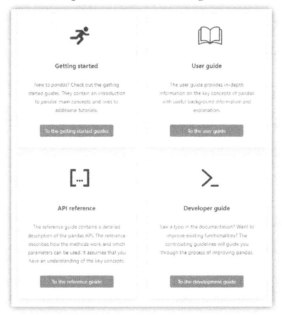

Figure 10.1: Official Pandas documentation web page

Furthermore, from the same page, a downloadable version of the documentation in PDF is available for those who prefer to read the documentation as a book (also printable), instead of following the topics through the hyperlinks between the various HTML pages. All the documentation provided by the official site occupies 3605 pages (as you can see by downloading the PDF).

The first section, entitled *Getting Started*, is an introduction to the use of the Pandas library, while the second, *User Guide*, is a complete guide to its use with all the topics covered in this book and much more – all enriched by a large number of examples to facilitate learning. The third section, *API Reference*, is the ability to search for all possible information starting from the name of the functions and attributes implemented within the Pandas library. This is, and will always be, a valuable tool to be taken into consideration whenever we work with Pandas. In fact, as we saw in the previous chapters, many functions of parsing some functions depend exclusively on the optional parameters passed as arguments, and some functions have so many that it is almost impossible to know them by heart. But the most interesting part is certainly the fourth section, entitled *Developer Guide*.

Participate in the development of the Pandas library

One of the possible ways could be to contribute to the development of this beautiful library. As you can see from the documentation in the Developer Guide section, the invitation is open to all those who think they are able to contribute in some way to the development or improvement of this library.

So, for those who feel inspired by this goal, they can first read the guide and then begin to enter the development environment by participating in the developer meetings that take place regularly (**https://pandas.pydata.org/docs/development /meeting.html**) and then contributing with programming on GitHub following the lines suggested by the milestones (**https://github.com/pandas-dev/pandas/ milestones**). See an example in *Figure 10.2*:

Figure 10.2: Pandas Development Milestones on GitHub

What can you learn after Pandas?

Now that you have completed the book and have found an opportunity to deepen the subject by documenting and practicing, you will certainly ask yourself – What is the next step? What to learn after Pandas?

Well, the answers to these questions depend a lot on what goals we set for ourselves from the start. In fact, our approach to the Pandas library will certainly be motivated by some reason. It may be that for study or professional reasons, we were suggested to learn this library, and therefore, we already carry out an activity relevant to data analysis. For other people who are recently approaching into the world of data analysis, they will want to find some suggestions on what goal can be proposed in front of them.

There are many domains in the scientific and professional world that open up after learning the Pandas library and its analysis techniques. But there are some avenues that are more obvious and plausible than others and I want to mention them in this chapter, as follows:

- Data Science
- Statistical analysis
- Machine Learning
- Image Processing and Deep Learning
- Big Data

Certainly you have heard of these great themes. It must be considered that the boundary between these them is not always so clear, and that the knowledge of one of these is often useful for the others. In fact, all these issues have a common basis – they work on data. Here, we have set ourselves from this common point by studying the Pandas bookcase. Pandas is, in fact, an excellent data analysis tool in the sense of acquiring data from the outside world, their manipulation, and their processing. The results of this analysis would then be used in the context of the topics mentioned. Another point in common is the Python language that Pandas works on. In fact, Python provides many libraries and tools that can be applied in each of the themes; it is, therefore, convenient to use Pandas as a tool compatible with these other libraries.

So, let's take a quick overview of the topics listed.

Data Science, to which the Data Scientist professional figure is closely linked, is one of the subjects of the 21st century. Many programmers and computer science students would like to apply their studies in this professional field, which is much talked about today. For anyone who has acquired an excellent knowledge of Pandas (after reading this book, of course), the choice to deepen their knowledge in the field of Data Science is practically the most obvious way.

Statistical Analysis is the most classic part of data analysis. Much of it was developed before the advent of programming languages and the use of computers and is based on mathematical foundations, that is, hypotheses and theorems whose validity has been demonstrated. This activity, closely related to Numerical Calculus, is perhaps the one that best complements the Pandas library.

Machine Learning is a recent evolution of data analysis that relies heavily on the ever-increasing power of computers. Here, the data analysis is carried out through the use of calculation models, powerful algorithms and, above all, learning by the system to ensure that it is able to make increasingly correct predictions. While the classic approach of studying data and their analysis is based on statistical models and techniques, acquired from theoretical studies and verified hypotheses, in Machine Learning, the techniques have an algorithmic and, often, empirical basis.

Image Processing and Deep Learning are currently on the crest of the wave. The recent rediscovery of neural networks in conjunction with the increasing power of computers, have led to the ability of machines to recognize data as a human brain would. In this case, the data are no longer numbers or strings collected in tables, but videos, images, and sounds taken directly from the real world and converted into processable data (numbers or strings) or directly into information. Even in Image Processing, as in Machine Learning, great use is made of calculation algorithms, which in Deep Learning, have evolved by replacing them with structures capable of learning from the input data and providing information at the output.

Big Data is another great possibility, for those who want to undertake the study and analysis of data; only in this case, you have to deal with a large amount of input data compared to our standards (datasets of various Gigabyte). Furthermore, here you also have to work with data flows, in which the information obtained will vary dynamically with the flow of data in real-time. It is, therefore, clear that the techniques and technologies necessary to work in this area will be much more complex and structured.

The Data Scientist

If our choice is to become a Data Scientist, we can certainly say that the Pandas library and the choice to work with Python has already made us reach a good level in this goal.

The knowledge of the Data Scientist

We must make this clear that Python is not the primary skill of a Data Scientist, but it is still a fundamental tool for obtaining results in a fast, modern, and interactive way, and this allows us to have multiple libraries that cover many areas.

Before establishing themselves as such, a Data Scientist must have acquired a fair knowledge of the theoretical principles of numerical calculus and then applied them in Statistics and Algebra (almost always matrix). Their mathematical knowledge must also include the study of algorithms and other techniques for calculation applied to computers.

Having then gained this knowledge through studies, they will then be able to put them into practice using a series of calculation tools, such as applications (Excel, Matlab, and Scilab) and programming languages (Python, R).

The Task of a Data Scientist

Having defined the knowledge that a Data Scientist must possess, let's define the task as well. Many may think that the goal of a Data Scientist is to develop new techniques, applications, or algorithms capable of processing data. Although Data Science is based on these tools, a Data Scientist's main job is to explore the data. All activities will focus on this task – exploring data to obtain information. It will then be the skill and knowledge of the Data Scientist that will establish which tools are the best to obtain these results.

The goals of a Data Scientist

With regards to the objective of the Data Scientist, the exploration of data must be aimed at processing information useful for the company we are working for or for the person responsible for the project to be able to make decisions. In the business environment, decisions are important, and these are increasingly made, thanks to the outcome of data analysis rather than purely by intuition.

Data Scientist and R

As far as the application field of data analysis is concerned, the other side of the coin is the programming language R. After studying this book, we can certainly ask ourselves – but if I know Pandas, is it necessary that I also learn R?

In many respects, they are similar – they are high-level languages that work in workspaces, they have specialized libraries to download from time to time, and for most of the things, they perform the same operations. So, it will seem totally useless to undertake a study of R if you know the Pandas library perfectly.

The time and resources available to the Data Scientist also limit the evaluation of whether to study R. Studying a new language and a new environment takes time and money, and moreover, achieving an excellent level of knowledge for both environments can be costly. In addition, many companies have only chosen one of the two environments to work on, and so if you purchased this book, it is very likely that a Python environment was the choice partly conditioned by your working environment.

Well, despite all that said, as a data scientist, it would be better to know both languages. The two environments with the two languages perform many similar operations, but they certainly do not do it in the same way. If you deepen the study of both, you might find that, in many respects, the two systems complement each other. Furthermore, the two systems work on completely different environments – R does not work on Python. In some cases, the choice of Python (Pandas) or R could be essential to achieve the intended objectives quickly and efficiently. Knowing which tool to use in a specific case is precisely what distinguishes an experienced Data Scientist. We must always focus on the fact that the goal of a Data Scientist is to extract information from the data, no matter what the chosen tool is, and to arrive at rapid and correct results in the most efficient way possible. Limiting yourself to the use of a single tool (even if we are talking about Pandas or even Python) can be restrictive in the long term. If we want to undertake a profession like that of a Data Scientist, we must always be ready to learn new technologies. The tools evolve over time and become obsolete, giving way to new technologies.

Statistical analysis with StatsModels

For those who like to stay in the field of classical statistics and want to deepen the analysis and calculation possibilities acquired with Pandas, an excellent solution is to start learning the StatsModels library (**https://www.statsmodels.org/stable/index.html**), as shown in *Figure 10.3*:

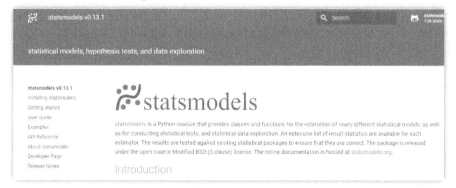

Figure 10.3: Statsmodels home page

StatsModels is a Python library that greatly extends Pandas's potential for the approach to statistical analysis and econometrics while continuing to make use of DataFrames as structured data. Econometrics is the science that uses mathematical and statistical methods to produce models to verify the validity of hypotheses in terms of economic policy. The wealth of statistical models, the possibility of being able to conduct tests, and the exploration of data make Statsmodels a powerful and indispensable tool in statistical analysis.

As the name of the library itself says, its power lies precisely in the quantity of the following models on which it is based:

- Linear models
- Discrete Choice models
- Generalized linear models
- State Space models

Such models have also been tested on other applications such as R.

In addition, Statsmodels also has internal analysis tools implemented that work exclusively on Time Series, including AR, ARMA, and VAR regressions.

The study of this library can, therefore, initially be a valid way to approach more complex methods starting from the basics learned with Pandas, acquiring a wide range of concepts and methods useful for a more professional mastery of statistical analysis.

Machine Learning with Scikit-learn

Parallel to the statistical approach of data analysis, there is Machine Learning. As we already mentioned, this subject is often put outside the skills of a Data Scientist, but in reality, it can add tools and knowledge to this professional figure.

Also, in this case, starting from the basics acquired with Pandas, one can approach Machine Learning to undertake this method of analysis, very often opposed to the statistical approach previously described. In fact, there is a widespread Python library in this regard – **scikit-learn** (**https://scikit-learn.org/stable/**) – which integrates perfectly with all other Python modules, including Pandas, as shown in *Figure 10.4*:

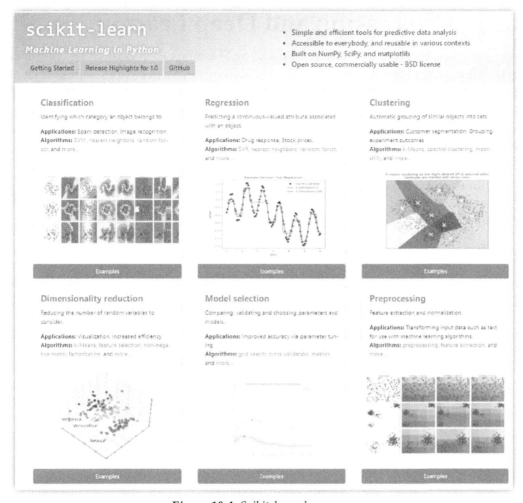

Figure 10.4: Scikit-learn home page

This library also provides a large number of usable models for Machine Learning divided into the following three application categories:

- Classification
- Regression
- Clustering

All these models are then subjected to learning, testing, and verification processes on different types of data structures, thus, allowing the analyst to be able to make predictions or obtain information on the importance of decision-making at the end.

Remembering that the purpose of a Data Analyst is precisely to explore data to obtain information useful for making decisions or predictions, it is clear that Machine Learning can also be a valid tool.

Image Processing and Deep Learning

Going even further in the direction followed by Machine Learning is Deep Learning, in which models capable of learning are replaced by neural networks. This branch of data analysis is the most pioneering one at the moment, but also the most studied. Numerical or textual data have been replaced by visual or sound inputs, which are interpreted by complex artificial neural structures capable of recognizing patterns and information, similar to what a human brain does. The results that are being obtained are exceptional, so much so that in **Image Processing**, the classic analytical algorithms are gradually being replaced by these structures of neural networks, as shown in *Figure 10.5*:

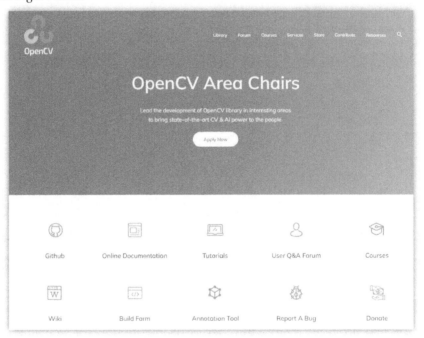

Figure 10.5: OpenCV Home Page

Again, continuing along this path can be very tempting. Python offers some very powerful libraries for this. OpenCV (**https://docs.opencv.org/4.x/index.html**), which stands for **Open-Source Computer Vision**, is a library originally implemented in C++, but a version of this has also been created in Python – OpenCV-Python. Computer Vision comprises a series of processes based on different algorithms that simulate human vision to recognize patterns in two-dimensional images.

In *Figure 10.6*, there is an example of the application of one of the many algorithms made available by the library to recognize the edge of some two-dimensional figures within an image:

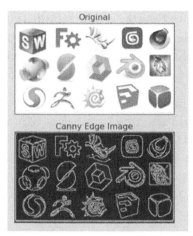

Figure 10.6: Example of image processing with OpenCV (edge detection)

With Deep Learning, we go even further, replacing algorithms with neural bases. There are many libraries in Python that deal with this subject, of which, the following four are the most used at the moment:

- Theano (**https://theano-pymc.readthedocs.io/**)
- TensorFlow (**https://www.tensorflow.org/**)
- Keras (**https://keras.io/**)
- PyTorch (**https://pytorch.org/**)

Refer to *Figure 10.7* for the PyTorch Home Page:

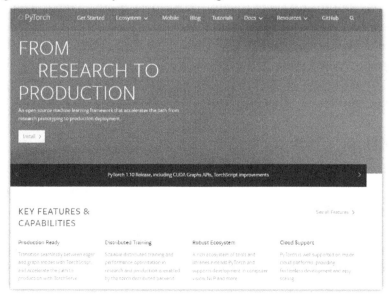

Figure 10.7: PyTorch Home Page

The computation necessary for Deep Learning requires very powerful infrastructures that go far beyond a simple laptop or personal computer. Each of these libraries works on different architectures that make use of different technologies; therefore, their choice will depend on our availability, or vice versa.

Consequently, Deep Learning libraries have very different characteristics, and a study of what they allow and what they do not is very important, before investing time and money on them. However, all of them provide, albeit in a different way, the possibility of creating artificial neural network structures and managing their functioning based on the flow of data, as shown in *Figure 10.8*:

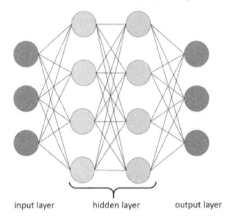

input layer   hidden layer   output layer

Figure 10.8: Artificial neural network

Similar to the study and construction of models (both statistical and machine learning), the construction of neural network structures is a very complex subject. Not all neural networks perform Deep Learning, to be such, they must be able to learn. Furthermore, not all structures built with these libraries are neural networks. So, like the models, the libraries will provide a series of Deep Learning structures that have already been studied and tested in carrying out particular tasks.

Big Data

An alternative to the previous choices may be to devote oneself to the study of Big Data. Although the Pandas library is a powerful tool, there is a certain limit to the size of the data it can handle. Big Data, therefore, includes all those technologies and processes that allow the management and study of huge amounts of data. These data are, in fact, hundreds of Gigabytes in size, too large to be managed entirely within the memory of a computer.

By deciding to upgrade the system through the use of distributed environments and with greater computing power, the results improve but at a high price. It was, therefore, decided to develop a series of *out-of-core* solutions, in which fractions of data are used which are loaded into memory and used only when necessary.

So even if Pandas is no longer useful in this field, he introduced us to this new field. In fact, there are Python libraries that manage Big Data and make use of DataFrame objects very similar to those used in this book. Among the various Python libraries available, I mention only the following few:

- Koalas (**https://koalas.readthedocs.io/en/latest/**)
- PySpark (**https://spark.apache.org/docs/latest/api/python/index.html**)
- Vaex (**https://vaex.io/**)

The first two libraries, Koalas and PySpark, were created to work exclusively with Apache Spark, a parallel processing framework on clusters of machines that allows you to work with large amounts of memory, faster and faster. This technology was created specifically to develop projects and applications for Big Data. Refer to *Figure 10.9* for the Apache Spark Home Page:

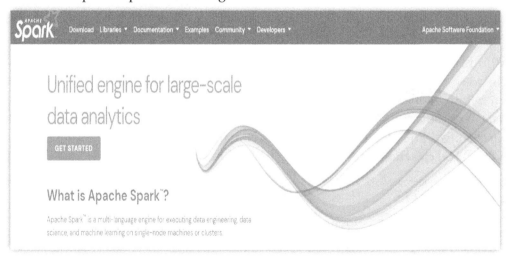

Figure 10.9: *Apache Spark home page*

Vaex, on the other hand, is a Python library for Big Data that is not specific to work in a particular environment, but universal, as their motto says, *"I aim to democratize big data and make it available to anyone, on any machine, at any scale."* Furthermore, with regards to its internal characteristics, it is considered by many to be *the Pandas library for Big Data*, given the great similarity of the DataFrames and the operations available on them.

The Data Engineer, a new professional figure

A professional figure that has recently developed in relation to Big Data is the **Data Engineer**. This figure has the task of verifying, controlling, developing, and evaluating solutions for Big Data. The Data Engineer must have the knowledge that allows them to manage the data analysis process on specific systems to work with Big Data. In fact, they are expert with data pipelines, able to design and implement data analysis systems on these architectures. Furthermore, he must be able to evaluate the sources and the quality of the data from which to acquire the Big Data (sites, social networks). So, what are the differences between a Data Engineer and a Data Scientist?

Data Engineering deals exclusively with all the collection, analysis, and management processes of Big Data. A Data Scientist (in the field of Big Data), remains the professional figure who deals with the exploration of the data provided by the Data Engineer, and obtains useful information.

Conclusion

With this chapter, we concluded our book on the Pandas library. In this chapter, you were able to have a quick presentation of some in-depth opportunities that can follow the Pandas library study. I took the opportunity to suggest some ways that cover different themes, and which constitute the *naturally* subsequent steps to expand one's knowledge in the field of data analysis. Staying within the scope of Python, you can choose from a wide range of libraries.

Questions

1. What could be your suggestions on future Pandas releases?
2. How important can it be for a Data Scientist to know applications that work on spreadsheets such as Excel?
3. Considering what you learned in this chapter, how much can the knowledge of Pandas affect the activities of a Data Scientist?
4. What could be the substantial differences between Machine Learning and Statistical Analysis?

Multiple Choice Questions

1. Which of these Python libraries is used for Machine Learning?

    A. StatsModels

    B. Scikit-learn

    C. PySpark

2. Which of these libraries is based on the Pandas library?

    A. StatsModels

    B. MatplitLib

    C. NumPy

3. What is the main task of a Data Scientist?

    A. Develop algorithms for data analysis

    B. Make use of libraries like Pandas and R

    C. Explore the data

4. What is Deep Learning based on?

    A. On learning models and algorithms

    B. On neural networks

    C. On structures and neural networks capable of learning

5. In Big Data, what is the characteristic that differentiates a Data Scientist from a Data Engineer?

    A. Extract useful information from data analysis

    B. Control and manage the structures that process the data

    C. Analyze data from Big Data sources

Answers

1: B; 2: A; 3: C; 4: C; 5: A

Key Terms

Data Science, Machine Learning, Deep Learning, Big Data, Data Engineer.

References/Further Readings

- https://pandas.pydata.org/docs/
- https://www.meccanismocomplesso.org/en/opencv-python-canny-edge-detection-2/
- https://www.meccanismocomplesso.org/en/deep-learning-2/
- https://www.meccanismocomplesso.org/en/first-steps-with-r/
- https://www.meccanismocomplesso.org/en/data-scientist-a-new-professional-role/

Index

A

aggregation, DataFrame
  agg() method, using 178-181
aligning, on DataFrames 231
  align() method, using 231, 232
  with Join modalities 232-234
align() method 231, 232
Anaconda 20
  command line shell 23, 24
  distribution 20, 21
  installing 21
  installing, on Linux systems 22, 23
  URL 20
Anaconda Individual Edition
  download link 21
Anaconda Navigator 22, 23
Apache Spark Home Page 399
append() method 199-201
applymap() method 172
apply() method
  chaining 169, 170
arithmetic operations, with DataFrames
  between subsets of different
    DataFrame 225-227
  between subsets of same
    DataFrame 224
  flexible binary arithmetic
    methods 216, 217

flexible binary methods and
    arithmetic operators 217-219
flexible binary methods,
    versus arithmetic operators 219-224
homogeneous DataFrames,
    as operands 210-212
non-homogeneous DataFrames,
    as operands 212-214
operations, between DataFrame
    and Series 214, 215
relative binary methods 227, 228

B

bar chart
  creating 353
Big Data 391, 398, 399
Boolean operations, DataFrame 228
  between two DataFrames 229
  flexible Boolean binary methods 230
box plot
  creating 356, 357

C

categorization, DataFrame 189
  category column, specifying 190-193
common operations, for correcting
    new imported DataFrame 317
  Axis Indexes, renaming 321-323

Data Duplicated 319-321
Data Replacing 318, 319
concat() function 202-204
Conda 23, 24
 environments, creating 24, 25
 environments, creating with
  different Python version 26, 27
 environments, exporting 27
 environments, managing 25
 packages, creating 27, 28
 packages, managing 28, 29

D

data
 saving, to file 262
data, adding to DataFrame 198
 append() method used 199-201
 concatenations, between DataFrame
  and Series 204, 205
 concat() function, used 202-204
 multiple concatenations 205
 multiple Series, appending 202
data analysis 7
 data cleaning 9
 data collection 8, 9
 data modeling 10
 data processing 9
 data scientist 7
 data transformation 9
 data visualization 10
 process 8-10
 tabular form, of data 10
data analysis environment
 basic procedure 16
 considerations 20
 Jupyter Notebooks installation 19, 20
 Pandas installation 18
 Python installation 16
 setting up 15, 16
database interaction, for data exchange 262
 SQLite installation 263, 264
 test data, creating on SQLite 264-266
Data Engineer 400
DataFrame 61

aggregation 178
aligning 231
arithmetic operations 210
as indexed data table 61
basic functionalities 88
Boolean operations 228
categorization 189
constructor arguments 64-67
creating, from list of Data Classes 80
creating, from list of dictionaries 79, 80
creating, from list of Named Tuples 81
creating, from ndarray dictionary 74
creating, from Numpy ndarray 70-72
creating, from record array 76-79
creating, from Series dictionary 72-74
creating, from structured array 76-79
DataFrame() constructor 62, 63
data viewing 88
editing 114
elements, accessing with
 iloc[] and loc[] 67-69
filtering 104
functions, applying 162
grouping 181
iteration 154, 155
MultiIndex DataFrame 81
pass-by-copy, with Dictionaries 75, 76
pivoting 153, 154
reindexing 137
selection 92
shifting 146
sorting 132
transforming 173
transposition 131
viewing, in Jupyter Notebook 63
ways of building 70
DataFrame() constructor 62, 63
data, from external files 238, 239
 content preview 242, 243
 graphical display, in Jupyter Notebook 242
 Microsoft Excel file, reading 244-247
 Microsoft Excel file, writing 244-247
 reading in CSV format 239-241
 to_csv() parameters 243, 244

writing in CSV format 239-241
data from web
    data, reading from HTML pages 247-250
    reading, from XML files 250-257
    reading, in binary format 260, 261
    reading, in JSON 257-260
    writing, from XML files 250-257
    writing, in binary format 260, 261
    writing, in JSON 257-260
data profiling 377-380
Data Scientist 390, 391
    goals 392
    knowledge 392
    R language 392
    task 392
data sources 266
data structures, Pandas 45
    DataFrame 61
    Series 46
data viewing, in DataFrame
    direct printing, of values 88-90
    head() method 91, 92
    tail() method 91, 92
Date Times 267-273
    values, importing from file 279-281
Deep Learning 391, 396-398
descriptive statistics 125
    calculating, with describe() method 125-127
    data standardization 130
    individual statistics, calculating 128
    skipna option 129

E

editing, in DataFrame
    column, adding 114, 115
    column, deleting 116, 117
    column, editing 117, 118
    column, inserting 116
    new columns, adding with assign() 123, 124
    row, deleting 122
    row, editing 118-121

F

filtering, in DataFrame 104
    application, of multiple conditions 108-110
    Boolean condition 104, 105
    Boolean reductions 110-112
    on columns 107, 108
    on lines 105-107
    with isin() 112, 113
functions, DataFrame 162
    applying, with apply() method 164-167
    applying, with pipe() method 167-169
    by aggregation functions 162
    by element functions 162
    levels of operability 162
    NumPy functions, applying 163, 164
    with arguments, applying with
        pipe() method 171

G

groupby() method 181-184
    for indexes 185-187
grouping, DataFrame
    apply() with groupby() 189
    groupby() method, using 181-184
    with aggregation 188, 189
    with transformation 187, 188

I

Image Processing 391, 396
Index() constructor 50, 51
INNER join 209, 210
integrated development environments
    (IDEs) 37
Internet of Things (IoT) 9
iteration 154
    methods 158-161
    row iterations, in DataFrames 161
    with for loops 155-157

J

JavaScript Object Notation (JSON) 257
join parameter alignment modes
    inner mode 233
    left mode 233

outer mode 233
right mode 234
Jupyter Notebook 29, 30
    creating 30-32
    installing 19, 20
    new Notebook, creating 32-36

K

Koalas 399

L

LEFT join 207, 208
line plot
    creating 347-350
lists 94

M

Machine Learning 391
    with scikit-learn 394, 395
map() method 172
matplotlib 346, 347
    bar chart, creating 353
    box plot, creating 356, 357
    data in DataFrame, using 357-368
    importing 19
    installing 19
    line plot, creating 347-350
    pie chart, creating 354, 355
    scatter plot, creating 350-352
merge() method 206
merging, DataFrames 206
    INNER join, applying 209, 210
    LEFT join, applying 207, 208
    merge() method, used 206
    OUTER join, applying 209
    RIGHT join, applying 208, 209
missing data
    handling 300
missing values
    counting 308, 309
    data types, converting 314-317
    dropping 309, 310
    Fill Backward 312

Fill Forward 311
filling in 310, 311
finding 308, 309
interpolation 313
working with 308
MultiIndex DataFrame 81
    creating, from dictionary of tuples 82-84

N

name attribute, of Series 51, 52
NaNs
    generating 301-303
    generating, with other operations 304-308

O

OpenCV
    reference 396
operations, for NaN generation 304-308
OUTER join 209

P

Pandas 1
    and DataFrames 13
    data structures 45
    features 4-6
    for data analysis 4
    importing 19
    installation, on Mac OS 18
    installation, on Windows 18
    library 2
    library timeline 3
    official documentation 388, 389
Pandas library
    development 389
Pandas Profiling 378
pie chart
    creating 354, 355
pip 18
pipe() method
    chaining 169, 170
pivoting
    performing 153, 154
PyPI 18

PySpark 399
Python 6
Python 3.x
    versus Python 2.7 16, 17
Python installation 16
Python workspace
    creating in Replit, for data analysis 38-41
PyTorch Home Page 397

R

reindexing 137-139
    reference DataFrame, using 140, 141
Replit 37
    development environment 37, 38
    Python workspace, creating
        for data analysis 38-41
    URL 37
reporting phase
    data profiling 377-380
    examples 376, 377
    in HTML 380- 384
    in PDF 380-384
reshape 149
    performing, with stack() method 149-152
    performing, with unstack() method 149-152
RIGHT join 208, 209
R language 392, 393

S

scatter plot
    creating 350-352
scikit-learn
    home page 395
    URL 394
seaborn
    importing 19
    installing 19
    working with 369-376
selection, DataFrame
    by labels, with loc[] operator 98-100
    by location, with iloc[] operator 100, 101
    by value, with at[] 102
    by value, with iat[] 102

indexer ix[] 101, 102
    on dtype 102-104
    scalars, as return values 94
    selection by subsetting 92
    Series, as return values 94
    subsetting by index 93, 94
    subsetting by position 93, 94
    with indexers 95- 98
    with indexing operators 95-98
Series 46
    as sequence of data 46-50
    creating, from 2-element array list 60, 61
    creating, from dictionary 58-60
    creating, from list of tuples 60
    creating, from NumPy array 53-57
    creating, from scalar value 57, 58
    Index() constructor 50, 51
    name attribute 51, 52
    Series() constructor 52, 53
    ways of building 52
Series() constructor 52, 53
shifting 146
    with shift() method 146-149
slices 94
sorting, DataFrame 132
    by labels 133, 134
    by values 135, 136
Sparse DataFrame 324, 325
spreadsheets 11
SQLite database
    installing 263
SQL tables
    from databases 12, 13
stack() method 149
Statistical Analysis 391
    with StatsModels 393, 394
subsetting
    via indexing 93
    via integer positioning 93

T

tabular form, of data 10, 11
    Pandas and Dataframes 13
    spreadsheet 11

SQL tables, from databases 12
text data
  alphanumeric, separating from
    numeric characters in column 290-292
  characters, adding to rows of
    column 293, 294
  methods, for concatenating text
    columns 289, 290
  methods, for correcting string
    characters 284-287
  methods, for splitting strings 287-289
  methods, searching in strings 295
  recognition methods, between alphanumeric
    and numeric characters 294
  working with 281-284
TIDY data 299, 325
  basic principles 325, 326
  columns, containing multiple
    variables 334-336
  columns, containing values 330, 331
  columns, with multiple variables 339-342
  example, with melt() method 329
  example, with stack() method 327, 328
  groups of variables, in columns 338, 339
  methods, for inversion of stacked
    data 326, 327

variables, in rows and columns 336-338
variables, in same column 331-334
time data
  array of time values, creating 276
  Date Times 267-273
  Date Time values, importing
    from file 279-281
  Time Deltas 273-275
  Timestamp array, creating 277-279
  working with 267
Time Deltas 273-275
Timestamp array
  generating 276-279
to_csv() parameters 243
transforming, DataFrame 178
  MultiIndex DataFrame, reducing to
    DataFrame 175, 176
  with transform() method 173-175
transform() method 173-175
  single column, at a time 177, 178
transposition, DataFrame 131, 132

U

unstack() method 149